D0450043

MAKING AMERICA WORK AGAIN

MAKING AMERICA WORK AGAIN

J. Morton Davis

HC
106.8
D37
1983

EERL Withdrawn
Surplus/Duplicate

Crown Publishers, Inc. New York

Copyright © 1983 by J. Morton Davis
All rights reserved. No part of this book may be
reproduced or transmitted in any form or by any
means, electronic or mechanical, including pho-
tocopying, recording, or by any information storage and retrieval system, without permission in
writing from the publisher.

Published by Crown Publishers, Inc., One Park
Avenue, New York, New York 10016, and si-
multaneously in Canada by General Publishing
Company Limited.

Manufactured in the United States of America

**Library of Congress Cataloging in Publication
Data**
Davis, J. Morton.

    Making America work again.
    Includes index.
    1. United States—Economic policy—1981–
I. Title.
HC106.8.D37   1983   338.973   83–7706
ISBN: 0–517–55117–9

Design by Dana Sloan

10 9 8 7 6 5 4 3 2 1

First Edition

To Rozy who is, simply,
my wife—my life

Contents

Part Three
**NATIONAL ECONOMIC PLANNING:
A NEW FRONTIER**

Acknowledgments

I would like to thank the friends, colleagues, and critics who contributed to this work. My special debt of gratitude is to Dr. Evelyn Geller, without whose collaboration this book could not have been written. A number of scholars who read all or parts of this manuscript in early drafts provided incisive criticism and were, though not necessarily in agreement with all of my views, extremely helpful and constructive in innumerable ways; they include Milton Friedman, Charles Haar, Walter Heller, Lawrence Klein, Robert Lekachman, Harold Proshansky, Leonard Silk, and Paul Wachtel. I received stimulation and encouragement throughout from Dr. Philip David and Thomas Hexner.

My thanks go to Fran Di Monda and Alison Brown for their assistance with the manuscript through its various stages of production.

Finally, I am endlessly grateful to my wife, Rozy, and my daughters, Esti, Ruki, Rivky, and Laya, for their inspiration and forebearance during the time in which this book was written.

Foreword

J. Morton Davis, drawing upon his own experience as a successful entrepreneur and a wide variety of published sources, has in vivid language offered an incisive analysis of the disordered American economy and a set of fresh responses to unemployment, inflation, and poorly chosen national priorities. A member of a minority within the business community, Mr. Davis advocates democratic national planning as a sensible strategy. Readers of this highly intelligent book will be reminded of Felix Rohatyn, another vigorous exponent of coherent national policy.

Not the least of the services this work is likely to offer is stimulus to controversy. Just as examples, I might say that I consider the target of full employment more attainable than does Mr. Davis and I am inclined to impute more blame to American management for the poor performance of the economy than does Mr. Davis. Nevertheless, as Reaganomics loses the diminishing band of true believers, public discussion will almost certainly focus not on the contrast between authoritarian central planning on the Soviet model (which no one wants) and "free" markets that exist only in the textbooks of economists, but on the nature of democratic, decentralized planning in a representative democracy. Mr. Davis's valuable book is a good start to a debate likely to become the leading issue of the 1984 presidential election.

Robert L. Lekachman,
Distinguished Professor of Economics,
City University of New York

Preface

Unemployment is at a 6 percent level.
The prime rate is running at 6.5 percent.
Inflation is at 5 percent.

Does this sound like the answer to our economic prayers? Take another guess. Once upon a time, in 1971, these figures were symptoms of a crisis. They signaled an emergency so drastic that President Nixon, the last person from whom such a move could have been expected, clamped wage and price controls on the economy and proclaimed himself a Keynesian.

We have come to live with more grievous conditions. Inflation in 1980 peaked at 18 percent. The prime rate, which topped 21 percent in 1981, dropped only to 16 or 15 percent in the 1981–82 recession, and in early 1983, with the rate of increase of inflation at approximately zero, the prime rate remained a double-digit 10.5 percent, a record figure for real interest rates. Unemployment, which has reached higher and higher plateaus, remains so high that it often hovers around 7 percent even in prosperity. We have never recovered from the supply shocks of the 1970s.

Back in 1970, Andrew Hacker, making what seemed an implausible claim, predicted "the end of the American era." Today, inflation is seen, with good reason, as the sign of a deeper malaise—a psychology of affluence and abundance colliding with an economy of dwindling resources. The easing of inflation confronts us even more sharply with the menace of limited growth.

Baffled by this turn of events, the voting public has shuttled from party to party, venting its frustration by shifting its weight to the promises of the opposition. Once Election Day has passed, these promises are not so much forgotten as transformed into pre-

xv

dictions—sanguine projections of economic growth that can later be dismissed as statistical errors. Even the Reagan administration, which has pursued its goals far more relentlessly than other administrations, has inspired as much bewilderment as admiration. The promised balanced budget has become a deficit that the wildest liberal economists would never have dreamed of or tolerated. The social safety net is being ripped open. The great innovation of supply-side economics has fallen on the sword of high interest rates, producing, in 1982, a record year for bankruptcies.

Economists have had a field day in analyzing these problems. Never have the destinies of so many been confided so blindly to so few.

I share the present disenchantment with our experts. When I first studied economics in college and graduate school, I found that much of what I read was complex, boring, unnecessarily heavy, and written as if for some secret cabal—as indeed much of it was and is, only for the society of intensively trained professional or quasi-professional economists. It was a catch-22 situation. To decipher the language, you had to be a highly trained expert. Yet to become a highly trained—or even a lowly trained—expert, you first had to decipher the esoteric code of the accomplished virtuosi.

Many students dealt with this situation by learning the codes but not the course. They spouted back the words, but never gained the understanding. Their pens and lips moved after the style of the professors, but their minds went to sleep. Perhaps not many dropped out, but most copped out. Later, when I taught economics myself, I found the secret language of the economists— an abundance of charts and graphs, presumably designed to assist in the learning process. But the graphs and charts were clearer than the concepts they were meant to illustrate, and the ideal equations seldom bore any correspondence to real life.

What I hope to do in the following pages is remove some of the mystification of economics and simplify its discussion, clarify the philosophy of economics, the politics of economics, and the realities of economics, by using the everyday language, the commonsense English of the common man. Once these ideas have been decoded, I will use them to examine the problems of the 1980s and show how we can learn from the policy mistakes that have littered the path of social and economic development, skewed our priorities, allowed our most productive incentives to atrophy, and produced the impasse of stagflation—inflation coupled with high unemployment—a condition that, according to standard economic theory, wasn't supposed to happen.

This book, drawn from the experience of the marketplace rather than the classroom, falls into three main parts: a demystification of economic theory, a hard look at history, and recommendations for policy. The first section, "Economics for Everyman," translates economic concepts into everyday language and illustrates their relevance to public policy. "From Roosevelt to Reagan" reviews the key events from the Depression through the early 1980s that have produced our problems in welfare, defense, and monetary and banking policy. Finally, "National Economic Planning: A New Frontier" presents my policy alternatives and describes their philosophical underpinnings. The last chapter provides a recapitulation of the elements that must be part of national economic planning. I approach my theme from the vantage point of a businessman and an investment banker. Each day as I provide venture and public capital to small and emerging companies, I immediately see the creation of new jobs, new products, new growth—increased productivity and improved competitiveness, vis-à-vis the Japanese, Germans, and others. I know capitalism can work, can produce new and unprecedented growth, new opportunities, new careers, and new exciting products to make our lives better, richer, fuller, and healthier. I know it can produce relatively full employment without the side effects of ravaging uncontrollable inflation. I know because I see immediately the positive impact of the capital I provide or help to provide. An MIT study pointed out that 80 percent of the new jobs and over 50 percent of the new products are generated by small companies (the kind I finance everyday). It is in the area of small companies, new companies, entrepreneurial management, with its creative exciting energy, its new uninhibited approaches, its pioneering research and development in the pursuit of new solutions and new products, that we can compete with the Japanese; not through protectionism of our older industries such as steel, autos, or textile. America has always been best in opening new frontiers, new dreams, new horizons, when it encourages education of its young, open-ended research, and the incentive to be rewarded magnificently as an individual by the success of one's effort and the dedication to the fulfillment of an idea or project that enhances the collective good.

Compensation and reward based on performance and achievement—these have been the secret of America's history of ever-increasing productivity, of an ever-improving, formerly unimagined, superior standard of living and the enviable success of capitalism. We must once again reintroduce the incentives, to our youth and to our entire populace, to work, to pursue excellence and achievement to make America work again as it once did, to make American capitalism with its unparalleled combination of maximum, almost unbridled, freedom and thrilling opportunity fulfill the potential envisioned by Adam Smith and the forefathers of our nation, and truly deliver the wonderful dream that America's reawakening and revival can surely once again produce.

I advocate government *planning,* which by establishing specific broad goals and priorities and then introducing those *incentives,* such as tax credits or greatest profits and rewards, that will stimulate the private sector and motivate the individual, can minimize bureaucracy and the role of government and take our economy to new undreamed-of heights and a better, healthier, happier standard of living for all Americans.

Making America Work Again presents the key elements for economic revival and success. Those seeking miracles will not find them here. Only children believe that wishes transform reality simply through the act of wishing. Only through planning and concerted action can we accomplish economic growth that will shape a better society, guarantee a brighter economic future and improved standards of living, and realize our potential for greatness.

But we must start at once. While I attempt to enlighten the reader about the nature and functioning of our economy I hope to advocate a plan of action that will enable all Americans to attain a larger share of the good things in life. Since we cannot rely, like President Reagan, on slogans or simplistic formulas (such as "supply-side economics") to achieve results, we must make plans and work to realize goals. We must recognize these goals for what they are: the products of an almost infinite set of complex *human* interactions and decisions. For example, we cannot regenerate capital investment by large givebacks—tax cuts for everybody—without producing enormous deficits, destructively high interest rates, and an erosion of business confidence, all of which are aggravated by record levels of defense spending.

The way to achieve realistic goals is to introduce a sequence of steps that will produce the desired objective. The best way to realize objectives is not through negative controls but through positive incentives.

No successful businessman would proceed toward the achievement of his company's goals without a well thought out, carefully analyzed and reanalyzed business *plan* including when, where, how, and by whom it will be implemented; what its costs will be and what incentives, in terms of prices, wages, investments, will be necessary to bring about the desired result. How the hell can we manage the "business affairs" of our country without employing at least as much concern and careful, intelligent planning as does the average businessman? Is the business of our country—which affects each and every one of our own daily lives and our children's future lives—less important? Certainly not! Then let's plan! Let's agree on a plan for the present and future success of our economy.

Paradoxically, it is the business community, which lives by careful, analytical planning, that has been most resistant to the concept of government planning. Businessmen feel that planning is a socialistic or communistic means of running a society (and therefore ipso facto must be horrible). They would deprive our own governmental system of the advantages of a tool they themselves must use to survive in the competitive environment. It is this fear of public-sector planning that has led to the ad hoc, short-term, politically expedient, and ultimately damaging nonplanning that has brought us to today's economic muddle of stagflation alternating with recession.

While it is true that the detailed five-year or seven-year plans of the Soviet Union, Eastern Europe, and China are essential to the operations of those totalitarian, rigidly controlled countries, and therefore correctly repulsive to our free-market democratic system, it must be recognized that it is the coercive, ambitious, and ineffective nature of such planning which makes those societies so onerous to us. The minutest detail of exactly what should be produced, who should produce it, and just where, and at what price, and in what quantity, is dictated by an ideological elite. Each individual citizen is told what education he will receive, what apartment he should occupy, what products he might consume, where he will work, etc. I, like other businessmen, in fact like all other Americans, find such inhibition of free choice repugnant—and would fight to my death to avoid such a narrowing and stifling condition. What's even worse is that such totalitarian planning doesn't work because it ignores human nature. The theories of the collectivist planners stifle ambition, imagination, and productivity and lead to the apathy, cynicism, and corruption that Mr. Andropov is attacking in Russia today.

I propose that we Americans face the necessity of making hard choices and institute *a workable plan for economic success* through our elected officials. Such planning will specify targeted incentives that will motivate the members of our society to act in their own long-range self-interest. This type of planning for predefined goals will substantially reduce or completely eliminate the need for government intrusion and the accompanying vast bureaucracy from direct involvement in our economy and our lives.

"Contrary to classical economic theory a free-trading system does not run itself; it requires a conscious act of political leadership," says Henry Kissinger in his article entitled "Saving the World Economy" (*Newsweek,* January 24, 1983, p. 46). In the real world the invisible hand of each man, who acts in his own self-interest but ultimately serves to achieve what is best for all, sometimes needs the guidance of a wise political (visible) hand to steer toward superior results. I am convinced we can achieve far more through intelligent planning—planning that we as a society need and want.

We do, in such a plan, have to determine an order of priorities. No country, no matter how wealthy or well motivated its citizenry, can achieve instantly all that it wants. We must design those incentives that will help the collective invisible hand of our free-market system achieve the successful implementation of ascending priorities in a hierarchy of increasingly ambitious overall societal goals.

Why am I so confident that this approach will work? Because I believe that the one thing we can truly count on, if nothing else, is man's self-interest. It has helped him survive in a hostile world. It has helped him produce the miracles of science, technology, agricultural productivity, and distribution we witness and benefit from so enormously today. So I know we can count on it in the future if we just design, after the planning stage, those incentives that will unleash this tremendous force for achievement. Through them we can bring forth almost any result we wish.

The Japanese have already demonstrated how effective overall planning can be in producing economic miracles of magnificent growth and increasing prosperity within a framework of a democratic free-enterprise system. They employ government and private-sector cooperative planning that recognizes both the interdependence of nations in a complex and fragile world economy as well as the competitive environment in which world trade functions. We must learn to plan under a cooperative public-private arrangement that is right for *our* society and system. Slavish imitation of the Japanese model would be a great mistake. Many elements of the "consensus" or "social contract" in Japan reflect a society radically different from ours.

Often the argument is made that we can't make it happen. Or that it would take too long so that by the time we implemented a given plan the problem may already be gone or on the way to a solution. For example, during the recession of late 1982 and early 1983 unemployment hit almost 11 percent. It was proposed that a jobs program be implemented and accelerated. The Reagan administration argued it would take too long to yield results and therefore should not be initiated; by the time results might be expected, went the argument, the economy would once again be growing and providing jobs without the need for such (wasteful) budget-inflating expenditures.

This position was taken even though such jobs might be immensely productive in that they might help build or rebuild some vitally useful and desirable community and national structures and infrastructures—bridges, mass transit, highways, sewers, tunnels, etc., many of which are in terrible, even dangerous, condition. Such jobs would also generate taxable income, and reduce public-assistance costs, such as unemployment insurance, welfare, and food stamps. One could also anticipate the less tangible but certainly real benefits that the dignity of a job can give to a jobless member of society.

Surely all of this is consistent with the Reagan administration's stated objectives of increasing production and productivity, putting our nation back to work, rebuilding our infrastructure, and perhaps most important of all, reducing the number of people on the government dole.

One may object that such a jobs program could not be implemented quickly enough to be useful. Yet in 1933–34, when the country was far poorer than it is today, the civil works administration put 4 million people to work on four hundred thousand projects in three months. If we really want to make things happen, we can. Moreover, we might note with some satisfaction that the government-sponsored WPA program created public works that we still enjoy and use today. Is it better to just give handouts and hope for an impending economic improvement that may come far too slowly, and in the process cost far more than is necessary in lost production and in government handout expenditures, or to start the catalytic process that might fire up the economy and bring about more quickly and surely the hoped-for improvement and expansion of the economy and its commensurate increase in job opportunity and productivity? As this book goes to press, President Reagan and Congress are working on putting a jobs program in operation, one that may prove to be too little, too late.

In response to this and many other issues, I wrote this book as an entrepreneur who has had to test economic theory every day in the cauldron of the marketplace, where mistakes are tallied up in millions of dollars. My position at the pivot of change, where invention and technology couple with private enterprise, has given me a privileged perspective on the forces that confirm or undermine economic prediction. My own future hinges on the answers to today's major questions: Can we have growth without inflation, or must we choose one and forgo the other? Can we combine what is best in our system—our economic and political freedom and our zest for innovation—with the best that other systems, including socialist regimes, offer, or at least promise: full employment and at least a minimal level of security?

My answer to both questions is optimistic. I am convinced that if we can identify and offer appropriate incentives, we can achieve, and get others to achieve, almost anything we wish. In the military forces, men risk their lives for medals that symbolize honor, courage, and patriotism. Athletes test the biological limits of the human body for the sake of recognition. Entrepreneurs build theaters and concert halls when given the right economic incentives.

The key is to fix our goals firmly and then decide what is needed to achieve what we want. If we want and need lower interest rates to achieve a true supply-side economic strategy, we must take the actions, and implement the incentives, that will immediately produce this desired effect. If we wish to defeat inflation and achieve a balanced budget and the expectations that come with it, we can set higher taxes on oil, liquor, and cigarettes, while we lower interest rates at the same time in order to encourage supply-side capital.

It need not take long to correct inflation and stagflation, although it took time to create them. I believe in elasticity. In the case of oil, the solution came more rapidly than we expected once we introduced higher prices and a free market—the incentives for conservation, additional exploration and production. The same decisiveness can produce swift results in bringing about the non-inflationary growth we all desire.

With the same foresight, incentives, and precise targeting, we can achieve salutary economic pluralism, too, combining the best of capitalism and socialism, laissez-faire and planning, growth and conservation, self-sufficiency and the security of the welfare safety net. We can combine a public-sector role with private-sector actions. We can transform apparent contradictions into mutually complementary political and economic programs that will make our economy succeed and so achieve a better quality of life for us all.

Part One

ECONOMICS
FOR
EVERYMAN

1

Our Precarious Prosperity

Our generation is caught up in a curious paradox. Our politicoeconomic system is perhaps the most enviable in the world. We force no one to remain within our borders, yet we suffer few defections and (despite all the criticism leveled against us) attract millions. Our workers today are as dedicated as those who once shaped this country out of wild forests and arid plains.

Yet we sense ourselves an endangered species. We seem to be on the brink of an "era of enduring shortages." For almost three-fourths of our population, the Land of Plenty is becoming the Land of Want.[1] The billions spent on defense do nothing to ease our apprehensions. We are haunted by the threat of nuclear destruction. Poisons pollute our rivers, our food, the air we breathe. We have been losing our lead—in productivity, growth, our share of exports, our standard of living, our quality of life. We are no longer Number 1.

Our response to these uncertainties has been a kind of frantic self-indulgence dictated by a short-term psychology and a culture of narcissism. It is reflected in the frenzied, inflationary credit buying—now. It is expressed in union demands for higher wages, pensions, fringe benefits, cost-of-living adjustments—now. Business executives, petulant at the sacrifices needed for long-term growth, fix their sights firmly on the next quarter's earnings.

GO-GO POLITICS AND NO-FAULT ECONOMICS

That short-term perspective has spilled over into our public lives. Presidents act like the go-go managers of yesteryear. Pressured to deliver now, they focus on short-term results. Elected leaders sway with every interest, while voters respond at the level of personal economics: "What's in it for me?"

The typical political leader today reminds you of a dog tugging at a leash, apparently leading its master because it is out in front. We know, of course, that the dog is really only responding, looking back intermittently to get an idea of where its master wants it to go. Similarly, our present leaders also seem to be "up front" yet are not leading any more than that dog is. They fail to demonstrate qualities that might inspire the citizens. They look to the next election, not what is best in the long run. Instead of using incentives to persuade industry to produce in the public interest, they have let business influence government to meet its own needs with highway programs, import quotas, and price supports.

Economists, too, have been guilty of pseudopopulism. Engaging in "no-fault" economics, they deal with the semantics of the problem, letting words rule. "Panic." "Financial crisis." "Recession." "Rolling readjustment." "A slowing of the secular growth trend." "A dip in the ever-rising GNP." "Stagflation." These are the catchwords dealt out in the daily press. By giving the disorder a new and less disturbing label, economists assure the people—the patients—that all is under control. Or, if it is not under control, then it must be accepted as inevitable. To index inflation, for example, is essentially to ratify its inevitability.

Obsessed with the short term, economists concern themselves with this quarter's gross national product (GNP), with this month's unemployment or productivity, with the current consumer or producer price indexes (CPI, PPI) and their impact on votes in upcoming elections. They are literally engaged in the politics of economics.

4

What we need instead are concepts geared to long-term goals, to changes that will permanently improve economic performance as it affects the quality of our lives. For that end to be achieved, economics must undergo a spiritual revival, a revision of its narrow and materialistic premises.

ACHIEVING HAPPY ECONOMICS

Where do we, as a country, want to be when we grow up—when we are 5,000 or 3,000 months (250 years) old? The answer hinges on our visions of where we want to be, on the setting of priorities among these goals, and on the design of alternative routes toward their achievement. It requires us all to ask: "Is what I am doing, or about to do, getting us closer to our objective?"

We want to ensure the Total Possible Satisfaction that the earth can offer: physical health, comfort in old age, self-fulfillment, cleaner air, and energy conservation, as well as full employment, price stability, and growth. We want to end disease, starvation, urban decay, and illiteracy. To achieve these ends we will need, as William James put it, the moral equivalent of war. Ironically, the periods of greatest zeal in pursuing those ends—the Depression, Lyndon Johnson's War on Poverty—ended in, or were accompanied by, war. The Marxists claim that war is the capitalists' only way out of economic depression. Are we doomed to prove them right, or can we muster the same discipline, energy, and capacity for sacrifice to wage war on our problems?

"Ask not what your country can do for you . . ." The reasons for the immediate appeal and lasting resonance of John Kennedy's exhortation are not hard to trace. We don't simply want our material needs provided for. We want to feel that our individual action can and does make a difference to our society. We need to have a sense of what we might be, in order to think best of ourselves as we are.

Witness the pride with which so many of us vote—despite the apparent meaninglessness of our single vote. Witness our behavior during the 1974 Arab boycott, our constructive and cooperative response to no Sunday gasoline, our success in energy conservation, our acquiescence in World War II price fixing, OPA, and rations. Then contrast the Vietnam War, which produced the worst inflation in our history because our leaders said, in effect, "We don't want you to sacrifice butter for guns. Even if you don't have a son going into the service, you may realize that there is a war on, and rebel against a war that is based on a fuzzy ideal, an undefined goal, a mixed commitment and a questionable rationale for our involvement."

Witness what political leaders have done to our army. Proud men once served at meager salaries, sacrificing material rewards and risking life and limb. Now we have neither patriots nor citizen inductees who would take pride in sacrifice. We have created paid mercenaries trained to kill when necessary. Perhaps the next step will be a piecework incentive: X dollars paid for each enemy killed, Y dollars for each one captured.

The propensity to sacrifice illustrates a key economic insight: Cost implies value. It represents what we are willing to give up in order to achieve something better. In fact, a greater cost may imply a greater value.

INCENTIVE PLANNING

The policies that I propose depart from those of both Democratic and Republican administrations. Past administrations have been addicted to transfer payments* and have created disincentives to work, to saving, to productivity, and to competition through subsidies and regulations that maintain income or price security for individuals, business firms, unions, and entire industries. The new Reaganomics, despite its productive challenges to old traditions, has not consistently pursued supply-side economics, relies too heavily on the old inflationary stimuli of accelerated defense spending, and has too strong an ideological commitment to deregulation for its own sake. I believe in competitive capitalism and a strong private sector, but do not see these as incompatible with either planning or the setting of long-term goals. The key to my program is planning through incentive rather than by

* For definitions of this and other specialized terms, see Glossary.

edict—planning that appeals to, but channels, voluntary activity and the impulse of self-interest.

We want to rely on, and preserve, the motives that have made laissez-faire capitalism the miracle of production and productivity it has demonstrated it can be. Under that system, each individual expresses his self-interest and coincidentally, even magically, promotes productivity and the material welfare of all.

Yet we cannot rely on unbridled self-interest alone. Adam Smith's invisible hand assumed self-interest within some minimal moral framework, either self-imposed or imposed by some higher institution like government. It thrived on dedicated labor, a healthy, inexhaustible competitiveness, superior effort, applied intelligence, and original technique.

Today the assumptions of that value framework have become suspect. A value crisis affects our moral and economic life. Corporations often exact exorbitant profits through price fixing, monopoly mergers, payoffs, and corruption of politicians. Professions like the AMA organize against the public interest. We have gun lobbies and defense lobbies. Unions strike for inordinate, damaging, and ultimately self-destructive settlements; police, hospital, transit, and airline workers strike. Union leaders rip off the pension funds they manage; witness the history of the Teamsters' Union.

Departing from Adam Smith's model of controlled self-interest and exuberant, competitive enterprise, our system of structural oligarchy and value anarchy generates new forms of petty cheating, freeloading, profiteering, and tax evasion, new schemes rather than new businesses, gray-flannel gangsters and adventurers rather than dynamic entrepreneurs.

We cannot restore the best features of laissez-faire models simply by eliminating governmental planning or even regulation. Some modification of pure laissez-faire must evolve, as it has in the past, to channel self-interested activity toward socially desirable goals.

Laissez-faire purists may object to government planning, invoking the classic issue of conflict between freedom and totalitarianism. Yet it is not planning but bureaucratic centralization that threatens our freedoms.

The issue of big government reminds me of George Bernard Shaw's famous interchange with a well-known actress. Shaw asked if she would become a certain man's mistress for a fabulous sum. Receiving her affirmative reply, he asked if she would grant the same favor for one pound. "What do you think I am?" she responded indignantly. "Madame," said Shaw, "that has already been established. Now we are merely determining the price."

The question is no longer whether government should influence the economy and the decisions of businessmen and consumers. It does! Through its actions on taxes, energy, investment tax credits, welfare payments, education, and monetary growth, and through its own direct spending on defense, health, education, welfare, and research, government is now by far the greatest influence on the individual and collective behavior of consumers and businessmen. Its actions and decisions create economic events. Its planning is implicit in every budget and every legislative action.

But because planning is perceived as a totalitarian strategy inimical to capitalism, we avoid intelligent and analytic national planning. We plan by default instead of design, without evaluating the impact of our plan, using expedient short-term criteria for arriving at our decisions. So we end up with piecemeal planning and no clear blueprint that establishes what we want to achieve, where we want to be five or ten years from now.

The result is a kind of anarchy that suggests freedom but fails to take into account the fact that we have values, goals, and priorities. Absolute freedom is anarchy; that is why we are organized in societies in the first place. There is no inherent threat in setting goals and monitoring our progress toward them. No skipper would proceed without charting his course, nor would any one expect General Motors to embark on a new venture without planning or design.

In baseball each year, a professional sports team reappraises, evaluates, and asks:

How can we work

    to win
    to build a better team

to do better than last year
to heighten our appeal
to win more fans and attendance
to be more profitable
to develop a system that ensures new talent for future teams'
    good performance
to help fans reach the stadium more easily
to provide tickets at more places
and so on.

Our government might do at least as much. It might ask, just as systematically, and without waiting for crises:
What kinds of planning, what kinds of incentives, are we using

to increase productivity
to achieve profitability
to maintain employment and reduce inflation
to solve our energy problems
to prevent cheating on Medicare
to discourage OPEC extortion
and so on.

If planning is important for a baseball team, it is far more essential to a country when our life styles and survival are at stake.

The philosophy I advocate is simple. Any organization wishing to succeed defines its objectives up front; then it creates a plan of action that tabulates its cash-flow needs, personnel, capital, and so on; finally, it designs into the plan the incentives that will motivate the members of the organization to achieve its objectives. Along the same lines, executive and legislative branches of our government should each appoint a blue-ribbon panel of outstanding citizens to define the nation's short- and long-term goals and priorities. Then the president and Congress can create the best plan to get the country from where it is to where it wants to be by designing the incentives that will induce its businessmen, wage earners, investors, educators, and scientists to get us there.

The closest our system comes to such a rational method is the annual budget. This is sometimes projected out for two, three, or even five years and almost inadvertently introduces different values and objectives. But it does not specifically define for the citizens or their leaders a set of goals and objectives and a program, a plan that all can understand and share and help implement.

Historically, government has dedicated the funds directly to achieving the specific program and carrying it out through a growing, often overwhelming, bureaucracy. The approach I endorse would involve the least government and the greatest leverage through incentives targeted at the private sector, so that the private sector produces the desired end result. Although the setting of goals and plans to fulfill them resembles the approaches of socialist systems, it reduces the government's role to that of designing ideal targeted incentives rather than creating the large budgetary expenditures and enormous bureaucracies that have marked our recent history.

This approach would get the most done with the least government. Not all actions would be positive or all decisions work out perfectly. Some consequences might prove negative. Not everything a president does will make all the people, or even a majority, happy all the time. Long-term interests may be served, and often are, by painful short-term actions. We endure them if we value the goals and believe these steps are needed to reach them.

Nor can we expect government to create an ideal society. "Don't look for happiness," says a character in *Lovers and Other Strangers*. "It will only make you miserable." The same can be said of our economic goals. We need to forget absolutes and abstractions and aspire to realistic goals.

> What is perfection?
> What is really worthwhile?
> What is crucial?
> What is achievable?

These questions set a structure of priorities. We can't satisfy all our desires. Some are even mutually exclusive. So let us concentrate on the more realizable aspirations. Defining goals implies priorities. Once we know what our priorities are, we can, in a world of scarcities, make logical choices that move us closer to achieving what we want most.

If we view our problems realistically, we will also recognize the assets we can bring to their analysis and solution. We are one of the most literate nations in history. And since knowledge is a major, perhaps the most important, ingredient in coping with problems, in inventing new technologies and products, and in discovering new cures, we can surely achieve a better quality of life.

ECONOMICS: INSIGHT OR MYSTIFICATION?

One of the first steps to take in analyzing our problems is to review, with some skepticism, the tools so popular today in the politics of economics. Government officials constantly invoke economic principles. We are lectured on the tradeoff between inflation and unemployment. Interest-rate policy makes front-page headlines. Yet can we judge which tradeoff is inevitable, and which is a backhand justification of policies that don't work? Can we say what the government's monetary policy does to the average person's wallet? Or why, in the face of our favorite economic theories, we have incessant stagflation?

We are told to equate economic health with our gross national product—our total output of goods and services as defined or validated solely by their dollar value. Rarely are we asked to question the composition of the GNP, to inquire what its activities contribute to our quality of life, or to ask which aspects of production have increased—aircraft, armaments, alcohol, tobacco, barbiturates, energy guzzlers, polluters? Perhaps producing less is sometimes better. A few economists have been measuring "net economic welfare" to gauge our quality of life. They deserve a better hearing.

We are given contradictory prescriptions for identical policy outcomes. Experts, who hardly agree among themselves, ask laymen to believe—at the same time—that a tight money supply will raise interest rates, and a loose money supply will raise inter-

11

est rates. Both explanations have been reported in the newspapers. We are told that increased demand will raise prices, and that increased demand will lower prices. Each of these statements is true at times, but which works when? Our experts and journalists fool us by citing only one effect and by ignoring feedback relationships.

We need to strip away the mysticism that lies behind these statements and behind political statistics from the unemployment rate and the Phillips curve, the inflation rate and the Laffer curve, to the gross national product and our measures of productivity. We need better insights into basic economic concepts and processes and the way governments interact to impede or change these processes.

Economics is useful because it permits us to explain a great variety of phenomena with a small number of simple concepts. But when these concepts are used inconsistently, the validity of economics itself is challenged and its usefulness impaired. Our economic soothsayers quantify what can't be quantified and make predictions about what cannot be foreseen. They have predicted nine of the last four recessions.

Economics can never be an exact science because it is rooted in human behavior, and in the infinite number of variables that affect individuals as they go about running the business that is their lives. It rests on human expectations, which are often self-fulfilling prophecies; on basic needs for clothing, food, shelter, and medicine; on fear and confidence; on feelings of progress, self-esteem, and self-realization; on work and hyperactivity; dependence and magnanimity; aggressiveness; anger at unfulfilled promises; cooperation and competition; caring.

Yet economics does not wend its way wherever it will. We know that alternative inputs produce probable—that is, predictable—alternative outputs. The high probability of a certain outcome suggests policies to be pursued, actions to be initiated to produce desired end results. We can expect neither absolute certainty nor quick and easy solutions; but we can anticipate some positive, predictable outcomes.

Because economics can be simple and logical, the ideas presented here will suggest certain solutions and modes of government and business behavior to the reader. Many, I believe, will (though they need not) concur with my own solutions. Some of my ideas will seem so self-evident that one wonders why they have not long since been made doctrine. Perhaps presenting any subject in its simplest format is not in the interest of those who have the exclusive license—via their complex language of specially defined words and constructions, formulas, graphs, and charts—to control it and to serve as its high priests, enjoying a kind of transcendental power over the rest of us. Economists, politicians, and political economists fall into this category.

Economics is like a chess game. It involves nothing absolutely new. But it requires the application of judgment, brilliance, insights, energy, dedication, experience, knowledge, feel, anticipation, courage, forcefulness, and timing to bring about the desired result. In chess and in economics, the tools and actions are limited; it is the timing and the sequence of actions that make the difference between challenge and boredom, victory and bungling defeat. This is true regardless of whether the players are capitalists, communists, socialists, or opportunists.

Economics is a game whose players and actions should be familiar to the public. In spectator sports, as in politics and international affairs, we deal with the motivation for action, the exciting surface sequences. Rewards for other activities—for example, the work of the Nobel Prize winners—cannot compete with the salaries of athletes, movie stars, or TV news commentators, partly because the sequence of their actions can't be simplified for showing on TV as a continuing competitive or artistic contest. If economists could show the fumbles and recoveries, the errors and home runs, the performance and dedication, knowledge and wisdom, the slow and artful discovery of the minutest clues, the articulation of details, step by step, in an unfolding mystery, then they might command the same interest, financial rewards, and vast following that public idols enjoy.

But economics is far more than a spectator sport. Whether we have less poverty, clearer air, good health, sufficient energy, whether we can attain the quality of life we need, all depend on its evolution, decisions, and outcomes. Knowing its insights and its limitations, analyzing its concepts and data, understanding the way its theories are used and abused, can help us regain some sense of control over our lives and the confidence and wisdom to plan the world we want.

NOTE

1. "Worry about rent and upkeep," (May 1974–April 1979) ". . . Our Wealth Is Limited" (1979), ". . . Age of Enduring Shortages" (1974–1978), "Land of Plenty . . . Land of Want" (1979), all Yankelovich, Skelly & White; Daniel Yankelovich, *Economic Policy and the Question of Political Will,* New York, Public Agenda Foundation, February 14, 1980, 42.

2

An Economic Primer

The central economic issue of our time is whether our system of free choice can work as the basis of a political order. Since the Depression, the survival of capitalism itself has rested on the development of planned economies. Yet much of our planning has been haphazard and inconsistent, bureaucratic yet piecemeal, and incapable of solving the incompatibilities of inflation and depression.

These problems are the subject of this book as a whole. In this chapter, I emphasize three economic concepts that should shape our public policies: scarcity, equilibrium, and marginality. Our central values of justice, equality, and freedom rest on scarcity—the central question of economics. How should scarce goods be distributed among the members of a society and by whose authority? The notion of equilibrium also has political overtones because the inherent instability of these equilibrium states in a free-market system is what has prompted economic planning. Finally, the concept of marginality shows how very small changes can have overwhelming consequences. Targeted incentive planning, which is based on marginality, is my alternative to the coercive planning that has characterized public policy in the contemporary "mixed" political economy.

Scarcity was hardly discovered by the Club of Rome, that group of social scientists whose report on limits to growth, because of the natural limitation of resources, shocked the sixties generation. Economics by definition has always dealt with shortages, limits to growth, and the alternative uses of scarce resources: how they are to be employed, how conserved, to whom distributed. The sudden "discoveries" resulting from the energy crisis and the Rome group's concern with limits to growth merely lend new urgency to a fundamental concern in economics.

Scarcity is the pivot of economic theory. Without it we would have no economic science—no issues of supply and demand, no prices, no study of alternatives, no inflation or depression. Without it we could hardly distinguish between political systems, since such systems differ mainly in the way they legislate the distribution of scarce goods: through state rationing and planning, or through the economic "votes" (dollars) of consumers, or through a combination of the two.

Our own society answers these policy questions largely in terms of the free market or free-choice system. Each day, individuals and businesses engage voluntarily in economic activities, buying and selling in markets that respond to consumers' wishes and needs as expressed in their dollar "votes." As consumers vote in millions of transactions, they direct resources toward the products and services they demand.

The free market is the sum of these countless independent decisions. It works because each consumer through his votes decides what will be produced, at what price, and in what quantities. His interests, meshing with the producer's self-interest, determine investment and output. The miracle of their coordination creates economic equilibrium. Their failure to mesh produces disequilibrium and havoc.

AN UNEASY BALANCE

Economists are addicted to the notion of equilibrium—an ideal theoretical state in which supply and demand are balanced by the mechanism of prices. High prices result in a surplus of unbought goods; the seller must either cut back on production or lower prices. Low prices lure customers who flood the market and bid prices up until a new equilibrium is reached at a higher price level. Eventually markets are balanced (or "cleared") so that no surpluses or shortages of goods or of labor remain.

Not all kinds or levels of equilibrium are ideal. The monopolist's maximum-profit equilibrium is exploitive, and Keynes blasted classical economics by demonstrating an underemployment equilibrium.[1] Yet many theorists hold to the notion of a self-correcting economic system with a tendency toward equilibrium—i.e., stability, rather than change—at levels of full production and full employment. That is, any deviation from full employment will be impermanent, because it will generate processes (for example, lower labor costs and lower prices, with their impact on increased labor and product demand) that cause the system to revert to the full-employment, full-production level.

At least in the long run. But in the long run, as Keynes said, we are all dead. In the meanwhile, fluctuations every day suggest that we are out of synch as often as we are in equilibrium. For *dis*equilibrium is inherent in all systems at all times. Invention and technology produce change that will uproot segments of the work force before they adjust and move to new industries. Nor can full employment be maintained more than briefly. For at that point, the purchasing power, confidence, and optimism generated by full employment increase demand and spur borrowing, producing even greater demand. At full employment levels, when output can no longer increase to accommodate these pressures, prices are inevitably driven up.

The classic example of this instability is the situation of farmers who overproduce. Each farmer decides independently to expand his crop to ensure high profits if, for example, this year's shortage has driven prices up. Yet the farmers' individual but cumulative decisions to grow a given crop at a given time create an inevitable oversupply that may even produce losses, so that the crop hardly seems worth growing again. Then a new cycle starts in which the crop will diminish in quantity, the price rise again, and the profits once more become attractive.

Similarly, in the full-production economy, a surge in capital investment (as in 1955–57 and 1964–72) will produce excess capacity, and the resulting profit squeeze will kill off private investment. "Any attempt to accumulate capital beyond the rate required by the annual growth in output will soon be unsuccessful."[2] Yet how can each investor making a separate decision know exactly how much capital accumulation or investment will meet the "rate required by the annual growth in output"? Given the sheeplike nature of most decision making, all investors will expand simultaneously at the peak of demand, when the outlook is buoyant and capacity obviously inadequate.

Like farmers who overproduce, these private investors or decision makers respond all at once to the same external stimuli, often achieving the opposite of what is needed and what they anticipate. The effort to relieve an apparent shortage creates excess capacity as investors move separately but simultaneously to satisfy demand. This is the fallacy of composition: what is true for the part, or the individual, may be false for the whole. Hence the old Wall Street adage: "When everybody is bullish [optimistic], it's time to sell."

In this sequence of events, whether it is soybeans or capital that is involved, an excess at one end of the range produces a reaction that moves toward the other extreme. These oscillations produce disequilibrium—the cycles of inflation, shortages, and underinvestment on the one hand; and of depression, oversupply, and unemployment on the other.

Disequilibrium is the major sin in economics, a source of pain and deprivation to members of the economic system. Inflation can be seen as one form of disequilibrium, the result of too much money chasing too few goods with attendant rising prices. Depression is another. It occurs when production outpaces consumer demand. The ensuing glut of inventory, curtailed business activity, and reduced need for labor grind employment and demand down to the final condition of depression.[3]

Inflation and depression are both imbalances. *Both* result in curtailed activity, rising unemployment, and diminished savings for the vast majority. Depression is immediately visible, hence easily responded to. The disequilibrium of inflation is less obvious since it occurs at full employment, when the economy seems healthiest. In fact, it may at first lead to more employment, higher sales, unreal higher wages, and confidence—to a sense of progress. But it is a brief and illusory euphoria. As the devastating German inflation of 1923 showed, the declining credibility of the currency erodes buying power and chokes confidence, damping business activity and creating vast unemployment.

Although the most severe depressions and inflations affect entire economies or nations, other forms touch only one sector of one economy. Some minor imbalance always exists in the economic system. It may be caused by a strike making a given product temporarily unavailable; by wages rising faster than prices, or vice versa; or by an external event, like the embargo of a vitally needed import or an inordinate rise in the price of energy. A drought in the farm belt may cause a shortage of wheat or feed and/or cattle, and thus the need for some to do without. Generally, the negative effects of these small imbalances are limited and temporary; the free-market price adjustment usually leads promptly to a new equilibrium of production and consumption.

This is not to suggest that minor imbalances cause no damage. Clearly they do, and the poorest and weakest segment of the population is deprived of essential goods. But the damage is limited in numbers and duration.

It is often the bunching of these small imbalances that produces the major disequilibrium of inflation or depression. A series of strikes or of wage hikes trying to catch rising prices (or vice versa) in several industries may propel the entire system into galloping inflation or spark the ultimate explosion of prices, ensuring the destruction of the currency, and the final crash of depression. The steep rise in oil prices and energy costs shows how a disequilibrium in one sector of the world economy can produce a major upheaval with its broad and devastating consequences.

THE PARADOX OF OVERPRODUCTION

Depression, the frightening halt of business and employment, presents a major theoretical paradox. By definition, if even one member of society is forcibly unemployed, it implies that society requires nothing more for him to produce, that all its needs must already be satisfied. It implies utopia.

Yet we all know that this logic is absurd and perverse. Society

always has a list of essential and unfulfilled needs, products needed but not being produced: decent housing, better water and sew-
erage systems, more medical schools and laboratories, upgraded
capital-goods facilities, modern and efficient mass transportation.
An "oversupply" of labor, or "excess" output, cannot be plausibly
rationalized even if output exceeds demand. For while overproduction seems to prevail, *under*production" exists simultaneously, in view of society's myriad unmet needs.

And that is precisely the case. The paradox of overproduction is
that society as a whole (and thus its members to varying degrees)
always has a substantial list of unmet needs that increased employment might help fulfill. Yet our "free choice" system, at least in
the short term, often creates an imbalance whereby too much of a
product that is not needed—that is, for which no demand exists—is produced, while some needed products are not produced.
It is this mismatch of production and allocation, and not excess
productivity, that creates "overproduction." It is a mismatch, and
not a labor surplus, that creates unemployment. We have a hint of
this mismatch in our help-wanted ads. Even when unemployment
is high, large numbers of jobs always go begging.

PLANNED AND FREE-CHOICE SYSTEMS

Since disequilibrium is the major threat to our economic system, our political leaders should be alert to the need to anticipate
and prevent these shocks and imbalances. If we cannot eliminate
simultaneous under- and overproduction, we can at least enhance
productivity and minimize the waste of labor—a resource that,
once not used, is irretrievably lost.

But our options are limited under our "free choice" system of
production, distribution, and consumption. Once we leave decisions about what to produce, inventory, and buy to individual
choice, we must tolerate some unpredictability. We cannot
achieve absolute equilibrium, if indeed any system can. Sometimes a producer, despite his best judgment, even after using extensive market research and other authoritative scientific
measures, will produce far more than the market requires. He will

be forced to adjust and retrench, or else suffer failure and perhaps bankruptcy. And cutting back usually means layoffs, though layoffs were certainly not among his intentions.

Communist or socialist regimes seem at first glance to be better equipped to solve these problems because of their tighter control and detailed planning of product prices and capital investment. In a planned economy, what is produced, distributed, and consumed is bureaucratically defined and dictated, along with each man's corresponding job training and employment. A central bureau decides and schedules just how much of every item people will consume in a lifetime, from baby nipples and TV sets to caskets and everything along the way. It also plans capital goods, from the smallest nuts and bolts to the machine oil that greases them, as well as agricultural products and every form of food grown and processed. Then, of course, after deciding what to produce, and how much and where and when, the central bureau still has to tell each one what work he has to do and when, and of course where he will live, too, and when and how and at what wage, so as to realize this perfectly planned production. The Soviet Union seems to have come closest to such a system.

Yet by what rationale can one argue that a government bureaucracy is better able to make these decisions and meet consumer's needs, much less assure absolute economic equilibrium? It is not necessarily in a position to make better estimates of market demand (especially without market-determined prices). The room for error is enormous. The most meticulous planning will still create periods of over- and/or underproduction with their attendant dislocations. No one can achieve an economic utopia. The nature of the economic disease may differ in planned societies, but similar, if not greater, disruptions are bound to occur. The recent Polish upheavals bear ample witness to that truth, and so do the continual Soviet grain shortages.

Finally, any Soviet success in controlling inflation or unemployment has been bought at the price of curtailed consumer (and even industrial) goods; of food shortages, of bottlenecks and massive bureaucratic red tape, and, perhaps most important, of freedom: political freedom, freedom to choose one's career or move

21

geographically, to vote with one's spending power for consumer products, to select one's daily behavior and life style.

Under our free-choice arrangement, the producer is at least driven by a more urgent imperative—the need to make the best possible decision for fear of failure as well as hope of success. He has something real to lose if he fails: his savings, investment, time, energy, and reputation. If he succeeds, he has something tangible to gain, in the way of profits and growth, that bears a *direct* relationship to his planning. A bureaucracy, lacking these rewards or penalties, cannot instill the same individual motivation to avoid waste, be efficient, aim at as precise an estimate of market demand as is humanly possible, and thus most effectively supply the wants and needs of society.

In the same way, any distributor, wholesaler, or retailer has the strongest possible motivation to determine what inventory to purchase and stock. His entire enterprise rests on that judgment. By definition, he wants to maximize his successes, minimize his failures, enhance his productivity, and increase the number on his payroll—in short, to expand.

Finally, the consumer cherishes his free choice. He prefers to decide, even whimsically at times, what he wants to buy, and when, where, how, and from whom.

In this way, as Adam Smith demonstrated in his classic analysis, each man acting in his selfish interest brings about what is best for all. Few Americans—producers, distributors, consumers, employees, or even "unemployees"—would exchange our free-choice system, with all its imperfections, for the economically secure but sterile alternative. If what each person desires or needs were planned for him, we might come closer to the full-employment equilibrium. But hardly anyone would be inclined to exert himself to achieve a desired life style, since he could not choose it through his own purchases. And without this incentive and exertion, even full employment would be accompanied by lower productivity, and probably, therefore, less total output as well, with a commensurately lower standard of living.

A totally planned system provides no feasible solution to our economic disruptions. The comprehensive and detailed programming of central planning must invariably go wrong. It attempts to deal with too many factors at once. In fact, the diffuse global strategies that have characterized our own social and economic policies share this defect.

By contrast, the planning I recommend consists in setting a group of targeted and ordered long-term goals and priorities, then generating the incentives that will impel us all to achieve them. This targeted approach would analyze each macro disequilibrium into its components, then address legislation and policies to each component, the small strategic differences that create imbalances in the first place. This sharply focused approach applies the logic of the margin.

MARGINALITY: THE ARITHMETIC OF ECONOMICS

Economics is based as much on *marginality* as it is on *scarcity*. Just as economic concepts would be irrelevant if goods existed in limitless abundance, so, too, there would be little need to understand economics if marginality did not affect prices, wages, hiring, and product availability, and hence our life styles.

What do I mean by "marginality"? I refer to that small degree, that slim extra margin, *above or below some amount that would theoretically (or in reality) result in a perfect balance, or equilibrium of supply and demand, of production and consumption, of availability and need.* The margin is the source of the disequilibrium. It may be that 1 percent (or a fraction thereof) of beef production that the consumer wants but that the farmer has not raised or brought to market. It may be that 1 percent of the engineering work force that industry needs but finds unavailable.

Like life-sustaining equipment (kidney machines, for example) whose limited availability determines life and death for patients, the small, sometimes infinitesimal, margin often has an impact far out of proportion to its slight absolute or relative quantity. It is that one extra person who climbs aboard an already crowded lifeboat and by that small incremental change causes all to drown. It is the proverbial straw that breaks the camel's back. At some strategic point, a minute quantitative change affects the entire configuration of events and produces disproportionate qualitative changes. It may have enormous, even world-shaking, impact.

Consider the price of sugar between 1973 and 1974. The total shortfall in production was slight (only about 7 percent in the United States and less than 3 percent in world production), and there never really was a genuine shortage, if one allows for what was stored in warehouses and so on. Yet the multiplier effect was enormous. Retail prices for sugar almost quintupled, while world sugar futures prices jumped from about $6\frac{1}{2}$ cents to 66 cents a pound—an elevenfold (1,100 percent) increase. Companies and housewives panicked, buying and hoarding all they could lay their hands on. Supermarkets were emptied.[4] A number of commodity firms, including the Sugar Exchange in Paris, went bankrupt. The cost of candy bars, ice cream, cake all skyrocketed. These were hardly sweet times for users or consumers of sugar, and all because of a shortage of less than 5 percent. Why?

The reason is that as any shortage, however small, develops, the first one who cannot get the commodity offers a bit more to obtain it. (In this case, increased demand in oil-producing countries sharpened the effects of that slim shortage.) The next person also offers a bit more, in an endless bidding contest that magnifies many times the dimensions of the actual shortage. The suppliers are of course quick to respond to opportunity and adjust their prices to the highest the market will bear. And generally, for fear that the shortage may get worse and may last longer (a fear often encouraged, of course, by suppliers), people buy and store more than they use or need and thus create an even greater immediate shortage and greater price rise.

Stock-market transactions also show the impact of changes on the margin. Each day only about one-tenth of 1 percent of all stocks available for trading on the New York Stock Exchange actually changes hands. In April 1980, an average 32.1 million shares were traded each day out of a potential 30.8 billion. Yet the value of the securities for *all* shareowners was determined by these activities of a very small marginal group holding a slim proportion of the available securities.

Marginality is the great secret of economics. It is the reason why programs succeed and fail. It is the reason why the OPEC countries have been able to demand and get exorbitant prices— over $30 a barrel of oil for the Saudis. Oil costs perhaps 50 cents a barrel to extract from the earth and exists in such abundance in the ground, for them and for others, that the OPEC countries could choke on it, or drown in it, were it not for their brilliant perception: to control the amount available to the West (a feat achieved by cooperation with others) by gearing production *to a margin just below the amount we have learned to depend on,* thus increasing our dependence upon them.

If we could truly grasp that simple economic insight, we could solve many problems of inflation and depression. We have begun to through conservation, taxes on oil, products to reduce consumption, or even direct rationing—that is, by using a margin of oil just below what the OPEC countries have come to *depend* on exporting, and on whose profits they have come to rely. This is the lesson the OPEC countries are finally learning.

To know economics, to understand economics, is to understand marginality and work with it vigorously and decisively. One often hears—and from expert government economic advisers who influence our daily lives—that if we cut the national budget to eliminate the deficit, the consumer price index will go down less than 2 percent by the end of the year. This nonsense stems from failure to take account of the multiplier effect of a marginal increase or reduction in the budget, of the enormous ensuing and accelerating impact it can have once the expectations of the members of society are influenced by that small marginal shift. The leverage in marginal economics is geometric.

If we could grasp the impact of the margin of a small, albeit even temporary, surplus in the government budget, as against a deficit, we could appreciate its role in helping to check inflation. A small change would have a great multiplier effect. It would immediately result in the government's spending less than it takes in in revenues. Thus, the government could immediately stop creating the money that it must in order to spend more than it takes in. This slim margin would immediately reduce the government's demands for goods and services and would stabilize, or, more likely, deflate the prices of these products. It would reduce government's demand for labor and personnel, deflating the wage scale. It would reduce government's insatiable demands on the credit markets, permitting interest rates to drop, hence cutting businesses' costs of money, which go into every product and service, and which have the multiplier effect, through the traditional markup that every businessman practices, of increasing prices by far more than the increase in interest rates. Lower interest rates would themselves have a multiplier effect and push prices down.

Marginality is the extra interest we presumably must pay to get the foreigner to invest, or rather, lend, his money here so that the dollar will be stronger. If we want a stronger dollar we should *not* simply pay more interest, which only requires us to print more dollars to pay that interest and in the long run actually weakens the dollar. If we feel we must get the Europeans or Japanese or Arabs to put their money into dollars by offering higher interest, let us simply pay that premium to targeted groups and not push up all interest rates for everyone, generating inflation for everyone, when we want only a marginal change. You don't use a nuclear bomb to capture two criminals holed up in an apartment.

The margin applies to unemployment policy as well. If the government finds that black youth unemployment is far too high, as indeed it seems to be, then it should address that margin of our unemployed. It should not try to produce so great a demand for labor that it finally absorbs unskilled, untrained, sometimes unreliable and even unwilling workers. If it should use such an imprecise macroeconomic approach rather than a targeted approach to a specified group, it would generate great demand for goods and services as well as for labor, propelling higher and accelerating wages for those already employed, along with the higher prices and inflation that are likely to result from such a government program—and without even assuring achievement of the goal.

Much of our social spending ignores the logic of the margin. In public spending, one reaches a margin of diminishing returns—ultimately, even negative returns—where the incremental investment (funds spent) does more damage than good. Welfare payments, carried beyond the point of mitigating acute want, produce a subsidized dependent class, and act as a disincentive to

26

those who might otherwise find useful employment. By giving buying power without increasing output, they generate an upward push on prices. Price supports extend depression policies into inflationary periods in which they are not only inapplicable but disastrous. Inflation indexing aggravates the condition through exaggerated adjustments to minor and unrepresentative changes.

The result has been not only inflation on an unprecedented scale but the combined disequilibriums of inflation and unemployment (a very real kind of depression), two conditions that we always thought counteracted each other. So ingrained is this new pattern in our economic system that we tally up a "misery index"—the sum of the rates of unemployment and inflation. To this condition, as the next chapters will show, each aspect of government spending has made its distinct contribution. And, for all of Reagan's efforts, the end is not yet in sight.

NOTES

1. See chapter 6.

2. Paul Samuelson, *Economics,* 11th ed., New York: McGraw Hill, 1979, p. 698.

3. My language here departs somewhat from textbook terminology, which does not define inflation or depression as disequilibriums. As noted above (page 17), Keynes posited an underemployment, or depression, equilibrium. The implication of classical economics and Say's law (chapter 6), however, is that unemployment and recession are disequilibriums because they are impermanent. The long-term equilibrium is one of full employment, while price signals serve as a self-correcting check on the disequilibrium of inflation. This is the perspective described on pages 16–17, which stresses the role of market-determined price changes in clearing markets—that is, maintaining the balance of supply and demand, the absence of surplus or shortages, that constitute economic equilibrium.

4. "Why Sugar Prices Are Zooming," *Business Week,* November 16, 1974, p. 113; *Wall Street Journal,* November 5, 1973, p. 36; November 22, 1974, p. 32, U.S. Bureau of the Census, *Statistical Abstract of the United States,* 1981, 102nd edition, Washington, D.C.: U.S. Government Printing Office, 1981, Table 1235, 692.

3

Structured Inflation: The New Poverty

Inflation has swung loose from the business cycle to become rooted in our economic system. Even in the trough of recession, the mere hint of recovery is enough to trigger our inflationary fears, although, logically, inflation was supposed to set in only as we approach peak capacity. Trouble is, "peak capacity" is no longer what it used to be. Government has tampered with its definition through policies of planned scarcity, undermining the competitive conditions that would tend to push prices down. Instead of mediating between capital and labor, sellers and buyers, it has operated in the interests of a variety of sellers. In effect, it has been in the same business as unions and monopolies. In this chapter, I explain some of the reasons why.

Suppose you sat down for lunch and the menu indicated your order would cost $20. Then, because an inflationary rise while you were eating pushed its price up, you were presented with a bill for $50 rather than the $20 you expected.

That's what happened in the legendary German inflation of 1923. Between 1913 and 1923, currency in circulation increased from 6,000 million to 92 trillion marks, or 15,300 times. From a base of 1 in July 1914, the wholesale price index moved to 2,785 in January 1923, to 194,000 by July, and to an unbelievable 726,000,000,000 by November. The price of coffee, or a few rolls, or a coat, often doubled in an hour; a loaf of bread cost 200 billion marks. People had to lug baskets of currency to buy simple necessities. Years later, the dread of another hyperinflation impelled the German government to insist on deflationary measures in a period of high unemployment. By thus increasing unemployment in a time of depression, it laid the ground for even worse social unrest, so that Germany's old, cultivated middle class, which had been ravaged by inflation, became a breeding ground for Nazism. [1]

Inflation is not always catastrophic. If its growth is slow and consistent, hence predictable, it does little damage to the economy, except perhaps to retired persons on fixed pensions. Businessmen can still plan expansion and estimate their capital needs and costs.

Inflation is as old as currency; it has been a recurring theme in American history. The American Revolution was launched on a flood of paper money. Andrew Jackson's battle with the banks, the Greenbacks issued during the Civil War, the free-silver controversy—all reflect our fears of inflation and the eternal conflict between debtors and creditors. The 1930s Depression desensitized us to the problems of inflation, but it has taken top priority since the late 1960s, as "creeping" inflation became "jogging," then "galloping," and finally, soaring or orbiting, inflation. In 1966 irate housewives picketed food stores across the country. In 1971 an inflation rate of only 5 percent impelled Nixon to abandon his laissez-faire, noninterventionist approach. Solemnly announcing, "I am now a Keynesian," Nixon resorted to wage-price controls that ultimately let prices run away faster when they were lifted in 1973. Since 1973, the oil embargo and mounting energy costs have brought on double-digit inflation. Until 1979, Americans could console themselves that their real earning power was still rising, despite inflation and declining GNP growth; since that date they can no longer afford that rationalization.

Not all work groups have been affected by inflation in the same way. The rich have had capital as well as earnings losses, as securities, especially bond prices, have plummeted while the interest, already eaten up by inflation, has been taxed. Middle-class professionals have endured both inflation and tax-bracket creep. Families with incomes from $10,000 to $25,000 spend 70 percent of their income on necessities like food, housing, health care, and energy, items that have gone up nearly half again as much as the consumer price index itself. Inflation, however, has helped those whose income is *completely* indexed to the price level: military and federal retirees, unionized workers whose contracts are completely indexed to the price level and who have had substantial wage increases in the 1970s, and Social Security beneficiaries.[2]

In this new age of anxiety, people have lost faith in their destiny, in the dream of mobility, in the ability of government to control events. That anxiety gnaws at all levels of the social structure. Capital investors avoid taking risks because of the unpredictability of their efforts. The gains of wage earners and managers are washed away. "Middle-class altruism," the sponsorship on which most social reform ultimately rests, is destroyed in the quest for financial stability. As savers lose and spenders profit, the notion spreads that those who adhere to American values are being cheated. The result can be vulnerability to totalitarianism, with its spurious promise of a solution.

THE GILT-EDGED RIPOFF

What is inflation? Better still, what causes inflation?

Inflation historically has been described as too many dollars chasing too few goods, forcing prices up without increasing the supply. So what? If all the players were the same and each got his hands on more dollars in amounts proportionate to those he had before, there might be little damage above the need to deal in larger numbers and perhaps carry more currency or larger denominations around.

But the players do change. Older people must leave the work force. Dependent on their painfully accumulated nest eggs, they watch their savings disappear through an invisible confiscation. These citizens, the backbone of our economic system, spent their lives believing, as they were encouraged to, that by working and by diligently hoarding whatever earnings they did not need for their immediate needs or desires, they could store this delayed purchasing power in the form of dollars, U.S. Treasuries, or savings accounts, in so-called "riskless" investments, to assure them a reasonable, if not exciting, retirement.

Let us analyze a specific case. Mr. George Frazier, now retired, lives in Arizona with his wife. In 1974, at age sixty-one, finding himself in weakened health, he sold the small Massachusetts superette that he and his wife had been running, from early morning to late evening, for almost twenty-five years. He received $60,000 for his inventory and goodwill. That sum, along with $90,000 that he and his wife had laid aside for their old age, was their nest egg, the reward for some forty years of hard work and good citizenship. Moving to their new home, which they bought for $30,000, they were left with $120,000. A nice sum in 1974.

Since this fund represented all they would have to live on in their remaining years, they were advised to buy risk-free, long-term U.S. Treasury bonds with a 6 percent yield. This would assure them an income of $7,200 a year for twenty-five years till 1999, when the bonds would mature. Since they had paid for their home in cash, the $7,200 a year ($140 a week) seemed more than adequate.

Let us freeze the camera in early 1980. The Fraziers find themselves scrimping and scraping, even with Social Security payments to supplement their savings. Worse still, they ask themselves, what if our buying power continues to fall? Where will we be in a year, or two years, three years? The inflation rate had averaged about 6.6 percent a year from 1975 on (after a spell of double-digit inflation in 1974); in 1980 it climbed to 18 percent.

To add to their misery, they find, as they try to cash in some bonds to meet their current needs, that current bond yields are much higher. As a result, the bonds they bought for $120,000 are worth only about 60 cents on the dollar if they are not held to maturity. (They will be worth even less by mid-1981.) Since any lender wants an interest return on his investment that will protect his buying power against inflation and yield some moderate return (about 3 percent above the prevailing inflation rate), Mr. Frazier, to compete with current interest rates, must offer his bonds to yield at least 12 percent. This reduces their value to only $600 per bond, or $72,000.

What a ripoff! The U.S. government, which seemed the safest place for his irreplaceable funds, sold him $120,000 in "gilt-edged" bonds whose guarantee made him believe he would have $120,000 in buying power whenever he might need it. Instead, he can get back only 60 percent, or $72,000. To make things worse, that $72,000 investment is itself worth less than 61.5 cents on the dollar in terms of present purchasing power—or $44,280. Inflation has reduced his 1974 $120,000 nest egg to a value of $44,280.

Surely no one believing in the equity of our political system could have planned such a scenario. How did this uncontrollable inflation come about? We look at the unfolding process and answer:

> too much demand, too little supply
> or vice versa—too much credit availability
> too little productivity
> too large a federal budget deficit
> too many excessive wage increases, or price increases
> too many shortages
> too large a money supply

All of the above are true. But saying that hardly answers the question and provides few clues on how to avoid or ease inflation.

STAGFLATION: SELLERS' WELFARE

Theoretically, a price increase can be a self-correcting mechanism, readjusting supply and demand. Unless it is made to widen a profit margin, it is really an antidote, a form of rationing that produces a new equilibrium. It is a warning that either demand should be reduced or supply increased—preferably the latter. In this case inflation functions as an economic stimulus. *Only when neither demand nor supply is affected by the price rise does inflation persist, accelerate, and become a disease.*[3] How does this happen?

The reason is that the rules of the economic game have changed. It used to be that as labor demand slowed and unemployment increased, wage rates also declined or leveled off. With lower labor costs, demand for labor increased to create a new equilibrium at close to full employment levels. This self-correcting process was almost an iron law of economics.

Yet in the 1970s, despite unemployment mounting to 7, 8, and over 9 percent, negotiated wage rates continued to rise. In 1976 and 1977, increases in real wages matched or exceeded increases in 1965 and 1966, though unemployment was almost twice as high as it had been. Even in the first half of 1980, first-year wage settlements in major labor contracts were 8.5 percent, not including cost-of-living raises and fringe benefits that would likely bring these to 10 percent a year.[4] Only in 1981 did these demands finally show signs of leveling off, reverting to the classical pattern.

The same with prices. Theoretically, prices should never rise. If demand for one's product decreases, one should (assuming demand elasticity) adjust prices downward to stimulate additional demand, producing a new supply-demand equilibrium at a lower price level. If, on the other hand, total demand increases for one's product, then surely no price increase is necessary, for with increased sales, unit costs will come down and profits increase at the same price level. Economic logic suggests even more—that increased demand will provide a reason for lowering prices of manufactured products.

Yet what happens is the opposite. When demand increases, producers don't pass on the savings from increased production. Instead, they take advantage of the increased demand and raise prices to enhance their profits; so that when high unemployment should push down demand, prices continue to soar. Producers administer prices instead of lowering them to stimulate demand as a means of regenerating profits. They bring prices to ever higher levels to maintain or increase their revenues and profits. Then fewer unit sales are needed to cover the fixed overhead and meet the profit objective. Everyone wants the same revenue, or even more, for less output. So the operable proposition becomes: prices will *always* rise, whether demand is up or down.

The same logic applies to inflation. The classic view was that inflation was produced by too many dollars—too much demand—chasing too few goods. Inflation could occur, however, only when the economy's productive plant operated at full capacity or profitability. At levels below capacity, increased demand could be satisfied with increased output at constant prices that would still enhance total profits. When supply could *not* be increased, prices would go up to ration demand, creating a new demand-supply equilibrium. At this point prices would again stabilize, and inflation would be halted.

Economists today, however, say that we are not suffering from demand-pull inflation, because the economy is *not* working at full capacity. Demand *could* be met with existing plant, equipment, and labor. Since the supply side is not fully used, inflation must stem from some other cause.

According to the "cost-push" theory, higher costs are pushing prices up. As the costs to industry of wages and materials increase, they must be passed along in higher prices. Union pressure may force up money wages beyond increases in labor productivity, necessitating either a profit squeeze or a price hike; or unions and corporations, which are both large enough to influence the market rather than be governed by it, may be administering prices. The rising costs of oil and other raw materials have also played an important part in this trend. Where labor was largely the factor behind price increases in 1970–71, food shortages produced the severe 1972–73 and 1977–79 inflations, and energy costs have been prominent factors since 1973.[5]

This situation seems theoretically different from the classical definition of excess demand raising prices. Yet if demand did not persist for the goods at the higher price, the new price could not be sustained; or, if it were sustained, fewer and fewer goods would be sold at that price. Rising costs alone could not raise prices if people did not have the dollars to bid up the prevailing supply. Cost-push inflation can take place only under conditions that are consistent with the classical economist's definition of demand exceeding supply at prevailing prices. The classical, well-thought-out, and still rational theory seems to hold.

What is not explained, nevertheless, is how the condition can exist—the paradox of rising prices in the face of unused capacity; the persistence of excess resources, idle manpower, and plant and equipment operating below capacity, all of which could generate the supply needed to keep prices stable; and the source of this stubborn, inelastic demand that maintains high prices despite the large or increasing number of unemployed.

Something is wrong. Under conditions of idle capacity and a vast pool of unemployed, classical theory predicts stable or falling prices, not rising prices and inflation.[6] "Cost-push" inflation *is*, then, an alternative to, not just an elaboration of, the classical theory.

But wait. Before we dismiss classical economics, which seemed for so long to be factually sound and rational, let's check the facts and try to explain the paradox. Perhaps there is little or no real unemployment at these levels, despite the statistics.

THE SEMANTICS OF "IDLE CAPACITY"

What is idle capacity? If a well-equipped modern plant existed behind enemy lines and was unavailable for use, it would not be *effectively* available, even if it were idle. It would not be an example of idle capacity. If a wealthy eccentric bought a modern plant, fully equipped and magnificently maintained by a crew of workers for his own idiosyncratic pleasure, but refused to use it for productive purposes, then, despite its capacity to produce, it would not be considered part of the economy's idle capacity. In our free-enterprise society, a decision *not* to use *potentially* productive capacity cannot connote idle capacity.

Similarly, if a farmer is paid by the government to keep his acreage fallow, his land does not constitute idle capacity, because it is unavailable for production. Indeed, for the farmer who is being paid not to produce, the most "productive" use of his land is to keep it fallow! Potential or technological capacity is not idle capacity, and it may well be that more careful analysis and precise definition will show that we really are operating at full capacity.

Take unemployment. Over the past decade, the Bureau of Labor Statistics tells us, between 5 and almost 10 percent of the labor force has been unemployed—a figure unprecedented since the

Depression. Given the normal allowance for error in any body of data, statistics don't really lie. Our claims of what statistics reflect or suggest may be false, but that is quite a different issue.

Our unemployment statistics suggest an ever-increasing supply of unused manpower that could augment the labor force, create the supply to meet demand, and tame inflation if we chose to call upon it. But we must determine whether these manpower resources are really available to the economy.

BEHIND THE UNEMPLOYMENT FIGURES

Who are and what are the unemployed? Is someone sixty-six years old, in good health and of reasonable intelligence, receiving a Social Security check that says he must not work, unemployed? No. We don't include him in our unemployment figures, though he is potentially employable.

Similarly, someone who, through various government subsidies, is paid more for not working than he would be if he were at work may be defined as part of the unemployed work force. Yet under these conditions he is not available (though it may be by his own preference) to join the productive labor force and thereby provide the needed supply. Quite the contrary: he has been aligned on the demand side of the equation and given power, via unemployment benefits, welfare subsidies, food stamps, and the like, to push prices up.

An invalid who is incapable of useful production is not included among the statistics of the unemployed, and rightly so. Yet, in terms of productivity, many unemployed are hardly more capable than handicapped persons, having little or no education, training, experience or, indeed, willingness to engage in anything that might modify or improve their status. Others are too undisciplined to show up on time or to work effectively, even if they make a minimal effort to be productive within the operating framework of a company. Still others who are psychotic or alcoholic deserve our sympathy but do not really belong among the official unemployed, even if they collect unemployment insurance or say they would like to work.

Another kind of worker may want only a specific job that may exceed his capacity to perform. If such individuals agree to be productive only under virtually prohibitive conditions, they are not really available. And if they are subsidized, why shouldn't they hold out indefinitely for what they want?

Ironically, the minimum wage also operates to keep people— particularly young people—from holding down jobs. Adolescents, who constitute about a fourth of the total unemployed "potential" work force, are neither unwilling nor unable to work. They may be unskilled and immature, but in general they are not likely to overestimate their abilities or to demand high wages; nor are they organized. They know that they need to learn and are eager for the opportunity to learn. Yet this eager surplus labor force is held back from work by minimum wage laws that are supported by older workers and organized labor precisely to keep adolescent labor from competing with them and driving wages down.

Since the minimum-wage law was expanded in 1966, jobs covered by it have jumped from under 40 percent to two-thirds of existing jobs, and the minimum wage itself has been constantly raised. From 1977 to 1981 it went up 50 percent—from $2.30 to $3.35.[7] The result: a teenage unemployment rate that has grown both absolutely and in proportion to adult unemployment. The way youngsters (especially black youth) line up to apply for a few federally subsidized jobs suggests that this "idle" capacity would be well used were it not for laws that discourage employers from hiring and training inexperienced youths.[8]

On top of the official unemployed are those who do not figure among our statistics, who are not defined as part of the work force. Some are supported by subsidies other than unemployment insurance; others are structurally unemployed, lacking skills needed in the job market. Still others are discouraged workers who no longer actually seek work because, according to one hardly incontestable explanation, they don't expect to find it. If these workers alone were added to the unemployment statistics they would increase the totals by *over one third.* In January through March 1980, when unemployment was 6.1 percent, the addition of discouraged workers, along with some part-time workers and job seekers, to the official jobless rate would have raised it by 2.6 percentage points to an estimated 8.7 percent. For the most part, these workers are not in government public works, public service, or youth training and employment programs. "Mainly," according to one report, "the Government helps such people survive by providing welfare payments and food stamps, not bringing them into the labor force."[9]

Certainly not all the unemployed are undisciplined, unskilled, or kept off the market. Many are between jobs, in the process of moving, or uprooted by changes in technology, styling, the relocation of their company, or a profit squeeze. A labor force as large as ours will always have frictional (between-job) and cyclical unemployment. Most unemployment at "full-employment" levels is by definition frictional.

Yet once we consider the many who are encouraged not to work, or who cannot or prefer not to work for various reasons, or whose skills and productive potential are limited, we may find that we cannot so easily tap a reserve work force to provide the labor supply that would fend off inflation. We may be near or at the full employment of our "productive" labor force, in contrast to that segment significant in numbers but limited in productive potential. This may be why the slightest increase in demand raises wage rates and prices.

ADMINISTERED SCARCITY

If this analysis is correct, if we are indeed at or near full employment of our productive labor force, then the classical theory of inflation is confirmed and requires no semantic refinement like "cost-push." But the opposite seems true. The demand for higher wages—a significant factor in cost-push—succeeds because we are, in effect, operating at essentially full capacity. In such an environment, sellers of raw materials get away with introducing higher costs because the economy, given so many external limitations imposed on the free-market system by government, big business, and unions, *is* operating at full capacity at prevailing prices. We may even ask whether union workers who refuse, through featherbedding, to produce, or who resist changes in production that will enhance efficiency, or who insist on wage rates that sometimes preclude profitability, or who strike for sometimes impossible conditions—we may ask whether they are not in effect unavailable for work.

The withholding of labor services, directly or indirectly, is hardly confined to unions or nonworkers. In New York City, licensing limits taxicabs to a supply well below what would be set by a free market. Professional associations like the American Medical Association manipulate a shortage of doctors and thus of critical health services, restricting output and maintaining high medical prices.

The costs of raw materials, commodities, and some manufactured goods also illustrate the same administered scarcity. Our oil shortages and price distortions stem from OPEC decisions to control output and prices. Witness actions in 1980 and 1981 to cut back production (rather than lower prices) when too much crude oil "glutted" the world market—though the costs of imported oil had already multiplied over twenty times since the early 1970s. Similarly, auto companies respond to a saturated market or even competition by raising prices and living with huge inventories. A variety of government strategies keep the prices of food and other materials from falling to their market levels. They range from dairy price supports and tobacco subsidies to duties and import fees, quotas and antidumping laws applied to wheat, corn, beef, sugar, steel, and manufactured products. A 1980 study of five products found that import restrictions forced American consumers to pay over $2 billion a year in higher prices for these products alone. [10] The 1981 farm bill, it was estimated, would cost taxpayers almost $4 billion a year for four years and raise consumer prices for milk and peanuts in the bargain. [11]

Crop supports present the classic case of politically produced shortages, though they are defended in terms of the "paradoxical" situation of the farmer. It is a centuries-old truism that farmers receive smaller total revenues with good harvests than with bad because demand is relatively inelastic. People will not buy significantly larger quantities of food when prices are low, or when they earn more, or in times of prosperity. Farmers lose if supply increases, even if demand remains constant, and if prices go down. If demand drops, they suffer even more than industrial workers, as they did in the Great Depression.

39

By the same token, the farmer suffers if he is more productive. In industry, productivity results in prosperity—higher income and wages, and hence higher consumption. So long as demand increases more than output, the balance is still in favor of the producer. Yet in the case of farming, the opposite occurs. Demand expands less quickly than output. With the resulting surplus, prices and profits drop and unemployment results.

To prevent these outcomes, the government has bolstered agriculture with subsidies, with guaranteed purchases of farm output at stable prices, and with sponsored research. These policies stem largely from the agricultural depressions of the 1920s and 1930s, when the notions of price and income parity were developed. Price parity, which compares what the farmer gets for his products and what he pays for manufactured goods, was developed to measure the farmer's hardship, and programs maintaining price parity have tried to keep this ratio stable. Since price parity ensures neither a market nor adequate revenues, income parity measures the ratio of farmers' income, or standard of living, to that of city dwellers. Government policy does not merely stabilize prices. It tries to raise farm incomes. To bolster both prices and income, government agencies buy agricultural products at prices above market, set acreage restrictions and marketing quotas, and pay farmers not to produce, or, alternatively, to store grain, until prices rise to a certain level. [12]

Though it is argued that without price supports and guaranteed sales agriculture would be permanently depressed, one may question depression policies that are carried pointlessly into years of prosperity. On the one hand, land is kept idle to keep prices high. On the other hand, more labor is used than is actually needed, for the simple reason that price supports make overproduction economically useful to the seller. Inventories rise. Every year produces a bumper crop with constantly rising subsidies with no benefit to the consumer, [13] while farmers enjoy guaranteed profits at higher prices than they could otherwise obtain and effectively block any program that threatens to reduce their profits. With a vested interest in maintaining inflation, the farm lobby has persistently fought the notion of a government emergency stockpile, blatantly arguing that there would be a temptation to sell the grain at home to depress food prices in times of high inflation. Only in 1980, when the Agriculture Department bought grain originally targeted for the Soviet Union, did farm resistance break down. And this occurred because of an immediate payoff: the government bought the grain at higher than free-market prices, and guaranteed that the supply would not be used to keep domestic prices from rising. A government grain reserve was approved with the proviso that it would be tapped only to meet extraordinary needs in countries abroad, not to fight inflation at home.[14]

Federal price supports have a double inflationary effect. They push prices up (or at least don't let them fall) and at the same time increase the federal deficit. As a result the consumer is faced with a situation even worse than labor's idle capacity. What we have is a case of planned overproduction (a sure cure for inflation under other circumstances), encouraged and in effect politically defined as underproduction. With this restraint of trade, there can be no "idle" capacity.

It is questionable, also, whether the farmer's situation is really unique, when import quotas keep available resources off the market, or when a saturated and depressed industry, like the auto industry, receives government supports that keep its resources from being allocated to more socially useful activities. Under different political circumstances, these unsold resources or inventories would help alleviate our runaway inflation.

Even monetary policies that stress high interest rates encourage the overproduction of money and credit (whose abundance *should* make money cheap) at high cost. By maintaining overproduction at high cost, the government in effect provides price parity or subsidies for bankers.

Our government, then, is geared to the interests of a variety of sellers, who are always driving prices up, with little concern for the needs of buyers—a formula guaranteed to produce continuing inflation.

If all sellers, whether of labor or of property services or of goods, negotiate and determine their prices to try to get among them all more than

100 percent of the total national product, then the result cannot help but be a frustrating upward push of the price level—a case of sellers' inflation.[15]

Calling this cost-push inflation, however, not only misses the point but obscures it. The consumer is suffering today from demand-pull inflation, often in areas of low-demand elasticity, because of artificially produced shortages in which the government and private-sector groups have collaborated. In the meanwhile the government, which could intervene to halt this endless cycle, has by its welfare benefits, cost-of-living increases, and multiple price subsidies not only exaggerated the effects of stagflation, but increased the number of players with a stake in its perpetuation.

THE REGULATOR HAS GONE WILD

Inflation is an indicator of lack of discipline. It occurs initially when a major segment of the economy—government, labor, or business—is unleashed from some general balance of spending, production, and pricing. When one segment tears loose, the others try, not unjustifiably, to catch up, and we are off on an upward spiral that can be halted, it seems, only by depression.

If anyone is to prevent, correct, or check this process, it must be the government, the only agent empowered to act as mediator. The government may not have started this process, but it is responsible in large measure for its present dimensions. The success and survival of free enterprise rest on selfishness, on the effort of each team, each player—business and labor, union and management, employer and employee—to get all he can out of the economic game. Although the system rests on competition, which keeps prices down, the motive of each actor is to raise his income, his price, his revenues. In a capitalistic system, the essence of economic behavior is a bias on the part of every member toward higher prices and wages, toward more consumer goods, more services—and more leisure—all at the same time. The corollary is stickiness, or resistance on the part of all the economic actors to lower wages and prices, even in slack or recessionary periods in which classical economic logic would dictate falling wages and prices. Absent some specific external action, the natural tendency then is toward inflation of prices and wages and a natural line of resistance against their deflation.

If we want the players to do their best for the system, we cannot tell them not to be selfish, not to fight to get the most for their relative efforts. If we can accept this—and I believe we must, lest we opt for a totalitarian, rather than a self-directed, self-motivated system—then we cannot change the basic motivation of self-interest under which business and labor function.

Only government, elected and selected by the people to represent their interests, can act as regulator, or gyroscope, in the economic workings of the system to produce the requisite changes. It must be the aloof and unselfish, albeit highly involved, arbitrator or referee, in order to make the economic league function and perform efficiently, with a maximum of socially desired productivity and a minimum of disruptiveness. The role of government is not to change human nature, which, properly mobilized and motivated, can, under capitalism, create the most highly productive society ever achieved. Its role is rather to channel human nature so it can be all that it might be.

Somewhere along the line the government has gone wrong. In the early stages of our history as a nation, government intruded as little as possible in daily economic workings, acting largely as protector of private property and of its citizens from domestic abuse and external attack. It provided courts and an army to execute these functions.

Had society and business remained simple, this arrangement might have been ideal. But new situations and growth itself generate unforeseen problems demanding attention, adaptations, and structural changes. This was the case with the young republic. As barter decreased in business transactions and currency became essential to the conduct of commerce and our evolving industry, the role of currency issued by private banks became far too critical to permit the system to be left to the vagaries of small, often undercapitalized, sometimes dishonest, and completely uncontrolled banks. The government was compelled, for the good of all its citizens—business, labor, consumers, savers, and investors—to establish a national bank and banking system in the face of sharp

43

resistance. Much later, after recurring monetary panic, financial disruption, and economic depression, the Federal Reserve System was established in 1913.

In these efforts, government had to become more active in business. Once it took on that role, like it or not, it was forced to make decisions about the amount of money to issue. Unwittingly, almost unintentionally, it became a major player in economic life. Its actions in tightening or loosening the money supply could bring about higher or lower prices, a favorable or a difficult business climate, demand for products, business success or failure, employment or unemployment, inflation or recession and even severe depression. No longer did business or labor alone determine the workings, the success or failure, of the economy.

Similarly, as corporate enterprise and organized labor became major structural forces in the economy, government, representing the people's interest, had to intrude as arbitrator and mediator of these two powerful economic forces, introducing antitrust and fair-labor laws. Throughout the Progressive era and on, the government was a counteracting influence to these massive economic forces. The major players in the economic game remained business and labor. Except, perhaps, in international trade (e.g., through tariffs and the like), government retained a minor economic role.

With the crash of 1929 and the succeeding depression, the government undertook new economic roles and projects and introduced new economic structures, modifying the core laissez-faire ideology under which it had been operating as well as the market's role as regulator. Its programs, for all the good they did (and most economists agree that they did much good and much that needed doing) not only strengthened the government, but made it perhaps the most important entity in the economic game. They did so through the projects of the New Deal, the bureaucratic structures it created, the roles and responsibilities it assumed. As a result of those initial acts and the structures that have since evolved, government has mushroomed to become the nation's largest single spender, employer, consumer, and employee. Its bureaucracy, combined with its vast monetary and fiscal power, make it the major actor in the economy.

That being the case, how can government remain the aloof, disinterested umpire of a game in which it is the major player? It has developed its own needs to be filled, its own specific goals that it will not forgo or postpone. Instead of moderating and damping inflationary fuels, it generates and adds to these catalysts.

We have lost the one participant whose special role was to have provided us the moderation, stability, and equilibrium of a system within which business and labor could function effectively and efficiently. There is no discipline, there is no gyroscope. The regulator is gone. *The regulator itself has gone wild.*

NOTES

1. William Guttmann and Patricia Meehan, *The Great Inflation:* Germany 1919–1923 (Wimbledon, London: Gordon & Gremonesi, Ltd.), 1975, 43–86, 238–259; Scientific Market Analysis, *The Nightmare German Inflation* (Lynatrace, Inc., March 1978), 1–3; John Kenneth Galbraith, *Money: Whence It Came, Where It Went* (Boston: Houghton Mifflin, 1975), 162–163.

2. Gerald R. Rosen, "Inflation: the Big Losers," *Dun's Review,* April 1979, 76.

3. Economists who plot demand and supply curves or schedules term this insensitivity to price changes a shift *of* the demand curve because some factor other than price is affecting demand. A change in demand caused by something other than a price change would also be defined as a shift of the demand curve. By contrast, a change in demand that *is* caused by a price change is called a shift *along* a demand curve. These pages point up the complexity and paradoxes of these relationships and the way they are affected by nonmarket conditions.

4. "Labor Raises at 5-Year High," *New York Times,* August 7, 1980, D3; Census Bureau, *Statistical Abstract,* 1981, Table 688,410.

5. John B. Shoven, "Inflation: Views on the Problem and Policies for Its Control," in *Critical Choices for Americans,* vol. 5: *Trade, Inflation, and Ethics* (Lexington, Mass.: 197); John F. Early, Craig Howell, and Andrew Clem, "Double-Digit Inflation Today and in 1973–1974: A Comparison," *Monthly Labor Review,* May 1980, 3–20.

6. Assuming money supply is constant. With monetary expansion we can have inflation even when there is excess capacity. See chapters 4, 8.

7. Census Bureau, *Statistical Abstract,* 1981, Table 684, 408.

8. James F. Ragan, Jr., "The Failure of the Minimum Wage Law," *Challenge,* May–June 1978, 61–65.

9. Philip Shabecoff, "Uncounted Jobless: No Work, No Hope," *New York Times,* May 18, 1980, Sec. 4, 4.

10. "Cost of Import Curbs Found to Outweigh Benefits," *New York Times,* August 4, 1980, D3. The products were textiles, sugar, TV sets, radios, and nonrubber shoes.

11. "Conferees Agree to a Compromise on Farm Measure," by Seth King, *New York Times,* December 9, 1981, A1.

12. "Carter Orders $1 Billion Increases in Crop Support," *New York Times,* July 29, 1980, D11.

13. "Corn Belt Fears Impact of Cutoff in Grain Trade," *New York Times,* January 8, 1980, D1; "Carter Orders $1 Billion Increase in Crop Support," *New York Times,* July 29, 1980, D1, D11. Some government programs will pay these supports only if farmers cut back production, in this way at least preventing an *oversupply* at inflated prices, though farmers are still being paid, in effect, not to produce.

14. "At Last, a Grain Reserve," *New York Times* editorial, August 4, 1980, A20.

15. A. P. Lerner, cited in Samuelson, *Economics,* 11th ed., 771.

4

Socialism
without Tears

No one would deny today that the state should shield its citizens from potential catastrophe. We tend to forget, however, the limits and assumptions of that mandate. The pioneer sociologist William Graham Sumner observed that the state can give nothing to anyone without taking from someone else, from someone who has produced enough to save. Government can be generous to the poor and the debilitated only because someone responding to prevailing incentives is producing more than he needs or is required to produce. It is this surplus that is potentially available for the good of others. Without that highly motivated producer, the state would never be in a position to allocate to those in need. Redistribution in the name of equality can only reduce this base and result in a diminished life style, a smaller pie, a smaller gross national product, for all.

The ideological question we now face is hardly that of capitalism versus socialism—for taxation is already the functional equivalent of owning the means of production, and perhaps a more effective one. It is the question of how to retain the incentives of free enterprise that have led to its unparalleled capacity for creativity and inventiveness. It is the question of how to forge a national interest out of a welter of competing interest groups. It is the question of how to preserve the salutary elements of our laissez-faire system by nourishing the incentive to work while protecting the weak and limiting the power of the ruthless. It is the question of planning without shackling controls.

CAPITALISTIC SOCIALISM: TAXES, BUDGETS, AND DEFICITS

Our country seems to have developed its own version of socialism. This form, which we might call "capitalistic socialism," differs sharply from that of the socialist regime. It does not require that the federal government own industry or the means of production. It operates through other strategies, particularly taxation, by means of which the government "owns" the income of producers rather than the means of production. Socialist governments take over the means of production and distribute part of the profits to those responsible for production. Our government takes whatever share of profits and collective income it chooses to appropriate, which gives its capitalists the illusion of ownership and entitlement to the profits produced by their labors.

This arrangement can even be seen as a superior form of socialism. Why bother to acquire the means of production when you can accomplish the same result incrementally, without the revolutionary upheaval or the confiscatory actions that taking on ownership would entail? In this form of "evolutionary" socialism, the government with its tax dollars usurps the bulk of the economic vote and determines what will be produced. It thus becomes very much like the communist planner. It does so directly, through its purchases and subsidies, and indirectly, by competing successfully for borrowed funds in the capital markets, thus driving up interest rates and the cost of private-sector activity. The government also fixes, or helps determine, prices in many key sectors of our economy: railroad rates, airlines (until recently), postal services, and utilities. By controlling credit through its monetary policy, it affects the level of consumption. And it is more efficient, too, since it still has the option of using or permitting free-market pricing wherever it sees fit.

Finally, through taxation rather than outright ownership, the government avoids the labor and consumer unrest that have produced periodic crises in regimes like that of Poland.[1] As critics of socialism have long realized, the socialist revolution does not eliminate stratification or the ruling class.[2] Every society has discontents that must be either accommodated or repressed; no society is devoid of class conflict. Capitalism has been able to accommodate class conflict remarkably well, largely through economic growth, the welfare state, and negotiated conflict between capital and labor. Our working class today is more conservative than either the New Left intellectuals or the well-meaning but self-serving public-sector professionals. And whatever revolutionary potential it may retain is not directed, as it is in communist regimes, against the state.

The colossal size of the government role shows up in its budgets, taxes, and deficits. In 1961 the federal budget was only $98 billion. By 1971 it had reached $193 billion. Ten years later, in the period of presumed retrenchment that followed the heyday of the Great Society, it topped $657 billion. This figure does not include about $21 billion in off-budget outlays or $57 billion in on- and off-budget government loans. Federal spending in 1981 came to 23 percent of the entire gross national product, and spending at all levels of government to over a third.[3]

Taxes—the costs of government—have skyrocketed along with spending. In 1980 the average, not wealthy, taxpayer paid his entire earnings from New Year's Day until May in government taxes. Until the Reagan revisions, a married couple's marginal tax rate—the *differential* rate for earnings above the lowest bracket—rose sharply up to the first $50,000 of joint income earned by a working couple and leveled off after that.[4]

The Reagan administration's tax cuts have checked this upward climb but not the government's spending levels, which have merely been shuffled from social services to defense spending. In fact, having cut taxes without net budget cuts and pushed the federal debt ceiling to well over $1 trillion, Reagan's policies are producing over twice the record $60-billion deficit that his own analysts predicted. Instead of achieving the promised balanced budget, they have entrenched the huge deficits of the 1970s and the large public-sector role that Reagan promised to diminish.

THE BALANCING ACT: THE GREATEST SHOW IN TOWN

Part of the illusion by which government maintains its huge spending levels without unpopular taxes is through the public debt. In 1979, the total federal debt was $900 billion ($300 billion in state and local debt are not included) out of a total $4.3 trillion of debt, when the gross national product itself was $2.4 trillion.[5] In the 1983 budget submitted by Reagan to Congress, the deficit was $91.5 billion dollars (an underestimation); when the government's credit operations were considered, its credit needs came to $204.7 billion—almost one-third of Reagan's 1983 $757.6 billion "on-budget" budget, and about one-fifth the government's total debt, incurred in one year alone.[6] The actual deficit in 1983, according to Alice Rivlin of the Congressional Budget Office, was expected to top $160 billion.

Surprisingly, deficits this size are a fairly recent tradition. It was a long-held tenet that a government budget deficit, not unlike a business in the red, or a family in an overspent condition, was not only undesirable but unthinkable to the citizenry, and hence to politicians. All costs likely to unbalance the budget were avoided.

This commitment to frugality was suspended only in times of war. War throws economic expediency into the background, involving government and citizens in a struggle for survival, for life itself; and so we ignore its costs. War-related deficits are seen as essential but "temporary"—extraordinary expenses irrelevant to basic economic policy.

Historical analysis, however, shows that wartime spending has permanently magnified the public debt. Because taxes then were anathema, the American Revolution was financed with paper money and loans. The Civil War outlays exceeded all government spending in the entire history of the nation up to that time and brought the public debt to almost $2.9 billion, its highest point until 1917. In World War I, two-thirds of the costs were financed by loans, and the national debt, which had totaled only $1 billion before the war, jumped to $26.6 billion by August 1919. Within two years after the war's end, the federal government's interest charge alone was greater than the entire prewar cost of running the government. With World War II, the public debt jumped from $48.9 billion in 1941 to $258.7 billion in 1945.[7]

Wars thus produce inflation and a permanent increase in the public debt and the interest paid on it. Yet our economy survives and sometimes flourishes.

THE EVOLUTION OF THE BUDGET DEFICIT: ITS ACCEPTANCE AND INCREASING POPULARITY

Inevitably, politicians have observed that these enormous surges in deficit spending have produced no major catastrophes. On the contrary, they seem to produce a salutary condition in which all are employed and productive, business booms, and the vast military-industrial complex flourishes.

Gradually, deficits become immeasurably seductive. No one seems to suffer from deficit spending. Everyone gains. Budget decisions, not to mention political life, become more simple and rewarding. A politician can vote for everything that is good, or that appears good, or that voters demand because they think it is good. Or, even if it is not good, it is surely politically desirable because the voters want it. No need to make difficult choices among alternatives that are restricted by spending ceilings and expected revenues.

Of course, the politicians' hireling economists verify and seek to support the politically popular position, rather than deriving the abstract logical deductions that their discipline requires. Political sponsors of such theoretical rigor are absent; there is no direct payoff in such an enterprise. He who pays the piper picks the tune.

Under these circumstances, the notion of a balanced budget begins to seem outdated, conservative, and unnecessarily regressive.

51

A balanced budget inhibits exciting new programs. It impedes progress. It restricts growth. It creates unnecessary hardships, both for constituents who want more dollars injected into the system and for politicians who resist constraints on the grandeur of their vast and benevolent intentions.

The evolving acceptance, even popularity, of the budget deficit has been bipartisan. Both Nixon and Ford, adherents of a school, almost a religion, that hallowed the sanctity of the balanced budget, became spontaneous Keynesians, at least where deficit spending was concerned. Indeed, they were opportunistic and bastard Keynesians, for Keynes endorsed both deficits and surpluses as counter-cyclical measures.

It was not as serious students of Keynes that Nixon and Ford were converted. That doctrine merely suited their immediate political needs. Under Nixon, from 1970 to 1971, the deficit jumped from $2.8 billion to $22 billion, setting a precedent we have been unable to break. Not only debt levels but income-security payments in the Nixon-Ford years beggared the liberal largesse of the 1960s; they jumped from 21.9 percent to 34.8 percent of the national budget between 1970 and 1976. One wonders if Nixon and Ford would not have converted to Hinduism or even (heaven forfend) communism, had that been the way the wind would blow aspiring politicians into office.

THE FULL-EMPLOYMENT BUDGET AND THE ECONOMIC HOUDINIS

In the process of reversing their earlier ideas, Nixon and Ford introduced terms and concepts to rationalize their conversion and make it seem that they evolved, rather than rebelled, into it. When Nixon unveiled his first large deficit budget, it was not called a deficit budget—it was a "balanced" "full-employment" budget. By that fiction, *if* everyone were employed and paying his or her income taxes on that basis; and *if* all companies were earning the profits that they would presumably earn *if* everyone were employed and spending his money normally; and *if* these companies in turn were paying income taxes on those projected earnings, *then* the budget would be balanced. So, Nixon said, let us spend as if the government revenues were going to be what they would be *if* this wished-for magical situation were indeed the case.

The economic logic used to rationalize and buttress this "full-employment" budget was that perhaps, if we spent as if we did have full employment, then full employment would *ipso facto* come about. The Economic Magicians who concocted this potion to support what (we must assume) Nixon and/or his conservative compatriots and long-time "balanced budget" devotees would ordinarily never have swallowed, or advocated to the public without checking on their own rhetoric, were every bit as brilliant and creative as the Crafty Weavers of the Emperor's New Clothes.

Analytically, the "full-employment budget" is a fiction that is useful for comparing fiscal policies in a way that comparing actual budgets themselves does not permit. In recessions, we always have lower revenues and higher government outlays, no matter how conservative our policy. By comparing two policies at the same level of the business cycle—at full-employment levels—the "full-employment budget" presumably weeds out the distorting effects of economic cycles, to show which programs are more or less expansionary, producing larger deficits or surpluses at comparable levels of employment.[8]

True, the Nixon budget *could* have generated a surplus at that mythic level of full employment. But the budget that he *replaced* would have generated an even larger full-employment surplus.[9] Nor did the theorists' full-employment budget ever imply that spending at these levels could itself generate full employment. It is the surplus, not the full-employment level, that is important for comparisons.

As it was used by politicians, the full-employment budget was just a step in a process, part of a political magic act designed to make it seem that what in fact isn't, is. And the magic act was diverting, intellectually entertaining. It appeared to hurt no one, gave joy to many, and made everything seem perfect and beautiful. The full-employment budget became the magic finale in this evolutionary process of embracing the deficit, which has led to the totally unbalanced behavior of our political leaders today, and made projecting utopian statistics a matter of routine. Carter, too, Messiah-like, predicted a $60-billion surplus by the end of his term, on the highly overoptimistic assumption of a 5 percent un-employment rate and a 5 percent inflation rate throughout. Reagan stormed when his first sanguine projections were questioned and has since been developing alibis. His advisers have even maintained that a balanced budget was never a major goal.

What a far cry this embrace of the deficit has been from the agonized spending on critical needs once made in response to such critical upheavals as wars and military involvements, or dictated by the need to alleviate depression and misery and generate employment and business activity. These outlays were in most cases justified and unavoidable. The New Deal Keynesian deficits had merit and were justified as temporary deviations from a more desirable norm. They were to be balanced and even corrected by forthcoming surpluses as soon as the emergency or crisis was over. At least these earlier deficit budgets were simply that—*budgets in deficit* to deal with extraordinary critical situations that gave the country little, or no, choice. Like other periodic catastrophes that life produces, they were seen as inescapable: they had to be confronted. And, as with other catastrophes, the damage was to be repaired once the danger had passed. Moreover, the earlier administrations at least called budget deficits just that. They called a spade a spade, and did not try to make it disappear with some deft sleight of hand; they did not have the effrontery to call a massive deficit budget a "balanced" full-employment budget.

Keynes himself had no such commitment to deficit spending. He saw a fluctuating role for government involvement and advocated offsetting surpluses in times of prosperity. Since deficit spending was a temporary depression strategy, it would be balanced out in prosperity. The two strategies, deficit and surplus, were to be used alternately to smooth the inevitably disruptive business cycles of capitalism. Thus government spending as a proportion of GNP would rise in depression but decline as the economy revived. When the demand gap eased as crises subsided, the government would reduce its role.

In practice, however, the government's share of GNP only rises. As business slows down in depression, business's share decreases, quite understandably. But the government doesn't slow down in recovery. After each recession, its share of GNP has become larger.[10] In 1960 and 1965, federal outlays were about 18 percent of GNP. In the 1970 recession they rose to 20.5 percent but never fell back completely. They remained between 21 and 20 percent until 1974, when they dropped slightly to 19.8 percent. In the next year's recession, federal spending rose to 22.4 percent of GNP, then to 22.6 percent in 1976, and has since remained at levels of 22 and 23 percent.[11] The pattern is a countercyclical increase in recession that plateaus at close-to-recession levels, only to rise further in the next dip, destroying the likelihood of a balanced, or even reduced, budget.

Since 1971 we have seen deficits ranging from $49 billion to $66 billion, then, under Reagan, well over $100 billion. The 1984 deficit is projected at $200 billion. Between 1974 and 1980, the deficits alone totaled more than the entire 1974 federal budget, and the deficit in 1984 will be larger than all the deficits from 1950 to 1975 combined.

Two popular myths are belied by these figures. First is the notion that the public turned "conservative" in the early 1970s. Whatever the public rhetoric or the mood of the media, policies became, if anything, more liberal. The second is the notion that the Republican Party would make much of a difference. Given our geographic basis of representation and our two-party system, we expect that appeals to the broad electorate will play down real policy differences. But surely few expected that conservatives would violate their basic tenets, particularly in the 1970s, when liberal Republicans disappeared or changed their colors, and when Democrats turned right, aping Republican policies—Carter promising fiscal conservatism, Governor Hugh Carey (New York) pressing for a balanced budget, Democratic politicians turning to the private sector for solutions to social problems.

Reagan seemed finally to be breaking these precedents, but made the blunder of cutting taxes without cutting spending enough to pay for the tax cuts. Using the same utopian economic projections as his predecessors, Reagan was seduced by supply-side theory, the conservative version of Keynesian public spending,[12] forgetting the supply-siders' indifference to a deficit. The result continues to be heavier Treasury borrowing that crowds out the private sector and raises interest rates sky high, while canceling out the investment incentive the supply-siders rely upon.

TRANSFER PAYMENTS: PSEUDO-KEYNESIAN STRATEGIES

Along with the increase in spending and debt has come an alarming explosion in transfer payments. This category of benefits includes unemployment insurance, Social Security, pension payments, welfare, and disability, as well as subsidies to farmers and the merchant marine.[13] Although their rise was sparked in part by the ideology of the Great Society, benefits were maintained and expanded long after the Republicans gained power in 1969. Why? And where is their real damage?

Transfer payments have been attacked as socialistic because they redistribute income. They have also been defended as compatible with capitalism because the purchasing power they generate creates "orders and jobs for free private enterprise 'on the second round.' . . . The production induced by this process is both privately produced and privately consumed."[14] They help pull us out of depression by stimulating the private sector. But that debate hardly touches the economic problems that these subsidies create.

When Keynes endorsed deficit spending as a form of pump-priming, he hardly had transfers to individuals in mind. He may have felt that some income redistribution would be useful in depression, because the lower classes consumed proportionally more and saved less of their income, but his main focus was on public works. He held strongly that *among the options* for government spending, public works, which added to the supply of jobs and goods and services, were far superior to the dole. In fact, he calculated the benefits of public works spending *in terms* of the increase in jobs that would save the government payments for public relief.[15]

Although he wrote in the context of prosperity, John Kenneth Galbraith, in *The Affluent Society* (1958), endorsed similar policies for government. He saw the solution to residual poverty in government funding of public works and public education services—

transportation, parks, schools, libraries—that would benefit the entire community and the poor in the process. These investments in goods and services differ sharply from transfer payments. They constitute productive public spending, and add to the total supply of goods and services in the economy. One may argue about the extent to which government, rather than the private sector, should provide these goods and services. But that is a political question. In economic terms, public goods are part of our system of exchange of goods and services; public works add to our assets.

By contrast, subsidized consumption—the widow's pension, the veteran's check, the blind person's disability payment—may be *socially* desirable, but no services are rendered for the benefits received. The payments may be required because of the malfunctioning of the economic system, which makes unemployment insurance necessary; or because physical affliction or social inequities keep the elderly from the labor market; or because, after a lifetime in the labor force, and years of contributions to pension and Social Security funds, a worker should retire with an income. Yet because no services are rendered for the benefits received, these payments (whether public or private) are nonproductive, not part of the system of *exchange* of goods and services. In a purely economic sense they are gifts.

Transfer payments are not economically useless. They may contribute to economic stability or even growth, since, by maintaining aggregate demand, they create orders and jobs for others. Hence their automatic stabilizing function in depressions. But that contribution does not stem from the *initial* benefit. It operates "on the second round," after excess supplies have been used up by this stimulated demand and producers can start to work again, and only if the supply of goods and services does indeed increase. If such an increase is not forthcoming, if transfer payments merely increase consumption without increasing production, the result is inflationary.

In the light of these distinctions, the *form* or structure of public spending is more important than the level of outlays in assessing fiscal policy. If you look at post–World War II figures in terms of these distinctions, some disturbing trends come to light. Between 1955 and 1978, federal spending more than doubled in constant dollars; almost all that increase was in transfer payments and grants in and to state and local governments. Transfer payments alone increased from 18.2 percent to 40.9 percent of the total budget. As a proportion of GNP, transfer payments between 1956 and 1978 grew from 4.1 percent to 10.7 percent (or $224 billion in 1978). In the meanwhile, government purchases of goods and services barely changed.[16] They did not drop in *absolute* terms; but they have declined sharply as a proportion of a vastly increased federal budget.[17]

Who gains from these transfer payments? Not merely, or even mainly, the poor. Though over half the income of the poorest fifth of our population comes in the form of transfer payments, the largest programs, Social Security and veterans' benefits, go chiefly to the middle class. No less than 60 percent of the population—the bottom three-fifths—has received some government benefits that redistribute income, and noncash benefits make these gains larger.[18]

INTEREST-GROUP TYRANNY

Benefit programs are often defended as "automatic stabilizers" that maintain demand and hence act as countercyclical forces. Their effects, however, exaggerate inflationary tendencies because they align individuals on the demand side of the demand-supply equation. The recipients are given purchasing power to buy goods without adding goods and services that would augment the supplies of what they buy. Most of these benefits—Social Security, for example—are automatically indexed to inflation in the bargain, a fact that further serves to drive prices up.[19]

Since these effects are hardly stabilizing, and since they hardly constitute the only, or even the best, way to maintain demand, their usefulness seems to be more political than economic, a way to satisfy voters.

Transfer payments are a favorite mechanism for reallocating our nation's economic wealth. First, progressive taxation appropriates income or wealth for the government. Transfer payments, consuming an ever-increasing share of the government payout, redistribute that income. Finally, indexing augments the buying power of transfer payments while inflation and higher tax brackets eat up the income of productive workers.

Our political system serves, in effect, to counteract not only depression but the workings of our economic system. The trend may be inherent in democratic regimes. The man is rare who would not vote himself a greater share of the aggregate income, and the votes of the many outweigh those of the exceptional few. This leveling tendency of majorities has been encouraged by politicians eager to gain points in the next voters' popularity poll. Given our ethic of instant gratification, it is not surprising that the quick fix of expediency will be the prevailing political response to every economic problem and the measure of a successful program.

This pseudopopulism has been underscored by an ideology that in the 1960s and 1970s defined public responsibility as "accountability" to a variety of interest groups, groups that were urged to organize so that they could lobby and be represented. Using labels like "maximum feasible participation" or *Fortune*'s "creative federalism," this ideology ignored James Madison's insight that interest groups, or factions, work against the public interest and should be controlled, not catered to. Instead, federal agencies were designed to serve, not the public, but the groups they should have been controlling. Programs became sources of patronage; and, since all interests and interest groups were considered essentially equal, the notions of values and moral legitimacy were undermined. The public interest became the sum, or net balance, of competing interests, and not something above them all.[20]

This ideology helps explain why the Great Society programs outlasted their liberal sponsors. Under Nixon they expanded phenomenally, and with them the deficit. The reason for this bipartisan support should be obvious. Benefit programs create new loyalties, stronger interest groups, and constituencies, just as they create bureaucracies to serve them. Government employs a fourth of all clerical workers, 34.5 percent of male professionals, and half the female professionals in this country. Their employment hinges on strong government.

Although these benefit programs claim, and have, admirable objectives, it would be naive to ignore the element of insatiability in their dynamics and expansion. Political analysts, journalists, and opinion pollsters tend to think that when interest groups realize their goals and interests, their discontent will vanish. More often, however, success leads to demands for more of the same, or to new goals that may differ in surface content but have a latent, functional resemblance to the old ones.[21] Many of these programs start out as small, almost pilot, projects, then gather constituencies that include not only beneficiaries for whom they were not originally intended, but an assortment of associated vendors. The food stamp program is a good example. It gathered students under its umbrella for some years, and still appeals to farmers and grocers who have a vested interest in its expansion.

Politicians have catered to demands for benefit programs in the name of interest-group liberalism and other slogans intended to evoke sympathy with our central goals and values—care for the needy, the old, the disabled, and the unemployed, as well as for the ideal of equality.

To support these insatiable demands without risking unpopular taxation, government has not only magnified its debt, but has also "borrowed" the money from the central bank, which pays for or "buys" the Treasury's debt by increasing the money supply—creating money out of nothing. The result of this juggling has been inflation for all of us, but a bonanza for the government. During the period 1926–1978, according to a 1979 report by the Financial Analysts Research Foundation, the ex post "real" interest rate in Treasury bills averaged only zero percent and the ex post real rate on long-term government bonds averaged only 0.6 percent. The authors' calculations that "the real rate of interest historically has been zero percent" differ explicitly from the Federal Reserve Board's estimate that the real rate of interest has been 3 to 4 percent.[22] As government debt mounts, the government itself takes its place among the major actors with a vested interest in inflation.

If our politicians' Spock-like solicitude were carried to its ultimate conclusion, what might our economic system look like? What if the vast *majority* insisted on unemployment insurance of indefinite duration, and on a welfare system that provided a comfortable life style to every citizen irrespective of contribution? Our politicians would have to vote it in—or they would be voted out.

There is surely some kind of insanity in the notion that intelligent men would vote for policies they clearly thought destructive of our system. Yet if most citizens voted to be supported comfortably, and felt inconvenienced at having to work at a job, or in a place, or at a time not quite of their choice, their will could be enacted into law. Then those who worked (even assuming that they could or would be willing to produce enough for all the others) would be heavily taxed to pay the vast amounts of dollars needed for all the others. Eventually, working members would be intelligent enough either to rebel or to wise up, *quit* the work force, and themselves join in the system of subsidies. Such heavy taxation to support a system of limitless charity would eventually destroy the motivation to produce.

Moreover, if some of the prouder members of the working group felt too ashamed to defect to the ranks of the subsidized, Congress could always call it (as it does) the "guaranteed income" program, reducing resistance along with ignominy, and providing the priceless bonus of abundant leisure so cherished by all Americans. One can imagine the slogans emerging from such a campaign: "Don't knock it till you try it! Join the Guaranteed Income group and see the U.S.A.!"

One would expect that no politician, no matter how desperate for votes, would support a program that must go bankrupt or ultimately debase all money as it uses the government printing press to finance it. Yet at least one program suggests that we cannot afford such hopes: Social Security, which has won popularity without remotely paying for its costs, ever taking in more types of beneficiaries and requiring fewer working years. Between 1952 and 1981, it grew three times as fast as the GNP, and faster than inflation, especially since it was indexed.[23] Its income-to-payout ratio, based on even the least conservative actuarial assumptions, is an example of bankruptcy in the making.

Although Social Security taxes are increased almost annually in an effort to cope with part of the vast shortfall, these increases still do not generate the income to meet the payouts, especially with inflationary and ever-larger cost-of-living adjustments. Like a person running up a down escalator, we fall ever further behind. Congressmen and other political leaders know about this dilem-

ma; but because Social Security is popular and taxes politically unpopular, they have ignored the impending tragedy.

The system is almost Malthusian in its design. Diminishing
numbers of people will have to pay, or be willing to pay, the costs
of carrying ever larger numbers of people at ever greater dollar
benefits. Even now, half the applicants for Social Security benefits
apply before age sixty-five, when we should perhaps be abolishing
mandatory retirement before age seventy. Ultimately the system
must collapse, and those now paying to provide for their old age
"security" will find nothing in the till for them.

Our political sages, acting in collaboration with their economic
soothsayers, hardly need mathematical models to see the simple
arithmetic of disaster. Yet their behavior has been reinforced by
Congress's fierce resistance to Social Security reforms or cutbacks,
even on the brink of crisis.

Is it impossible, then, to suppose that politicians may also introduce a "welfare" or "guaranteed income" system that will guarantee every citizen who wants it a comfortable life style? It would
be even more popular, and more democratic, than Social Security,
which is limited to voters over sixty-two. What better guarantee
of the pursuit of happiness for all Americans?

I'd buy it myself, but for the fact that the system rests on the
same illusions as the infamous Ponzi scheme of the 1920s. Charles
Ponzi promised his shareholders a 25 percent return every three
months on a grandiose South Sea "venture," and used for his payments, not income from the enterprise (his initial capital went to
advertise the venture), but the funds received from new investors.
As long as his clientele kept expanding, the project seemed to
work; as soon as it leveled off, the scheme collapsed.

Like the thousands who wasted their hard-earned savings on
Ponzi's scheme, the hopeful beneficiaries of Social Security must
ultimately be disappointed. The system has no economic merit or
logic. In the short run, like Ponzi's idea, it seems to work and
sounds marvelous; people think it feasible. They cannot understand or explain its logic. But, since it seems to work and is endorsed by the brightest experts, they are lulled into a passive
acceptance of what they must know, intuitively, cannot be.

Our Social Security program, much of our current welfare and unemployment insurance problem, and our acceptance of a no-longer-creeping inflation, stem from our docile, more hopeful than rational, acceptance of the impossible, our denial that some day our Ponzi government can make no more "real" payments. The money created to pay for them will no longer be worth the paper it is printed on to anyone, not even those who still do productive work. There may not be much left in our political economy of what was once sacred classical economics, but one truism prevails, and will, as long as man inhabits the physical world: there really is no such thing as a free lunch. Someone has to pay. And someone has already paid for it with the investment of his tangible effort.

A SPURIOUS EQUALITY

Hard as it may be to accept in a country that insists on equality as much as ours, equality through economic redistribution is not a viable goal. Our Constitution guarantees equal treatment before the law, but not equality of ability, motivation, and contribution, while in nature nothing is exactly equal to anything else. Differences in the quality and availability of services and products, between the more and the less productive, must be acknowledged through some mode of social measurement and evaluation—through tangible gain, success, or wealth that accrues to achievement—if we are to inspire effort, energy, hard work and long hours, personal sacrifice of alternative leisure pleasures, savings and investment, the forgoing of current spending and gratification for the sake of some future return, and the dedication of intelligence and talent to socially desirable tasks.

Success is often described as the result of accident and opportunity rather than effort, creativity, and dedication. Part of this argument is sound. But "luck" cannot explain the many forces—particularly individual ability and stubborn perseverance—that lie behind the richness of our productivity and that enhance or catalyze the *potential* for luck itself.

Studies of scientific creativity disclose that a few scientists do the lion's share of the research, publish more articles, and make most of the discoveries from which the entire scientific community and society benefit. In entertainment and in sports, a few star performers reap huge rewards for activities that benefit the many. In our society as a whole, a constant flow of new products, techniques, ideas, foods, games, leisure activities, and technological and medical advances are produced for the many by the few.

Imagine, then, a situation in which the prizes and incomes of a few tennis champions or actors were divided equally among all the tennis players, or among all actors down to performers in bit parts. It would kill the incentive to succeed not only for the stars but for aspiring actors, who would see that their quest for distinction would be leveled to the point where their achievement would be indistinguishable from the average. In the end, everyone who might delight in their performance would be deprived.

Great Britain, with its enormous tax burden on high earnings, demonstrates the fallacies of such a policy. Years of income redistribution have worsened the economy and exhausted its potential sources of revenue. Government spending in 1975 came to 60 percent of Britain's gross national product. Even the Labour government, several years before Margaret Thatcher's election, had to cut social services and provide incentives to regenerate industry in order to compete once more in the world trade and capital markets.

In the United States, many citizens who see that billions in taxes serve an array of special interests have become cynical. "There is no longer any public perception of fairness and evenhandedness in the tax system," says Paul N. Strassels, author of *All You Need to Know About the IRS,* and a former specialist in tax law for the revenue service. People in all walks of life try to circumvent the IRS's record-keeping network through the "underground economy." They thrive on cash transactions (checks made out to cash), barter, unreported tips, and items sold but tallied as inventory losses.[24]

Although the size of the underground economy is difficult to estimate (Joseph A. Pechman of the Brookings Institution says it can't be done), a 1979 IRS study that examined unreported income in 1976 concluded that the underground economy amounted to about 7 percent of the gross national product, or $130 billion—$75 to $100 billion in legal but unreported activities, and $25 to $35 billion in illegal activities such as drugs, illegal gambling, and prostitution. In 1981, the IRS estimated that the figure would be $210 billion. Outside estimates peg the underground economy at 10 (sometimes 20) percent of GNP. The increased demand for currency is taken by some to indicate that the underground sector is growing. If any of these estimates is true, the underground economy is larger than the defense industry, which in those years came to 5 percent of GNP, and larger than auto sales, which come to about 4 percent of GNP. And it is continuing to grow.[25]

On top of this underground economy is a system of legal loopholes, shelters, hedges, and other tax dodges that range from investments in cattle and films and subsidized real estate to purchases of collectibles. These loopholes have flourished as a result of high marginal tax rates,[26] and make a mockery of the "progressive" income tax system, despite the steep nominal increase from 14 to (until recently) 70 percent.

In the real world it is neither desirable nor possible to appropriate the wealth of the affluent. Redistribution itself would lower the average income to a point far below the income that the affluent now enjoy. Though some would gain in the process, they could never match their fantasies of having, not equality, but what the rich have. Second, to distribute equally without requiring commensurate effort and performance would be demoralizing and destructive. The system of subsidies that has evolved into an almost indiscriminate distribution of payments for nonproductivity not only demeans those who accept them but generates two disastrous side effects.

First, as these programs proliferate and the associated bureaucracies grow with them, the overburdened working population is disillusioned and loses the incentive to work, the impulse behind higher output. In the end, everyone is poorer.

And second, as the millions given purchasing power increase the demand for goods they have not shared in creating or augmenting, bidding for the products of a diminishing work force, they push up the prices of limited supplies. Inflation is an inevitable structural consequence of such policies.

No state, however powerful, can decree by fiat that everyone will have all he wants, or that his needs will be satisfied in measure equal to those of the most fortunate. At best, it can create a climate that fosters the incentive to produce all that is possible, and in such abundance that those who respond best will gain the most, while part of what they produce is redistributed to minimize suffering and provide some goods to others, including those who do not or cannot respond to economic incentives. On economic grounds alone they might be neglected; on humanitarian grounds they cannot be overlooked, for they are part of the family of man.

It is futile to attempt to reduce all to the least common denominator of economic achievement. Rather, the government should inspire each one to strive for equality with the highest level of excellence and success. It should demand maximum effort, intelligence, and ingenuity, and maximum output. Seeking the highest potential common denominator will generate the highest *minimal* level of well being, even if it entails an inevitable degree of inequality. The standard deviation in the distribution of rewards would be greater in such a society: but given the higher total output (GNP) and the higher average, the level of benefits at each point in the distribution would be higher.

America was built on the Horatio Alger promise—the notion that each of us, no matter how lowly our beginnings, can be a Rockefeller, an Edison, a Harriman, a Carnegie, a Graham Bell. It was not built on the assumption that each of us would enjoy absolute subsistence-level security from cradle to grave. People are born with varied physical and intellectual qualities that they must accept and make the most of; we must also accept inequality in economic achievement and reward as not only necessary but useful to individual and collective achievement. We may do as much damage in trying to destroy economic inequality as we might if we performed surgical operations to produce equal IQs. Perhaps nature has its purposes with which government had best not tamper, lest it destroy what is most worthwhile in the human race.

NOTES

1. The 1981 Polish crisis was the culmination of a long history of tension. For an earlier example of consumer unrest in Poland, see David Andelman,

"Eastern Europe: Consumer Unrest and Concessions," *New York Times,* December 25, 1977, IV, 4, in *Communism: End of the Monolith?* Evelyn Geller, ed., New York, H. W. Wilson, 1977, 55–59.

2. For a theoretical discussion, see Raymond Aron, "Social Class, Political Class, Ruling Class," in Reinhard Bendix and Semour M. Lipset, *Class, Status, and Power: Social Stratification in Comparative Perspective,* 2d ed., New York, Free Press, 1966, 201–10.

3. *Budget of the United States Government: Fiscal Year 1983,* 9–44, 9–62, 3–27; Census Bureau, *Statistical Abstract,* 1981, 276, 421.

4. Richard G. Lipsey and Peter O. Steiner, *Microeconomics,* 5th ed., New York, Harper & Row, 1979, 433; *Statistical Abstract,* 1981, 102d ed., table 422, 260.

5. Daniel Hamberg, *The U.S. Monetary System,* Boston, Little, Brown, 1981, 9; *Budget of U.S. Government: Fiscal Year 1982,* 3.

6. William Barry Furlong, "America's Other Budget," *New York Times Magazine,* February 21, 1982, 62.

7. Harold U. Faulkner, *American Economic History,* 7th ed., New York, Harper & Brothers, 1954, 138, 508–15, 709.

8. Laurence Klein criticizes this concept on the grounds that at full employment levels it is difficult to deal with or even estimate inflation. And if we don't know the degree of inflation, we can say very little about the budget surplus or deficit.

9. Cf. Rudiger Dornbusch and Stanley Fischer, *Microeconomics,* 2d ed., New York, McGraw-Hill, 1981, Chart 3–1, 85.

10. Census Bureau, *Statistical Abstract,* 1979, 100th ed., Figure 9.2, 253.

11. Ibid., Table 423, 254.

12. See chapter 9.

13. They also include interest payments on the government debt, which vary directly with interest-rate fluctuations, and by large amounts, as well as grants-in-aid to state and local governments.

14. Samuelson, *Economics,* 10th ed., New York: McGraw-Hill, 1976, 155.

15. Robert Lekachman, *The Age of Keynes,* New York, Random House, 1966, 44, 75.

16. Lester Thurow, *The Zero-Sum Society,* New York, Basic Books, 1980, 155–156; Lipsey and Steiner, *Microeconomics,* 442.

17. Grants-in-aid to state and local governments may be used, however, to purchase goods and services, such as police and fire protection.

18. Thurow, *Zero-Sum Society,* 156, 160, 279.

19. See chapter 5.

20. Theodore J. Lowi, *The End of Liberalism: The Second Republic of the United States,* 2nd ed., New York, W. W. Norton, 1979, xi–xvi, 42, 49.

21. Murray Edelman, *The Symbolic Uses of Politics,* Urbana, University of Illinois Press, 1964, 154–155.

22. Roger G. Ibbotson and Rex A. Sinquefield, *Stocks, Bonds, Bills, and Inflation: Historical Returns (1926–1978),* Charlottesville, Va., Financial Analysts Research Foundation, 1979, 30, 32, 41. Their estimates for real returns on corporate bonds are also low, 1.5 percent (p. 31).

23. Robert M. Ball, *Social Security: Today and Tomorrow,* New York, Columbia University Press, 1978, 18–19. Social Security payments were actually double-indexed, to inflation and to wages, which tend to rise; that distortion, however, has been partially eliminated.

24. Steve Lohr, "How Tax Evasion Has Grown," *New York Times,* March 15, 1981, Sec. 3, 1.

25. Ibid., 1, 15; Paul W. MacAvoy, "The Underground—No Recession There," *New York Times,* July 4, 1982, Sec. 3, 3.

26. George Gilder, "We Couldn't Have a Clearer Choice," *Inc.,* October 1980, 52.

Part Two

FROM
ROOSEVELT TO
REAGAN

5

The Rise and Fall of the Social-Service State

The welfare state is on trial. The election of Reagan in 1980 has challenged what seemed for almost fifty years to be the Western solution to the instability and recurring crises of capitalism. The desperation of both political parties, as they sought alternative solutions, showed how far the New Deal had strayed from its original goals. What started as a series of reforms for relieving distress has become a tangle of unwieldy programs geared to the redistribution of wealth. In the process we have mortgaged our future.

Social Security, conceived as a form of contingency insurance, has become Everyman's pension plan. Welfare, rather than solving the problems of poverty, has created a self-perpetuating subculture and siphoned off dollars that could have been spent for productive job training. Medicare and Medicaid have raised the demand for services and consequently expenses—while doing nothing to increase the supply of better services. Transfer payments, from Social Security through VA benefits and price supports, benefit the middle class and even wealthy segments of the population. Indexing, which automatically propels many of these benefits upward, merely feeds the monster inflation to which it presumably "adjusts."

71

Our budget, as a result, has become massive, unwieldy, and inflexible. Uncontrollable outlays like Social Security, along with revenue sharing and interest on the national debt, consumed 75 percent of the federal budget in 1981—all this exclusive of defense spending.

For fifty years the "modern mixed economy" represented the triumph of the discipline of economics. It was a textbook truism that "fiscal and monetary policies are today able to prevent the great depressions of the past."[1] Even more, the Keynesian synthesis resolved the old theoretical disputes. As Kenneth Boulding put it confidently back in 1956,

> *It has become hard to tell a liberal from a conservative. . . . The orthodox Marxist and the orthodox laissez-faire man are today stranded on their little self-contained islands while the great commerce of discourse has swept to other shores. Keynes has drawn the sting on the Marxist scorpion by showing that the instability of capitalism—its tendency to intermittent periods of underemployment—is a real defect which is capable of remedy by fairly simple means. The position of the conservatives who maintain that there is no defect in an unregulated market economy was made untenable by the Great Depression.*[2]

The recipe was: *not* to raise taxes, balance the budget, or stiffen interest rates in depression; and conversely, *not* to lower taxes, increase the deficit, or lower interest rates when faced with inflation.[3]

Of course the problem was not quite so simple even in 1956. Boulding saw clearly enough that a vigorous full-employment policy could raise prices, even permanently. "For whereas an overdose of inflationary government action will raise prices, deflationary government action may merely create unemployment if prices are sticky."[4] Economists of the day thought we could learn to live with inflation. On this point we are far more divided today.

An election has been fought on a philosophical challenge much deeper than those of previous years, yet the welfare state is still with us; it may be an ineradicable feature of our politicoeconomic landscape. One may ask, in fact, where it went wrong. It had succeeded in making the lot of the poor more livable, by relative standards, than that of their compeers in an earlier age, and in many parts of the world today. Was the welfare state inherently flawed in its original conception? Or have other forces diverted it from original goals? What remains valid about its goals and its mechanisms, and the Keynesian notions that it came to adopt?

Our welfare programs are in many respects an unexpected outcome of policies established in the Depression years to mitigate the effects of unemployment, severe illness, and old age. These were salutary steps whose objectives one could hardly contest. The intent of the New Deal was hardly to establish socialism, redistribute income, or substitute long-term security for a work ethic. Bismarck's Germany and Britain's first Lloyd George government had enacted social-security legislation long before our Social Security Act of 1935. The New Deal programs were based on the humanitarian recognition that even the most prudent of men had little protection against personal physical and economic misfortune. And they covered aid to business and agriculture, and work and training programs like the WPA and the CCC, as well as outright benefits.

Nor was this intervention based on the Keynesian theory of deficit spending to revive the economy. Not until 1938 were even Roosevelt's major advisers strongly influenced by Keynes. In fact, Roosevelt and Keynes alluded to each other with mild disparagement. In his first campaign, Roosevelt chided Hoover for incurring a deficit, and the deficits that his measures did incur were too modest to pull an economy out of depression. Indeed, in 1937, when unemployment did contract, Roosevelt deferred to his fiscal conservatives, cut public-works spending, and balanced the budget, producing (as Keynes predicted) the sharp recession of 1938. When the Roosevelt administration finally accepted deficit spending as a strategy to stimulate the economy, it was with reluctance and a promise to return to fiscal orthodoxy.[5]

A more ambitious step in social policy was taken with the Full Employment Act of 1946, which committed the government to maintaining high employment, at least in principle. Though it stopped short of open endorsement of deficit spending to maintain economic stability, and saw it as a preventive measure, the bill opened the way for the deficit spending that later became epidemic.

In the heyday of the post–World War II expansion, however, the problems of economic stability seemed to be academic. Poverty came to be seen as residual—undesirable yet manageable in what John Kenneth Galbraith called *The Affluent Society*. For Galbraith the solution to this residual, self-perpetuating poverty lay in investing in public goods—like health and education, transportation, parks, and libraries—that would serve entire communities and the poor as part of those communities.

By then the problems that now plague us were beginning to emerge: slow growth, European competition, and unemployment. Eisenhower's fiscal conservatism had done nothing to ease these problems, and had produced by 1959 the largest postwar deficit yet. Kennedy, though averse to deficits, was looking for new solutions. The result was Kennedy's supply-side economics: the expansionary tax cut and investment tax credit in 1961, Kennedy's theoretical critique of the balanced budget in 1962, and the stimulative tax cuts and investment tax credits proposed in 1963 and carried out by President Johnson even as he launched the War on Poverty.[6]

But could we do everything at once—cut taxes and increase spending on public goods? "Choices have to be made," wrote Robert Lekachman, prophetically enough, in 1966.

A presidential program which stresses substantial tax reductions simply cannot at the same time demand of Congress very large new programs of regional development, education, man-power training, public works, and urban reconstruction. . . . The politics of consensus—something for everybody—should not conceal the relative financial weights of the two varieties of action {tax favors and social programs}. It should be evident that after an initial flirtation with cautious structural devices, the Kennedy-Johnson administrations have quite literally placed their money on the stimulation of aggregate demand by means of successive tax reductions totaling far more than the new social outlays. . . .

How long will this emphasis continue to be appropriate? At this point in the argument, even the sturdiest defender of the aggregate de-mand hypothesis is likely to shiver in a chilling breeze of doubt.[7]

If combining these programs with the tax cuts was grandiose, combining them both with a war in Vietnam was disastrous. Worse yet, the War on Poverty programs tended to imply that poverty was a kind of disease. As the programs lurched out in all directions to meet all possible causes, their social-welfare ethos combined with an adversary posture to produce a "psychology of entitlement." As various groups learned the skills of mobilization, the notion of a public interest was lost in the welter of competing claims. "Logrolling was transformed from necessary evil to greater good."[8]

These movements were supported by many in the "new class" of public bureaucrats that emerged after World War II to manage the new, "affluent, highly technological, mildly paternalistic, post-industrial society." Idealistically, these professionals—lawyers, teachers, social workers, criminologists, and city planners—believed that it was the government's responsibility to solve all human problems. More pragmatically, one may say that, having chosen public-sector employment, they depended on an expanding government that found its justification in regulation of all economic activity. By the late 1970s, the public sector employed nearly a fifth of all American workers, over a third of all male professionals and half the professional women.[9]

Though these tendencies became apparent in the 1960s, they had begun much earlier, and they became even stronger after the Democratic administration was ousted in 1968. The reason is simple. The 1960s notions of accountability and maximum feasible participation only lent a new gloss to crass political opportunism. The War on Poverty only added to the repertoire of strategies by which politicians court the public. As David Stockman, head of Reagan's Office of Management and Budget, wrote in 1975, the federal government had been misused by liberals and conservatives, Republicans and Democrats, politicians and bureaucrats, to create self-perpetuating constituencies that would keep them in power. "What might have been the bright promise of the Great Society has been transformed into a flabby hodgepodge, funded without policy consistency or rigor, that increasingly looks like a great social pork barrel."[10]

THE POLITICAL-ECONOMIC CYCLE

The political expedience of these benefits is revealed strikingly in the timing of their increases, which follows what Edward R. Tufte has called, in his incisive study, the "electoral rhythm of economic performance." So closely have Social Security benefit increases been timed to elections that the increase came in October if Election Day fell the first week in November, and in early November if Election Day fell the second week in November. The larger check came with a statement conveying the president's regards. Tax hikes to cover these expenses have come, of course, the next year.[11]

Since Social Security increases were indexed to rise automatically with inflation, rather than by congressional action, the schedule has changed, with increases coming in July. But the efforts to capitalize on the increases continue. In July 1982 Democrats were outraged when a television ad ran showing a postman with a Social Security check and crediting Reagan with keeping his promises. Democrats prepared a commercial of their own.[12]

These increases have been part of a more general strategy to convey the appearance of economic health in election years through mechanisms that increase real disposable income in these years. Social Security, with over 30 million retirees' votes (and those of their spouses) hanging on it, is the most popular benefit; Veterans Administration payments come next. Other mechanisms for pumping up the economy include keeping unemployment levels low, legislating tax cuts, approving larger deficits, engineering gushes in the money supply, and juggling with the balance of payments.[13]

These strategies date back to the Depression years. Franklin Roosevelt was not above the political and election-year timing of federal programs. During the Truman, Kennedy, Johnson, Nixon, and Ford administrations, short-run growth in real disposable per capita income tended to swing up in election years and to drop in odd-numbered years. Eisenhower, who was committed to reducing inflation and maintaining a small and balanced budget, was an exception. But Vice-President Nixon, Arthur Burns, and Herbert Stein felt Republicans were losing elections because they eschewed such techniques[14]—and they seem to have mastered that lesson since.

Nixon's 1972 election-year strategies are a classic if exaggerated illustration of this pattern. In October 1972, increased Social Security checks reached voters with a note crediting the raise to Congress and President Nixon. Payments were raised 20 percent and were indexed to inflation in the bargain. Under the White House's "Responsiveness Program," which was stepped up before and dropped right after the election, veterans' benefits heaped up, reaching a peak of $14.1 billion in the 1972 election quarter (as against $10.8 billion in early 1971). Grants to local and state governments, the third largest category of transfer payments, increased in the election quarter and declined by $5 billion immediately after. About 75 million individuals, all of voting age, gained temporarily from the increased cash flow.

For equally political reasons, $23-billion deficits were run back-to-back in the two years just before the 1972 election. To control such unpleasant side effects as inflation, the GOP borrowed Democratic strategies and instituted wage and price controls. Nixon also generated expansionary pressures to counter an expected 6 percent unemployment rate, relying heavily on monetary policy for the juice for expansion. George Schultz, OMB director, felt that if an election were to be won, the Fed would have to increase the money supply at far more than the 4.2 percent average of 1969–70. In various speeches and off-the-record briefings, the range of 6 to 9 percent was clearly suggested. The Fed did accelerate money growth in 1971–72. Whether it was for the sake of the election is moot. In any event, the 1972 election was not unique. Historically, the money supply has increased faster in the two years before presidential elections than in the two years after. The relationship is especially strong when the Eisenhower years are excluded.[15]

Although the two parties do tend to carry out their own economic priorities, they become bipartisan in times of crisis. Hence the convergence in both parties of many so-called liberal platforms, to the consternation of professional economists and conservatives. Turnover doesn't change policies. They acquire a momentum and constituency of their own that sustains them through different administrations and puts pressure on their electors.[16]

WELFARE: INSTANT SOLUTIONS OR LONG-TERM BENEFITS?

Our welfare program is a sterling example of good intentions gone awry. The poor today no longer suffer the devastating consequences of depression that they did until the 1930s. No one dies for total lack of food, clothing, or shelter, or from consumptive TB, cholera epidemics, or the other infectious diseases that stemmed from lack of the medical facilities and services now commonly available. Gone are the sweat shops, child oppression, the 100-hour work week of the early Industrial Revolution. Subsistence needs are met with an array of food, medical, and rent subsidies, income security payments, and educational grants. Even welfare recipients have a standard of living matching that of all but the top 10 percent of the world's population.

More than that, most people own their own television sets and transistor radios. They have some funds for movies and other entertainment. They have access to free schools and libraries. In terms of sheer amount and variety, they have more information, entertainment, travel options, and choices in food, at little or no cost, than was ever available to any people in history, including kings and emperors. Today, as one elderly lady quipped, recession means having temporarily to do without the things our grandparents never dreamed of enjoying.

Our social conditions are far from what they might be. But "if poverty is a lack of basic needs," says labor economist Sar A. Levitan, "we have almost eliminated poverty in the United States." According to a 1977 Congressional Budget Office study, federal programs reduced the national rate of poverty by 60 percent in the

78

preceding decade. A fourth of American families would have been officially poor without these benefits, says Professor Edgar J. Browning, and "the average poor family in 1973 had an income about 30 percent above the poverty level" with them. [17]

Yet this achievement is not widely acknowledged. If our provisions for income security have increased, so has our consciousness of suffering, heightened and exaggerated by the media in their quest for visible pathos. Newspapers and television focus on the smaller tragedies of little people, on our elderly indigents, on families of ten living on unemployment and food stamps in urban slums.

Statistics have become a political football in debates over poverty. Statistics not necessarily created for interest groups and bureaucracies have certainly been used to good advantage by them. The statistics are also subject to a recurrent debate over whether noncash benefits should be included in the income of the poor—an inclusion that would reduce their numbers. Such a dispute arose in 1975 over discrepancies between the Congressional Budget Office and the Census Bureau, which did not count noncash benefits. A similar issue was raised again in early 1982. [18]

What is more, there has been a proliferation, over the past three decades, in both cash and noncash programs. Aid to Families with Dependent Children (AFDC) is the oldest and largest component. Other programs that have been added or expanded include Supplemental Social Security, which helps old, blind, and disabled people who have not worked long enough to qualify for work-related benefits; Medicaid; rent and other supplements; and state and local home relief for poor people without families.

Between 1950 and 1960 alone, the number of AFDC recipients increased enough to alarm President Kennedy—from 651,000 families, or 2.2 million individuals, to 803,000 families. By 1976, 3.6 million families or 11.2 million individuals were receiving this aid—about 7 percent of the U.S. population. In large cities like New York, Los Angeles, and Baltimore, where poor populations are concentrated, AFDC rolls *quadrupled* between 1960 and 1970, increasing from 2.6 percent to 11 percent of the cities' populations, and then, by 1976, to 15 to 20 percent in

Hartford, New Haven, and New York City.[19] Social-service professionals estimate that about a tenth of all children in this country receive AFDC help.

Welfare costs also quadrupled, from $3.3 billion to $14.4 billion, between 1960 and 1970. AFDC costs alone quintupled, from $1 billion to $5 billion, then more than doubled again in the next eight years to reach $10.7 billion in 1978. Medical assistance costs multiplied *one thousand* times between 1960 and 1970—from $6 million to $5.9 billion, and then to an incredible $17.1 billion in 1977.[20]

What has propelled this explosion? Was a vast group in desperate need, or have we encouraged this growth? One of its causes has been the movement of black and Hispanic populations into the cities, where they swell the public-assistance rolls. Although cities have tried to check this influx with residency requirements, such restrictions have been declared unconstitutional, so that cities sustain migrant populations who have never contributed to their economies. Cities without a regional tax base are hit worst.[21] In the forty-one largest U.S. cities, welfare costs by 1970 consumed 11 percent of city budgets. In New York City, they came to 23 percent of the budget.

Another cause is the growth in the number of families headed by women. This group did not participate in the economic expansion of the 1960s. Furthermore, the situation of women was different in the 1960s from what it had been in the 1930s, when AFDC was launched. In the 1930s, the legislation permitted women to care for their children; work was scarce and welfare was a strategy that kept women off the job market. In the 1960s, however, when working mothers were becoming increasingly prevalent and acceptable, more women than ever before went on welfare. And though welfare families are smaller than they used to be (over half of AFDC families have only one or two children), the number of illegitimate children has increased. In 1977 just over a third of all AFDC children were illegitimate.[22] Even if the stereotypes of single-parent families are dismissed and the right to privacy conceded, illegitimacy remains a public concern if children who are neither planned nor provided for become subjects of public support. According to Rand and other studies, the structure of welfare itself discourages marriage. An AFDC mother and a father living separately on relief may be able to get a larger total benefit.[23] Thus the program encourages the very problem to which it is a response: the female-headed household.

Demographic changes alone do not explain the explosion in enrollment rates. Politicians and bureaucrats have acquired a vested interest in the expansion of the system. Radical analysts hold that the Democratic administration in the 1960s sought to regain its urban voting base by importing funds and jobs into the cities to underwrite political machines with their own form of patronage and political spoils.

Great Society programs "gave money to ghetto organizations which then used the money to harass city agencies. . . . Later the new programs helped organize the ghetto poor to picket the welfare department or to boycott the school system. . . . As it turned out, blacks made their largest tangible gains from this process through the public-welfare system."[24] But this gain came mainly because other groups were not competing for a share of relief. City revenues did not decline—in fact, they rose astronomically. But costs rose more, benefiting not the poor so much as the bureaucrats who served them; the vendors who sold to them; and the organized occupations who made a virtual run upon the treasury in the name of professionalism. New York City spends some $600 million as its local share (about 30 percent) of total welfare costs in the city; but over half goes not to poor people but for administration.[25] Lenient administration also contributed to the upsurge, as offensive home inspections (to determine if there was really no man in the home) were given up in several states.

Nor should militance be underestimated as a factor. "The feeling during that period was . . . 'Don't let a riot start.' Clients came in droves. . . . You couldn't arrest them, you had to let them stay all night or give them money. We gave them money."[26]

It is ironic that when the reasonable bare minimum subsistence level is provided, welfare serves as a disincentive to work. As Levitan points out, other factors may have been necessary conditions for the increase in welfare, but "in the final analysis, the decision to seek assistance was primarily stimulated by the increasing attractiveness of AFDC relative to other sources of income."[27] AFDC payments between 1963 and 1971 increased faster than the spendable earnings of all private employees—67 percent as against only 42 percent—whereas in the preceding period both had increased at about the same rate. Increases in food care and medical benefits have tilted the balance even more in favor of welfare. In 1976 a family of four received $5,556, excluding available rent supplements; in New York City the figure was $6,314. "In most big cities," comments Levitan, "two full weeks' work would be necessary to match monthly cash payments alone for a young mother with one child. When the food stamps, health care, and perhaps public housing benefits are added, the necessary income must also increase."[28] The disincentive becomes more apparent when one considers the time, the carfare that must be spent, the lunches eaten outside, and the clothes and grooming that are necessary when the option of work is taken.

This is not to say that most, or even many, welfare recipients deliberately seek welfare, or that they move to regions with the largest benefits in order to abuse the system. Research studies differ so in sampling, time periods, region, and other factors that consistent results are hard to synthesize. Welfare recipients may start out seeking work. Or they may move in and out of the labor force. But the proportion who work intermittently varies with the study, ranging from nine out of ten to one out of five. There is also tremendous turnover in the welfare rolls.

Nevertheless, a disincentive to work shows up in some of the statistics, especially in long-term and "lifetime" (six to ten years) cases. Between 1971 and 1975, Jodie Allen of the Department of Labor has testified, the proportion of the caseload on welfare for over three years increased from 31 to 45 percent.[29] From 1972 to 1977, lifetime cases went up 50 percent, from 12.1 to 18.1 percent of all cases, while short-term categories remained stable or declined. Over one third in 1977 had been on welfare between four and ten years.[30]

The cause of welfare may be poverty, but welfare has hardly

been the key to its solution. The result is apparent in many of our cities, which function like reservations, inhabited by a superfluous population that is nourished by funds from outside, and by the administrators of public funds who serve as their caretakers.[31]

The work disincentive also shows up in comparisons of states whose benefits are low and eligibility requirements harsh. In Alabama, Florida, and Mississippi, where welfare payments come to no more than half a family's "basic needs," about half the mothers work at least part of the year. Labor-force participation—that is, the incentive to work—is greater where benefits are low but permit recipients who work to keep some of their earnings than where full needs are paid.[32]

The effects of cutbacks highlight the importance of incentives. In the late 1970s, welfare rolls leveled off. Welfare officials claim it resulted from crackdowns on fraud, stricter requirements, and efficiency—a significant reflection on the ability of bureaucracies to budget when they must. Others, however, maintain that the relevant population was simply saturated. And workfare requirements in several states (New York, New Jersey, Connecticut) also forced some off the welfare rolls.

These are harsh disincentives, but they provide an object lesson in overambitious social planning. As vested interests acquire a stake in the expansion of programs, the programs are diluted and their original function is distorted. It is one thing to assist those in real need. But if the price imposed on those who make it work is ignored, attention shifts from the purpose of the program to its cost.

Over and above the mandate of feasibility is the requirement of justice. If a program is distorted by adversary ideologies, by demands that offer in return no contribution to society's array of current needs, the consequences can only be self-destructive. They produce a hostile, subsidized underclass, discouraging both the working poor who earn little more, as well as all those who must lose an ever-larger share of their hard-earned income. Those who carry the burden of the programs, who at first identify with and support their goals and implementation, become so overwhelmed that they refuse to supply an ever-growing army of recipients—

even to the point of denying the truly needy, for whom all would agree these programs are not only desirable, but essential in a civilized society.

THE MIDDLE-CLASS SAFETY NET

Despite its growth, welfare alone comprises a fairly small proportion of total transfer payments. As William E. Simon, no apologist for AFDC, has observed: "When one looks at the actual sum of money being given to this group of people, one can scarcely conclude that AFDC is breaking the back of the U.S. budget." Welfare payments themselves come to only 1 percent of the gross national product.[33]

Most of our social benefits go not to the hard-core poor but to "entitlement" programs for the middle class. The largest by far are the Social Security retirement and disability programs, but the category includes also veterans' benefits, the federal employees and railroad workers' pensions, unemployment assistance, and Medicare. For *none* of these benefits is financial *need* a criterion. Though half (49 percent) of the federal budget now consists of payments to individuals, only 8.5 percent of its total spending is laid out on the basis of financial need.[34]

Between 1956 and 1978, income security payments grew from 2.7 to 10.7 percent of the GNP. The mammoth OASDI (Old Age, Survivors', and Disability Insurance), the largest program in the budget, alone amounted to 5 percent of the GNP by 1982. In 1983, 35 percent of the budget will consist of income-security payments, 26 percent for Social Security and Medicare alone.[35]

SOCIAL SECURITY: A SACRED COW—MILKED DRY

Old Age, Survivors' and Disability Insurance (OASDI) has come to symbolize security in old age for millions of Americans. For millions it is the only source of income in old age, since private pension plans cover only about half the work force, where OASDI now covers over 90 percent of all workers. Its huge administration employs nearly 90,000 persons at 1,300 district offices across the country. It accounts for nearly two-thirds of the personnel of the Department of Health, Education, and Welfare, and pays $1 for every $3 spent by all the rest of the federal government.[36]

Between 1952 and 1981, Social Security grew more than three times as fast as the GNP. In 1982 Social Security and disability payments alone were estimated at $167 billion, as against $146 billion for 1981. Between 1968 and 1977, its benefits grew by 130 percent as prices rose only 75 percent, "so that the real value of the benefit increased about 55 percent," while it was indexed to rise with inflation. As a result, in part, of these increases the mean per capita income of the elderly is about that of the rest of the population—more, if noncash benefits like food stamps and Medicare are included—even though the proportion of the elderly who are poor is slightly higher than that of the rest of the population.[37]

Though the Social Security system often passes as a public pension plan, forcing people to save for their old age, it differs from pensions in several respects. First, workers pay not for their own retirement, but to support the *current* generation of retirees. When they retire, they in turn will be supported by the next generation. Second, retirement payments vary with the worker's income level. Low-income workers get back a larger percentage of their earnings than high-income workers, though their absolute benefits are lower. Third, the Social Security system is indexed for inflation where most pension plans and annuities are not.

In an important respect, however, Social Security resembles other insurance schemes. In insurance, unlike savings, there is no direct relationship between your contributions and your benefit payments. Insurance is based on the principle of averages. Your benefits, when they are paid to you, are paid by others who assumed the same risk but did not die or become ill. You may pay all your life, but if you never suffer the loss against which you are insured, you never receive the benefit. Yet if you are ill or die the day after you take out a policy, you or your family receive full benefits.

Although there must be a pragmatic relationship between the individual's premium and degree of risk involved, even private insurance and pension plans support the goal of providing a certain level of protection for *all* members of the group, even though some (the older, for example) benefit more. In Social Security, this group goal has so overshadowed the pragmatic criterion that the system is imperiled.

Private firms cover "risk"—the need to finance future administrative and benefit costs—by keeping enough reserves on hand to meet a test of liquidation. Reserves must be large enough to cover fully all future obligations to the insured. This is the test of actuarial soundness.

By contrast, the government doesn't have to maintain these reserves because it can rely on compulsory future taxes. It balances its future obligations against future taxes. Its actuarial deficit is the amount of money the government would need to have on hand today, earning interest, to cover the shortfalls that present tax and benefit rates would generate over the next seventy-five years. Its reserves have fallen well below the amounts required for even a reasonable contingency fund (for example, only 39 percent of estimated old-age benefits, and 25 percent for disability). Although some economists have called for higher reserve financing, reserves have not generally been thought to be necessary for actuarial soundness in a government-backed insurance scheme.[38]

At least not until lately. For many years, the two major trust funds, the old-age and disability funds, built up their small reserves because payouts were lower than taxes, and invested these reserves in government securities, both Treasury bonds and notes and special issues sold only to the trust funds.

In 1976, however, OASDI outlays began to exceed its receipts, eating into its small reserve balance at rates that threaten depletion by 1984. The probabilities have changed: the number of retirees and retirement years balanced against the number of paying workers and the number of working and taxpaying hours or years they work and pay in. In 1940 the ratio of workers to older "dependents" was 5 to 1; in 1980 it was 3 to 1. By 2030 the ratio is expected to be 2 to 1.

This drain on the fund was hardly envisaged when Social Security was passed. The retirement age was sixty-five, early retirement was not a practice, and the life expectancy was sixty-two.

Thus it was expected that benefits would be paid only to a very small proportion of the potential beneficiaries who paid in.

The system has not kept pace with demographic and social change or with the consequences of its own policies. The demographic change involves the increased life expectancy of the elderly, the post–World War II baby boom, and the next generation's baby bust. Longevity of course lengthens the period of retirement. Although the ratio of retirees to workers may be offset for a while by the baby-boom generation, a huge tax hike will be needed early in the twenty-first century, when the baby-boom generation retires with high longevity prospects, and will have to be sustained by the relatively small baby-bust generation. Declining marriage rates, later marriages, fewer children per family all sharpen the problem. Former HEW Secretary Joseph Califano has said that spending for the aged alone will take up 35 percent of the budget by the year 2000, and 65 percent by 2025.[39]

However, these long-range implications do not explain why bankruptcy is threatened as early as 1984. Early retirement, which puts more people on Social Security, and the gross expansion of the system itself are largely to blame. At various times since 1950, more categories of workers were made eligible: part of the welfare burden was given to Social Security; and the minimum number of working years required to qualify for minimum lifetime benefits was reduced to as low as six. As of 1978, it was about ten years.[40]

Finally, the politically popular rise in the level of benefits, especially since 1972, when legislation was passed to index Social Security automatically to cost-of-living increases, has changed the payout-revenue balance. Social Security has more than kept up with inflation. In 1970 the average monthly benefit to a retired worker—in *1978* dollars—was $201. In 1978 the benefit was $263. When noncash benefits such as Medicare are added, the benefits are even higher.[41]

Taxes have increased sharply to pay for these benefits, especially in the 1970s. In 1960 the taxable wage base—the portion of income that could be taxed for Social Security—was $4,800, and the combined tax rate for employer and employee only 6 percent.

In 1972 they were $9,000 and 10.4 percent. Since 1972, the taxable wage base has risen to $29,700 in 1981, and the tax rate to 13.3 percent.[42] Further increases in the tax rate and the wage base (or ceiling) are scheduled through the 1990s, some say to a tax rate of almost 25 percent. By 2005, when there may be one beneficiary to every two workers,[43] Social Security tax rates may have to increase to 50 percent to keep the program going.

This prospect has begun to create intergenerational disputes, as working people protest the need to support an older generation, even though they, too, will be putting a heavier strain on their successors. A system with one aged dependent for every three contributors is hardly viable, especially when you add other dependents—the child population, the student population, the numbers on unemployment (7–9 percent of our work force) and the numbers on welfare (7 percent of our population).

The main problem with the program, however, seems more immediate. The present "reduced" benefits are really benefits that were added in 1956 for men and in 1961 for women, as a bonus for early retirement at age sixty-two. Half the applicants for Social Security apply before age sixty-five. In 1978, more males received reduced benefits than received full benefits, and five times as many were on reduced rather than full benefits.[44]

Meanwhile, that worrisome baby-boom generation is at its prime, energetically at work. It should be ample enough in numbers and productivity for another thirty years, building up reserves to support itself in compensation for having failed to spawn a generation that might do so. And yet even now, with a baby-boom generation sustaining a presumably much smaller one, the Social Security fund is being drained at a rate that signals imminent crisis. Our problems of entitlement and eligibility lie not in the twenty-first century. They fester in the here and now.

INDEXING: AN ECONOMIC DEATHTRAP

Ironically, indexing, which originated as a hedge against inflation, has been functioning more as its precipitant. That has become apparent in the productivity and employment crises in several important industries, notably the auto industry (chapter 11).

In the public sector, indexing has had even worse effects. As the consumer price index rises, many benefits are simply pulled up: Social Security, federal-employee, and veterans' benefits. These outlays totaled about $200 billion, or almost a third of a $600-billion-plus budget, in 1980. When that $200 billion is indexed, say, at 13 percent, the automatic increase comes to $26 billion a year, and it takes a $26-billion cut in other parts of the budget just to balance it out.[45]

The inflationary effect of indexing is augmented by the CPI itself, which is a faulty measure of the cost of living. It gives too much weight to mortgage rates and housing costs, a one-time purchase that many regard as an investment rather than a consumption item. When in 1980, the CPI averaged 13.5 percent, the GNP deflator, which adjusts the value of the gross national product for inflation, was registering only 9 percent.[46] The "bundle of goods" on which the CPI is based, unlike the GNP deflator, has lags in representing new amenities that come to represent the improved quality of life for most of us.

For some time, economists, over the opposition of unions and other interest groups, have been urging that some other measure of inflation, like the GNP deflator, be used. Other suggestions include removing the home-purchase component from the CPI; measuring the actual interest paid currently on *all* mortgages, not just the most recent rates; using a measure of rental rather than of purchased housing; and replacing the "fixed market basket of goods," representing what consumers bought in 1972–73, with a *current* market basket based on the latest spending patterns from the quarterly survey that the Bureau of Labor Statistics now conducts. According to Philip Cagan and Geoffrey Moore, the latter measure would give the bureau the option of using an index "long advocated by economists as the best measure of the cost of living: an average of an index based on a fixed market basket (the existing CPI) with one based on a current market basket."[47]

However, no measure of inflation will wholly eliminate the destructive features of indexing, which, like inflation, feeds upon itself, creating a ratchet effect. Nonrecurring events, like droughts and mortgage-interest costs on new homes, are fed into the CPI, producing the chain reactions of commodity price and wage and benefit increases. If farm prices drop, but not as much as the "seasonal adjustment" factor "assumed" by the CPI, they register as an increase![48] This distortion is seen clearly in the inflation-influenced parity adjustments of agricultural farm prices, whose prices are adjusted twice a year and then included in the CPI, thereby guaranteeing justification of the next increase. With the vast portion of our budget (including defense) now indexed for inflation, our "social safety net" has become an economic death-trap.

TOWARD SANITY IN OUR
SOCIAL SPENDING

Our social-welfare design, whose momentum began with Roosevelt's New Deal, and whose heights were reached with Johnson's Great Society, was in its aspirations a worthwhile and in many ways an essential movement. Yet in its later stages, it became too impatient, aggressive, and grandiose in its expectations, its goals, and especially its costs, both direct and indirect, and through its disincentives to work and productivity. It became counterproductive.

It was like a winning army that moves forward, winning each battle as it moves aggressively toward its goal, and then suddenly, by trying too quickly to achieve too much, outruns its supply trains. As it moves beyond the capacity for the required support to keep up with it, it suddenly faces not only the failure to achieve its goal, but, worse still, the loss of all that it has achieved so far, and even, perhaps, its own total destruction. Similarly, by trying to achieve too much—eliminating poverty, malnutrition, the financial burdens of sickness and infirmity, the threat to security posed by aging, the wage losses of unemployment—and by trying to raise everyone's standard of living without requiring some minimum measure of performance, the government tried to deliver more than our reach would allow.

Reality dictates that an army cannot outdistance its supply without paying the price of potential devastation and destruction. Nor can a society, irrespective of its ideals, introduce programs that outdistance its supply without paying some analogous price.

No one, ultimately, can promise what is not deliverable except under certain prescribed circumstances. Tenured professors are learning that tenure is operable only if the funds are there. Whatever the implicit promise and the faculty's legitimate claims to assured positions, the lack of resources makes the promise meaningless. Similarly, government cannot promise security at some prescribed minimal standard of living without a productive base population turning out enough goods and services to make that standard of living deliverable. Government can issue all the promises, all the currency, even all the edicts or threats or legislation it wishes. If it cannot motivate its people to produce the GNP to meet the need, it cannot fulfill the promise of economic security.

As the pendulum swings back, however, it is important once more not to be led astray by absolutist notions, ideological slogans, or political semantics. The entire range of abstractions now being used to define social policy—deregulation, returning power to the states, supply-side strategies—may in turn be misleading, and may carry new public policies beyond *their* margin of effectiveness, producing counterreactions and the opposite of their intent.

Budget-cutting alone is no answer. And even that has been offset by the shift of funds from social to defense spending, by tax cuts and exemptions that forfeited whatever revenue the budget cuts might have raised. Besides, these mechanical adjustments do not provide for our major requirement.

TARGETS FOR PLANNING

Our major need at present is for a social policy that will focus spending on the truly needy and on the particular problems to be solved, without extending these programs to areas where they are irrelevant and even harmful. Here are some examples of diffusion in our programs and some ways in which spending can be targeted with greater precision.

1. **The application of our price indexes is too broad.** To reflect the sources of inflation more precisely, adjustments for inflationary housing and mortgage costs should be confined to those areas alone, not extended to a host of benefits for users to whom

91

they are irrelevant. Most Social Security beneficiaries who have their own homes have already paid off their mortgages. Thus neither housing nor mortgage costs have any relevance to their spending. The CPI should not be used so religiously or mechanically to calculate cost-of-living adjustments.

Nor is there any reason why temporary events and fluctuations should be permanently injected into indexing formulas, rather than treated as nonrecurring deviations. In August 1980, the wholesale price index went up because of a one-time episode, a drought. That cost should not have been built into cost-of-living adjustments, a policy that only fuels and accelerates the spiral. Instead, the government should apply emergency aid to those areas as a one-time solution to the problem. **Nonrecurring events should be treated as "deviant adjustments" in the way that nonrecurring events or activities are tabulated "under the line" in corporate earnings statements, so that they don't inflate (or deflate) actual earnings. Seasonal adjustments should be factored into, and not discounted, in the CPI. Present measurement disregards decreases and exaggerates increases in that index.**

2. Social Security should be revamped to focus on the margin of the truly needy. This means an entirely new philosophy for the system. Current proposals are more limited. They include: running Social Security on actuarial principles; gradually raising the retirement age; taking Medicare off the payroll tax; cutting benefits for early retirement; using a less exaggerated inflation index than the CPI; gearing increases to wage increases; taxing Social Security benefits above a given income floor; cutting back survivors' benefits; eliminating double-dipping on pensions; using a value-added or sales tax to finance it; reducing all benefits; shifting over to the welfare system almost all benefits to those poor who have not worked; and virtually eliminating the minimum benefits that go to those with just a few years of qualifying work.

All of these measures, while useful, fail to address the central problem. Social Security should be seen as an *insurance* program, not as a compulsory pension plan, in terms of which it provides inadequate benefits in any case. Protection is needed for the elderly without private pensions—fewer than half the workers in private industry have such coverage—and for single women workers and widows. Women suffer doubly because their wages, from which Social Security benefits are calculated, are much lower than those of men.[49] But millions of others are amply provided for, and for them Social Security is merely a bonus. There is no reason to give it to those who subscribed to the system as a precaution against poverty, a threat that fortunately for them never materialized.

By the ironies of our present system, I will be as much entitled to these benefits, despite my millions in assets, as the individual dependent on Social Security alone. During my earlier working years, I enjoyed the security and comfort of knowing that these benefits would be there if I ever needed them. In fact, I could undertake greater risks because this "fail safe" existed if my undertakings failed. That assurance should be enough. Having been treated well by our economic system, I have no need for these payments and should not receive them. If medical, automobile, or fire and theft insurance policies had to guarantee a payout to every client, the entire system of insurance would collapse.

3. **All pension benefits should be tightened.** President Reagan is one of thousands who are "double-dipping," collecting an old-age or retirement pension as a reward for his governorship of California while continuing in active work, after which he will receive another pension paid for by taxpayers. It is impossible to act on such situations retroactively, but some modification of the terms of these contracts is in order. The Social Security pensionee is highly limited in the active work he can engage in if he is to continue receiving benefits. Ironically, unearned income does not disqualify the pensionee while earned income does.

4. **Medicare benefits require a radically new approach.** The current program has made physicians astoundingly rich and has burdened the country with gigantic medical costs; it has all the disadvantages of socialism and none of its benefits. **By accelerating demand without doing anything about supply, it has raised prices in accordance with the classic inflation-producing model.** It has also discouraged the exercise of economic rationality. The beneficiary does not look for the best buy when the

government underwrites his or her medical costs. Doctors and hospitals routinely put patients through costly and unnecessary tests and treatments involving complex technologies simply to help amortize their expenses and increase their profits. Medicaid vendors issue cheap spectacles that don't last and continue to earn fees by their constant replacement.

We need expanded medical services and personnel—more doctors and the service competition that would stem from such a condition—not expanded medical subsidies. At present the supply of physicians remains inadequate, while government spending dramatically expands the demand for their services.

5. **The welfare system provides the most painful dilemma of social policy. We need a manpower policy in its place, not simple cutbacks.** The dilution of its programs cheats those who need them the most. The politics of welfare is something the street-smart learn and exploit, while those who have struggled all their lives on subsistence salaries without the opportunity to save, and consequently require public support, are cheated in two ways. The money that they deserve is diverted to others; and the crackdowns on fraud cheat those who need public support as much as they weed out abusers. The resultant bureaucratic red tape—and these crackdowns must result in bureaucratic red tape—bears down on the ones who truly cannot work, who become victims of ruthless manhunts. Those who are not politically adroit are shifted from bureau to bureau, to submit endless numbers of forms before they are really considered. Those who could be helped and rehabilitated become totally demoralized, while those who have learned to work the system enjoy the benefits. The dilemma is visible in the derelicts of New York City, who have no homes and do not qualify for any benefits. Indeed, one of these derelicts, an aged schizophrenic woman who was dropped from the welfare rolls because she missed the quarterly appointment with a welfare officer, froze to death on the city streets in the winter of 1982.

Welfare cannot really be reformed, no matter how much it is tinkered with, expanded, or contracted. It provides no constructive solution to the problems of the dependent poor. It merely creates a caste.

Welfare reforms, including job creation and work-incentive

programs, have been ineffectual. Recently employment and welfare programs were integrated, but much of the coordination is ritual. You register with welfare, go from them to the unemployment office, which has nothing for you, and repeat the routine periodically, while the system of job provision is barely changed.

Workfare, the twenty-hour-a-week work requirement for welfare recipients, is potentially useful, both in preventing abuse of welfare and in providing work. It has antecedents in the 1962 Kennedy proposal that placed welfare recipients in community jobs, and in the current work-incentive effort, which seeks to train and place adults on relief. Work incentive has been tried or adopted in Utah, Massachusetts, New Jersey, New York, and California, where Reagan instituted it. He has now established the requirement for federal welfare aid. Welfare recipients earn their benefits by serving as school crossing guards, baby sitters, nursery aides, park attendants, school lunch-room aides, and school-bus helpers.

Such programs have been criticized on various counts, including their administrative costs and the lack of placement possibilities. But the criticisms suggest that the program should be improved, not abandoned. The types of positions being created are often expendable, too much like the leaf-raking activities that have caused public works to be held in contempt.

It might be more productive to offer industry incentives to train employees and apprentices. Yet job training and job creation programs generate new problems. Union workers and civil servants oppose them. Administrators, understandably, employ those who will show the best results, but who probably would have gotten jobs on their own. Many welfare recipients are only marginally employable at best; they must compete (or refuse to compete) with immigrant labor (legal or illegal) for low-paying, menial jobs. The solution to these problems requires a manpower policy that takes our entire work force into account.

NOTES

1. Samuelson, *Economics,* 11th ed., 766.

2. Kenneth Boulding, *Beyond Economics: Essays on Society, Religion, and Ethics,* Ann Arbor, University of Michigan Press, 1968, 33.

3. Ibid., 34.

4. Boulding, *Beyond Economics,* 34.

5. Robert Lekachman, *The Age of Keynes,* New York, Random House, 1966, 112–20, 123.

6. Ibid., 194–97, 200–213, 271; Walter Heller, "Kennedy's Supply-Side Economics," *Challenge,* May–June, 1981, 14–18. For a more extensive analysis of Keynesianism and supply-side economics, see chapter 9.

7. Lekachman, *Age of Keynes,* 242–43.

8. Lowi, *End of Liberalism,* 55.

9. Irving Kristol, *Two Cheers for Capitalism,* New York, Basic Books, 1978, 15–16; Thurow, *Zero-Sum Society,* 163.

10. Quoted by Sidney Blumenthal, "David Stockman: The President's Cutting Edge," *New York Times Magazine,* March 15, 1981, 80.

11. Edward R. Tufte, *Political Control of the Economy,* Princeton, N.J., Princeton University Press, 1978, 34–44.

12. Adam Clymer, "Democrats Join the Battle of TV Ads," *New York Times,* July 16, 1982, A11.

13. Tufte, *Political Control of the Economy,* 15–45, esp. 36, 38, 50–57.

14. Gavin Wright, "The Political Economy of New Deal Spending: an Econometric Analysis," *Review of Economics and Statistics,* 56 (February 1974), 30–38; Tufte, *Political Control of the Economy,* 16–21, 45–48.

15. Tufte, *Political Control of the Economy,* 30–32, 48–54.

16. Ibid., 89.

17. Quoted by Harry Schwartz, "Is Poverty Abolished," *New York Times,* October 19, 1976, 39.

18. Ibid.; "Redefining Poverty: Some Interesting But Loaded Choices," *New York Times,* April 18, 1982, Sec. 4, 1; "The Poor Get More Numerous," *New York Times,* November 8, 1981, Sec. 4, 8E.

19. *Statistical Abstract,* 1979, 100th ed., Table 566, 352; Frances Fox Piven, "The Urban Crisis: Who Got What, and Why," in *The Fiscal Crisis of American Cities,* Roger E. Alcaly and David Mermelstein, eds., New York, Random House, Vintage Books, 1977, 139.

20. *Statistical Abstract,* 1979, 100th ed., Table 567, 352.

21. Piven, "Who Got What," 134–139; Charles L. Schultz et al., "Fiscal Problems of Cities," in *Fiscal Crisis of American Cities,* Alcaly and Mermelstein, eds., 200–201.

22. *Statistical Abstract,* 1979, 100th ed., Table 574, 357.

23. Leonard Greene, *Free Enterprise Without Poverty,* New York, W. W. Norton, 1981, 48–52.

24. Piven, "Who Got What," 138–39.

25. Piven, "Who Got What," 140–41; William K. Tabb, "Blaming the Victim," in *Fiscal Crisis of American Cities,* Roger E. Alcaly and David Mermelstein, eds., 315–36.

26. Cited by Sol Stern, "Computer Cards and Chaos," in *The Poverty Establishment,* Pamela Roby, ed., Englewood, Prentice-Hall, 1974, 118.

27. Sar A. Levitan, Martin Rein, and David Marwick, *Work and Welfare Go Together,* Baltimore, Johns Hopkins University Press, 1972, 19.

28. Levitan et al., *Work and Welfare,* 14. Since the Reagan cutbacks, liberal commentators and studies stress the disincentive to work when there is little difference between welfare benefits and earnings. See for example, the editorial "The People on the Edge," *New York Times,* January 17, 1982, Sec. 4, 22E, and Robert Pear, "Incentive for Not Working Is Found in Study of Budget," *New York Times,* February 25, 1982, A18.

29. Cited by Tom Bethel, "Treating Poverty: Wherein the Cure Gives Rise to The Disease," reprinted with revisions from *Harper's Magazine,* February 1980, by International Institute for Economic Research, Los Angeles, Green Hill Publishers, 1980.

30. *Statistical Abstract,* 1979, 100th ed., Table 574, 357.

31. Norton E. Long, "The City as Reservation," *Public Interest,* Fall 1971, 22–38.

32. Levitan et al., *Work and Welfare,* 66.

33. William E. Simon, *A Time for Truth,* New York, Reader's Digest Press, 1978, 218–19; Lester Thurow, "There Are Solutions to Our Economic Problems," *New York Times Magazine,* August 10, 1980, 30.

34. Peter G. Peterson, "No More Free Lunch for the Middle Class," *New York Times Magazine,* January 17, 1982, 40.

35. Thurow, *Zero-Sum Society,* 159; Office of Management and Budget, *Budget of the United States Government: Fiscal Year 1982,* 247; *Budget of the United States Government: Fiscal Year 1983,* 5–139; Ann Crittenden, "Most Experts Call Social Security Basically Sound," *New York Times,* June 9, 1982, B14.

36. Robert M. Ball, *Social Security: Today and Tomorrow,* New York, Columbia University Press, 1978, 308–09 (1977 data), 393.

37. *Budget of the U.S. Government: Fiscal Year 1982,* 247; Ball, *Social Security,* 18–19; Thurow, *Zero-Sum Society,* 159.

38. Michael Boskin, "How to Reform Social Security," *New York Times,* January 11, 1981, Sec. 3, 2; Simon, *A Time for Truth,* 219, 299; Ball, *Social Security,* 20.

39. Peterson, "No More Free Lunch," 56.

40. Ball, *Social Security,* 37.

41. *Statistical Abstract,* 1979, 100th ed., Tables 526 and 527, 330.

42. *Statistical Abstract,* 1979, 100th ed., Table 535, 335; Boskin, "How to Reform Social Security," 2.

43. *Statistical Abstract,* 1979, Table 536, 335.

44. *Statistical Abstract,* 1979, 100th ed., Table 540, 338.

45. Rudolph C. Penner, "Why Indexing Was a Big Mistake," *New York Times,* February 1, 1981, Sec. 3, 2.

46. *Statistical Abstract,* 1981, 102d ed., Table 767, 459.

47. Geoffrey H. Moore and Philip Cagan, "A Second Basket for the Consumer Price Index," *New York Times,* December 24, 1980, 16.

48. Jonathan Fuerbringer, "Ironing Out Seasonal Statistics," *New York Times,* June 24, 1982, D1, D9.

49. Ball, *Social Security,* 90, 91.

6

The Unemployment Game

*Give a man a fish and you feed
him for one day. Teach a man to
fish and you feed him for a lifetime.*

To ask how unemployment is theoretically conceivable is no
idle intellectual enterprise. From 1803 on, with surplus labor
staring them in the face, economists adhered to Jean-Baptiste
Say's (1767–1832) law of markets, "supply creates its own demand," according to which unemployment was impossible. Since
low wages gave employers an incentive to hire more workers and
increase their output and their profits, all workers could be employed at a low enough wage. Moreover, employers, by providing
jobs and income as they increased supply, generated matching increases in demand until economic equilibrium was reached at a
level of full employment and full production. Any unemployment
that did exist had to be voluntary or between-job (frictional), or
the result of union or government interference with the market.[1]

The major challenge to this thesis was presented by John May-
nard Keynes in 1936, when his pivotal *General Theory of Employ-*

ment, Interest, and Money appeared, adventitiously enough, in the midst of the Great Depression. Keynes argued that equilibrium could be reached at *any* level of employment; there was no theoretical reason to assume that any one level of employment was more likely to occur than any other. Nor was that level determined by wage negotiations. Involuntary joblessness could exist at even the lowest wages, because men could not get any work at any price if demand was absent and investors were pessimistic.

Central to his argument was his major contribution, the notion of aggregate demand. With it Keynes pointed up the fallacy of composition that had been built into earlier explanations: what was true for the part was not true for the whole. Say's law was valid when *one* employer reduced his costs—workers' wages—to expand his profits and output. But *all* employers could not benefit from a general reduction in wages. For when all wages fell, aggregate income and purchasing power fell too. Aggregate demand (spending) fell along with, and in proportion to, wages. And this drop reduced, in turn, the incentive to invest and produce. The result was an equilibrium of stagnation combined with chronic involuntary unemployment.[2]

In the era of "managed capitalism" that Keynes helped launch, this perspective has become dogma. Since the full-employment equilibrium does not occur automatically, through the private economy's self-adjusting mechanism, the government must intervene periodically to encourage investment and maintain employment, income, and demand.[3]

Both supply-side strategies and demand management are compatible with Keynesian theory, but they dictate different policy consequences. Each triggers a different side of the demand-supply equation, which is, after all, a relationship of mutual causality. Demand-side strategies have governed public policy for almost four decades now and have helped us avert depressions. But we have lived with unmanageable levels of inflation, while unemployment levels constantly creep upward. Now that supply-side theory has reentered into public discussion and textbooks stress the full-employment equilibrium,[4] it may be time to take another look at Say's notion that supply creates its own demand.

THE IMPOSSIBLE DREAM

Our approach to unemployment problems suffers today from the futile pursuit of an impossible dream—the myth of full employment and the notion that government can generate work for all. It is a worthy ideal, but it is based on depression assumptions that no longer obtain.

Traditional policies addressed cyclical unemployment—joblessness produced by fluctuations in the business cycle. Although these policies date back to the Depression, they were codified in 1946 in the historic Full Employment Act. At that time economists, seared by memories of the Depression, and expecting another depression like the one that had followed World War I, looked to the government to monitor and maintain economic health. The act was pushed through by the new Keynesian economists and the equally new liberal business group, the Committee for Economic Development, together with the National Farmers Union, over the opposition of the National Association of Manufacturers, the Chamber of Commerce, and the American Farm Bureau Federation. But splits within the business and farm groups weakened the bill, and it was passed largely as a symbolic measure in which the words "full employment" did not even appear. Its merit lay in the establishment of the prestigious Council of Economic Advisers and the Joint Committee on the Economic Report of the President. It also established the principle that government should intervene, through tax and spending policies, to maintain high levels of employment.[5]

As it happened, employment actually increased after World War II, and between 1945 and 1950 pent-up consumer demand pushed the consumer price index from 128.6 to 189.7. For seventeen years, from 1940 to 1957, the economy enjoyed a virtually unbroken period of nearly "full employment." Only during the mild slumps of 1948–49 and 1953–54 did the jobless rate go over 5 percent.[6] During this period, "full employment" was defined as a 4 percent level of unemployment (3 percent for adults), a figure that took into account "frictional" unemployment—that is, for those who were between jobs.

Unemployment resurfaced as a serious problem in the late 1950s, and it has never left us since. From the 1957—58 recession (with 6.8 percent joblessness) until 1964, it averaged 5.8 percent, sometimes rising to over 7 percent. Only in January 1966, when the Vietnam draft took many of the unemployed, did the rate fall back, to remain at 3—4 percent for over three years. It was during this period that the problem of structural or hard-core unemployment became apparent. In May 1969, with unemployment at a low 3.5 percent, nonwhites had 6.4 percent and teenagers 12.2 percent unemployment levels.[7]

The problem became endemic in the 1970s. Unemployment jumped to 6.2 percent in late 1970 with Nixon's anti-inflation efforts, but that figure is hardly considered high any more. From 1971 to 1973, the rate averaged 5.6 percent. In the 1974—75 depression, it averaged 8.5 percent; and even with recovery, it ranged from 7 to 8 percent through mid-1980 and was almost 11 percent in late 1982 and early 1983, showing an "unprecedented" pattern of "substantial" (6 percent or more) unemployment even in prosperity. More than that: employment has not been growing as quickly as the GNP; in other words, economic growth no longer seems to be the automatic solution to unemployment.[8]

Explanations vary. Some economists argue that we have never had full employment except in war. When World War II and the Korean and Vietnam years are subtracted from the halcyon seventeen-year period of prosperity, only five peacetime years of full employment are left.

Alarmed at these statistics, proponents of the controversial Humphrey-Hawkins Full Employment and Balanced Growth Plan Bill of 1978 (even in the weakened version that was finally passed) have responded with the old solutions and definitions. They still define "full" employment as no more than 3 percent adult (4 percent overall) unemployment, and they propose to reach that level by using government, if necessary, as employer of last resort.[9]

It may be, however, that our definitions of "full employment" should be refined. The 1977 *Economic Report of the President* and the Committee for Economic Development opt for 5 percent. "The reality is," a *Forbes* writer has put it, "that we will have to live with a rate of unemployment that would have been unacceptable in the recent past. This rate is probably in the neighborhood of 5.5 percent—trying to get it lower would set off an inflationary spiral."[10] This inflation-unemployment tradeoff is based on the simple notion that inflation sets in with full employment and that a certain degree of unemployment is necessary to check inflation or reverse the trend (see chapter 2). The trouble is that the tradeoff is becoming increasingly expensive and painful. We seem to need more and more unemployment to check inflation.

The debate goes to the heart of our political semantics and definitions. Unemployment statistics are not, after all, neutral or indisputable figures: implicit in them are value judgments and ideologies. On their number, nature, and implications hang not only the hopes of competing interest groups but billions of dollars in grants and subsidies, funds that might indeed help the poor, but that more often line the pockets of administrators or ensure the political advancement of advocates of the poor.

Depending on the way these figures are interpreted, unions can argue the desperate situation of the worker in the job market and demand stimulative measures regardless of the effect on inflation, deficits, or the damage to consumers or nonunion workers. Politicians can use the figures to call for vast pork-barrel programs to rescue their flagging constituencies. Advocates of the poor and minorities will consistently maintain that the figures are too modest. Each month senators and representatives pounce on the Commissioner of Labor Statistics report to see who can make the most political capital out of the data.[11] So disputable are the facts that the Bureau of Labor Statistics has described seven ways to count the unemployed.

The definition of *full employment* is equally political. Have we redefined the term to make unemployment seem more palatable as its levels go up? Or are we inflating the figures to create unwarranted alarm? What changes do these figures really reflect about the demography of work—the age, sex, ethnic, and educational makeup of our work force—on the one hand, and the structure of opportunities on the other?

THE DEMOGRAPHY OF WORK

Our unemployment figures today tell us something radically different about work and joblessness than did earlier statistics. They no longer describe cyclical unemployment alone, or even real unemployment as we once conceived it. Part of our problem is long-term and structural, stemming from automation, the obsolescence of skills, and the inability of workers to move to new job opportunities.

Another stems from the nature of work in an affluent society with rising expectations, in which job opportunities have not increased as fast as the numbers of women, teenagers, and minority people looking for work.

Still another significant aspect stems from our system of unemployment compensation and transfer payments itself. When these nontaxable benefits approach or exceed what wages might offer, workers are encouraged to be unemployed and to prolong the periods between jobs. Welfare payments, food stamps, and rent subsidies can also raise the level or duration of unemployment. Moreover, since employers' unemployment insurance taxes are not directly proportionate to their layoffs, some firms lay off more workers more often than they would if they had to pay the full costs of unemployment benefits, contributing to the pattern of induced or voluntary unemployment.

For different causes and motives, these factors have been responsible for variations that inflate, exaggerate, and destabilize the overall unemployment rate, oscillating around the levels of the stable mainstay of our labor force, the prime-age working male, and especially the married male.

Take the case of increasing female and teenage employment. In 1980, half the women of working age were members of the work force and made up 42 percent of the work force, in comparison to only 32 percent in 1960. Teenage (sixteen- to nineteen-year-old) work-force participation between 1960 and 1979 rose from 57 to 63 percent for males, and from 39 to 54 percent for females.[12] These groups contribute disproportionately to the unemployment figures.

The contrast is clearest when unemployment among women

and teenagers is compared with the rates for adult males, especially married males, and not with the overall levels. For the adult male, especially the married male, unemployment has been lower and less volatile than the overall rate. In 1969, when overall unemployment was at a low 3.5 percent, the rate for adult males, twenty years and older, was even lower, 2.1 percent, and for heads of families it was only 1.5 percent. For adult women it was 3.7 percent, more than 50 percent higher than the level for adult males. For female heads of families, the rate of 4.4 percent was over twice the 1.5 percent for married men. For teens, the unemployment rate of 12.2 percent was *almost six times* the adult male rate.

Similar disparities show up in recession. In the severe recession year of 1975, when the overall unemployment rate was 8.5 percent, the level for adult males was 8 percent and for married men only 5.1 percent. At the same time, the rate for teenagers was 19.9 percent, more than three times that for married men, while about 8 percent of female workers and 10 percent of female heads of families were unemployed.[13]

Unemployment has risen partly because these groups with "high unemployment rates" have grown in relative size in the work force. Women and teenagers are comparatively unstable elements in the labor force because they are usually not breadwinners with families to support, as are adult males. Adolescents generally live at home, while over half the women in the work force are married. For them, employment is far more optional, and their unemployment is often voluntary, if not indeed a preferred choice. They move in and out of jobs more often, just as they move in and out of the work force more often (though in the latter case they are not part of the official unemployment counts).

These groups inflate the unemployment counts partly because of the statistical peculiarities of the Bureau of Labor Statistics reporting. The BLS counts the unemployed in terms of several categories: job losers (those laid off); newcomers to the work force (those looking for a job the first time); and individuals returning to the work force after a period of absence. When women and teenagers enter or reenter the work force, they are defined statistically as "unemployed" because they are looking for work, even though they may never have worked before, do not really have to work, or are looking for work after a long absence. Although their job status is in no way different from what it has been, the result must be an increase in the number defined and counted as unemployed.

The increase in unemployment, however, is due to more than the changing makeup of the labor force and the increasing relative size of groups with high unemployment rates. As calculations by Philip Cagan of Columbia University indicate, unemployment *within* these groups has also risen relative to that for prime-age (twenty-five- to fifty-four-year-old) men.[14]

Teenage unemployment has risen disproportionately not only because more teens want work but because expanded minimum-wage laws and rising minimum-wage levels have pushed them off the market. Although these laws were intended to guarantee an income floor, they have had the opposite effect, since they discourage employers from hiring unskilled and marginally productive workers who can barely pay their own way, and who require constant supervision as well as on-the-job training. Despite strenuous denials of minimum-wage defenders, studies of teenage unemployment make clear that the laws increase joblessness in that group. Between 1957 and 1973, according to studies by Jacob Mincer that control for the effects of other variables, the minimum wage raised teenage unemployment for whites by 3.0 percentage points and for nonwhites by 5.7 percentage points. It increased unemployment of young workers aged twenty to twenty-four by about 1 percentage point. It raised the overall unemployment rate by 0.63 of a percentage point by 1974. The minimum wage also increased the minimum noninflationary unemployment rate for teens from about twice that for overall unemployment in 1955 and 1965 to about three times the overall figure by 1976.[15]

The statistical rise in female unemployment also reflects statutory changes. In 1972, new legislation was passed requiring mothers on welfare who could work to register for work. Although some found work, others were simply added to the unemployment statistics because they were "looking for work." After this legislation was passed, Cagan has estimated, the measured unemployment rate for such women increased by 5.8 percentage points. The increase added .2 of a percentage point to the overall rate.[16]

Women's higher unemployment rates tend to be offset by the fact that many cluster in service and white-collar jobs that are less cyclical than are manufacturing and blue-collar jobs; others withdraw from the labor force. In the 1981 recession, for example, female unemployment went up less than adult male—from 7.3 to 7.5 percent, compared with 7.5 to 8 percent for men. In 1974–75, however, their unemployment counts were fairly high, largely because women did not withdraw from the labor force as much as in earlier recessions. In general, unemployment rates for female heads of families run twice those for married men.[17]

New immigrants, legal and illegal, raise the jobless rates indirectly. They have tended to displace black workers not only because of labor-market conditions but for cultural and political reasons. They are willing to do work that American citizens disdain and may be able to decline because they have the alternative of receiving public subsidies. Immigrants may also be hired preferentially because, not having the full legal protection or benefits that citizens enjoy, they are in no position to complain about pay or working conditions. As one account has it, "In communities around the country, there is visual evidence of what has happened. Iranians are driving taxis. Asians and South Americans are doing restaurant work. Hispanics are picking vegetables and citrus fruits in fields and orchards where blacks once labored. The statistics show it, too. Unemployment is high for all poor minorities, but is highest for blacks."[18]

Immigrants, women, young people all enter a labor market in which they compete with other groups. Minority teenagers are predictable victims of this competition. They suffer not only from the influx of teenagers, women, and immigrants but also from the fact that lower-level jobs are often filled by college graduates who cannot find other work. As a result, the high unemployment figures for young people—the highest of all subgroups—are produced largely by rates for black youth, which run twice those for white youth; rates for black youth range from 33 percent to 40 percent, and in some cities, over 50 percent. Minority groups in general come next, then women, while male adult unemployment remains about half of that of minorities.[19]

UNEMPLOYMENT AND HARDSHIP:
A CLOSER LOOK

Clearly, unemployment carries different degrees of hardship. Adult males, especially married males, have often achieved and even surpassed the full-employment goal of 4 percent unemployment. This is why the 1982 rise in unemployment for this relatively stable group has been especially alarming. Many also have substantial protection against work instability. Members of large unions like the United Automobile Workers union receive substantial private unemployment benefits in addition to government aid. In the automobile, steel, and rubber industries, negotiated contracts provide for supplemental unemployment benefits, or "subs." Employers contribute a special fund for benefits to be paid to laid-off workers. A typical assembly line worker at General Motors plant may earn $9.55 an hour, or $382 a week, taking home $292.03. If he is laid off, he can receive $128 in government unemployment insurance and $135.93 in supplemental payments, a total of $264.93 a week, or almost as much as his take-home pay.

If these layoffs stem from international free-trade agreements, workers in automobile, steel, and other industries also receive compensatory tax-free "trade readjustment assistance." In 1980 union officials estimated that over $1 billion in such benefits would be distributed that year. That summer, some 310,000 laid-off workers in the auto industry alone became eligible for payments to offset unemployment caused by imported car sales. They could receive government subsidies of up to 70 percent of their normal wages for as long as eighteen months, plus UAW supplemental unemployment benefits of up to 90 percent of their usual pay. Since labor contracts bar double dipping (though the law does not), labor spokesmen said that most workers would use the government payments first and postpone their (private) supplemental unemployment benefits until the government payments were exhausted.[20]

In this fashion, a pivotal segment of our work force is shielded against cyclical declines. Each rise of one percentage point in the national unemployment rate—corresponding to 1 million more unemployed—makes available additional government benefits of $5.6 billion to $7 billion a year.

Other groups are cushioned in different ways. A sizable proportion of our households can claim more than one working member—a working wife or mother or teenaged child. In 1977, 85 percent of unemployed wives had working husbands, and 41 percent of unemployed husbands had working wives. Since about 60 percent of working women are married, they have or provide an economic cushion.[21] The economic impact of unemployment today is thus hardly comparable to what it was during the depression years, when the unemployed person was the male head of a household, the sole breadwinner, and the only source of income. Today the emotional content attached to and implicit in the word "unemployment" has been dramatically reduced—that, perhaps, explains why even at rates of unemployment approaching 11 percent social upheaval did not erupt in the 1982–83 depression.

White teenagers, but not blacks, have similar protection. Most live with a parent or adult relative. About two-thirds are looking for their first job or are returning to work after a voluntary absence. Almost half seek only part-time work. Their futures are not likely to be damaged for lack of immediate work. Although much is made of the fact that 46.1 percent of the unemployed are under twenty-four, few are heads of households and few seek adult responsibility. Even older youth, out of high school, are in a moratorium stage. Many leave school early, looking for "sex, adventure, and peer group activities," and they see jobs largely as ways of getting money for these activities. For a while, at least, they move in and out of temporary or impermanent jobs that require few skills before they settle into more regular employment. Firms looking for a supply of low-wage unskilled labor find them a plentiful and elastic source. "In fact, young people provide such a satisfactory source of labor that some secondary firms organize their production schedules to recruit them"—for example, by instituting special after-school production shifts.[22] They form, in effect, a voluntary reserve pool of the unemployed.

This life-style aspect of part-time or temporary work coupled with unemployment should not be underestimated. The attitude of many unemployed is like that of consumers. They seek very specific preconceived positions in return for the sacrifice of their freedom not to work. Many people enter the job market largely to achieve benefits available only to the unemployed. They work just long enough to achieve eligibility, then ask or induce their employers to lay them off so they can collect benefits; or they take the summer off, or they use their time for study. They claim to be available for work in order to be eligible for unemployment compensation.

These tax-free subsidies give the recipient discretionary leisure to dispose of at his or her pleasure. They eliminate the need not only to work, but to undertake the costs of commuting, buying clothes, and dressing in the manner that a job may impose. When the ancillary costs are considered, the cumulative benefits can compete advantageously with net take-home earned income.

Those most likely to use the system in this way are those whose take-home salaries are close to the benefits of unemployment compensation, such as students or low-wage workers, or whose salaries bring them into "high marginal tax brackets" (for example, "married women with well-paid spouses"). These groups "take advantage of unemployment insurance to accept and leave jobs and be unemployed more often."[23]

Students on research programs during the academic year may collect unemployment insurance in the summer months. Even the Census Bureau, hiring enumerators for *temporary* work, has been known to provide unemployment insurance once the work is over. These groups swell the forces of the so-called unemployed and artificially raise the jobless rate. The disincentive to work built into unemployment compensation bloats these figures to unrealistically high levels, so that even as the economy slows, the unemployment figure no longer rises as rapidly as it once did, since it is already so high in times of relative prosperity. In January 1981, jobless figures, at 7.4 percent, remained firm despite what was considered a contracting economy, a situation described as slightly increased unemployment accompanied by rising employment.[24]

So we have the sometimes paradoxical situation in which many unemployed can coexist with ample job openings. Our employment agencies and help-wanted ads abound in opportunity even as unemployment figures mount. In October 1976, with 7.9 percent unemployment, many leading employment agencies had two or three job openings for every qualified applicant. For those with the mind-set to seek available jobs, opportunity exists, even in what seems to be a declining job market.

About one percentage point of our unemployment rate stems from the misuse of the unemployment system through seasonal and temporary work or high turnover. Another estimated percentage point, possibly more, of so-called unemployment is accounted for by the underground economy—the unreported and sometimes illegal activities that provide more profit with less effort. Given these systematic opportunities, the full-employment rate may well accommodate 6, or even 7 percent unemployment, especially in so mobile, dynamic, and technologically fluid a society as ours. The present demographic structure and changing work preferences have made "frictional" unemployment, along with temporary and part-time work, more enduring, though not necessarily permanent, features of our economy.

Some economically marginal groups do lack a hedge against hardship: small-business people, home builders, farmers facing bankruptcy; young people without the work history to qualify for unemployment benefits, who may lose months and even years of valuable work experience; displaced groups like the steel workers of the defunct Youngstown, Ohio, plants; and those whose skills, developed over a lifetime, have become obsolete, at an age when their mobility is limited.

We do have severe unemployment problems in the case of minority youth with little economic security, for whom early unemployment threatens permanent blocked mobility. And we can hardly claim to have solved cyclical unemployment, when the devastating cutbacks and bankruptcies of 1981 have helped to extend unemployment to male heads of families.

Our most frightening unemployment problems, however, do not involve official unemployment statistics at all. "Discouraged" workers, those who no longer look for work because they feel they cannot find it, have multiplied since the 1970s, reaching approximately 1 million in April 1980.[25]

Finally, there has been an alarming drop in labor-force participation rates among men, particularly among older men, who have more generous retirement, Social Security, and pension benefits; and among adult black males, whose work-force participation declined from 80 percent to 71 percent between 1960 and 1978.[26]

These patterns show the devastating effects of a transfer-payment system that has helped create and maintain an underclass. According to Herbert Hill of the NAACP, an entire second generation of ghetto youth may never enter the labor force.[27] Caught between a subsidy system that is not geared to employment and training and the paucity of entry-level jobs,[28] even at the minimum wage, they have added to the burden of inflation coexisting with unused labor resources.

WHY CAN'T WE DO IT LIKE THE . . .

Other countries seem to have enjoyed not only lower unemployment rates but a better inflation-unemployment tradeoff. In the 1960s, when our unemployment rate averaged 4.8 percent, the average for seven Western European countries and Japan was 2.7 percent. Even in the decline of the 1970s their unemployment rates averaged 4 percent.[29] In 1976, when American and Canadian jobless rates were over 7 percent, Great Britain had 6.4 percent, France, Italy, and Germany about 4 percent, and Japan and Sweden only 2.1 percent and 0.6 percent, respectively. In Japan 4 percent unemployment would be defined as a crisis.

Germany and Japan both have a more efficient inflation-unemployment tradeoff than we do. Germany, with inflation in 1976 at only 5 percent, had an unemployment rate of 3.8 percent. Japan had about the same inflation rate as ours, but virtually no unemployment.

In Japan, a postwar tradition of corporate responsibility has been developed that is partly cultural, partly the result of bitter labor disputes in the 1950s, and that stresses job security and worker-management cooperation over wage increases and strikes.[30] Within that tradition, major employers assure the worker lifetime job security, standard wages and working conditions, and wage increases based on seniority. If a corporation were to break any of these rules, it would face tremendous loss of worker morale, government pressure, union resistance, and public indignation. The worker, in turn, promises to work for one firm all his life. And perhaps at least as importantly, not only to tolerate technological advancements and improvements in productivity, but to promote and encourage such efficiencies in order to achieve a competitive edge in international markets and thereby produce more domestic employment.

In America, this quasi-feudal arrangement would conflict with our values of mobility, opportunity, and the freedom to choose one's own fate, with all its risks but its possibilities, too. In Japan, the mutual commitment of employer and worker makes for greater productivity and industrial peace, since the worker's fortunes are meshed with his company's and his country's. For that reason, partisan union loyalty is weak. Unions tend in any case to be organized along company lines. [31]

On the other hand, the employer has almost complete authority to assign and reassign workers, whether to make best use of them in slack times, or to introduce new and more efficient equipment and changes in work activity. In America, this would impinge on the unions' jealous controls of work rules and assignments. There are also built-in sources of flexibility as far as work assignment is concerned. About a fifth of the work force are "temporary workers" (usually women) who can be dropped from the payroll when economic conditions demand it. Temporary work suspensions are sometimes permitted, with workers getting some pay from the employer and some from the government. Companies even "lend" workers to other firms during slack periods for as long as six months, the two companies sharing labor costs. The government also subsidizes firms to prevent layoffs. [32]

In contrast to American practices under which companies determine their own employment levels and layoffs with unemployment benefits dispensed largely by the government, the Japanese government support of income and job security operates at the company level. Unemployment insurance covers not the temporary suspensions but permanent dismissals for those without job security. The benefits can be extremely generous. They usually range from 60 percent of one's daily wage to a maximum of 80 percent for those in the lowest wage category and may be supplemented by family allowances. But their duration increases with age and with the length of time the recipient has worked in insured work during the preceding year; if less than a year, he receives benefits for only ninety days. *This policy reduces the incentive for the worker to remain unemployed.*

In Germany, unemployment until very recently has been relatively low for different reasons. Although job security is not institutionalized as it is in Japan, Germany did not suffer the same cyclical hazards as the United States because it had a flexible foreign migrant-labor pool. These groups swelled the work force during Europe's period of economic expansion. After the 1973 recession ended that boom, immigration was restricted and foreign workers were offered financial incentives to return home. As a result, the 2.5 million foreign workers of the pre–1973 period (out of about 10 million in all of Western Europe) were reduced to some 2 million by 1976.[33]

The jobless in Germany are well provided with unemployment benefits that come to 68 percent of a worker's last net earnings and are payable for up to a year. But, as in Japan, the longer a worker has lasted at his most recent job, the longer his benefits last. He must have worked at least twenty-six weeks to qualify for unemployment insurance, and then the benefits last only thirteen weeks. Forty weeks of work entitle him to twenty weeks of payments. Benefits for as much as a year are paid to those who have worked for two years on the last job.[34]

Germany also makes it easier for the unemployed worker to find another position. In a $180-million plan launched in November 1976, the government offered to offset the cost of commuting or moving to a new job, and to compensate an unemployed worker who was willing to take a job paying less than his former one, though no one was compelled to do either.[35]

There is a drawback to the foreign systems. European unemployment benefits, as a percent of after-tax earnings, are generally higher than their North American counterparts. As theory might dictate, the average *duration* of unemployment seems to be significantly greater abroad (and, more recently, in Canada), even though unemployment levels have tended to be lower.[36]

But the sources of unemployment in America are different. Our higher rates result not from a given number of people remaining unemployed for longer periods, but from greater flows of people in and out of employment. Our benefits may not be as high as the European, but they are available to a larger percentage of the labor force. Moreover, the largest category of U.S. unemployed since 1967 consists of layoffs, which occur far less often in Europe and Japan because of tradition and government and union constraints, as well as somewhat stricter work requirements for unemployment insurance.[37]

Despite statistically lower unemployment levels, Common Market countries share a crisis that resembles ours, particularly with respect to youth unemployment. Between 1973 and 1976, as two decades of economic expansion ended, the number of young people under twenty-five seeking work in Europe doubled; their unemployment rates varied from three times adult unemployment in France and Great Britain to nine times the adult rate in Italy. With overall unemployment at an average 4.75 percent, youth unemployment was 11 percent. Despite restrictions and financial inducements to leave, many foreign workers have remained to compete with indigenous labor, and the economies have not grown fast enough to absorb new recruits. More young people enter the labor market even as the number of jobs falls. Unions, in Europe as in the United States, protect those who already have jobs. Employees, once hired, are expensive to release because unions have exacted so many wage and social benefits that labor becomes a fixed-cost factor. Managers hesitate to hire new workers who will impose the same expensive obligations on them. When openings do arise, employers often try to acquire a machine rather than hire a worker.[38]

Common Market countries fear that they will soon face the disorders of adolescent and young-adult crime, violence, suicide, drug addiction, and prostitution that mark the lives of the least favored, least educated unemployed strata of American society. They fear also that persistent unemployment will erode popular confidence in democratic institutions and impel its victims to communism or to Nazism, as it did in the 1930s. Paris has seen demonstrations of unemployed youth chanting, "The only solution is revolution." Germany has seen a nascent neo-Nazi movement. Britain has been shocked by unprecedented riots, as well as by delinquency and other forms of crime. A Belgian employment officer maintains that jobs for youth are the "great moral issue facing our democracies."[39]

The demoralizing and inflammatory potential of unemployment is especially acute when young people first enter the work force and hence, in many respects, adult life. Denied the experience, discipline, and rewards that adults take for granted, they threaten to become unemployables. Foreigners have been blamed. Women have been blamed for having entered the work force and displaced young men, and because they fared better than men in the European recession of 1974–75—partly because they work in service sectors that are less subject to cyclical swings than are industrial jobs.[40]

Governments are attacking the problem in a variety of ways. Some replace earlier retirees with workers under thirty, or pay early retirees a substantial percentage of their last salary with government funds until they reach age sixty-five, when pensions will cover them. In some countries, workers normally retire at an earlier age. Japan's official retirement age is fifty-five, though workers may remain in the labor force. In Italy few workers continue past that age.[41]

Other strategies keep youth off the job market. Germany has extended the period of compulsory education. In Italy, where nearly half the unemployed are under twenty-five, a vast expansion of university enrollment has postponed entry into the work force, although the price has been political agitation from unemployed graduates.

Job-training programs have been initiated. Britain, France, Sweden, Germany, and Holland have incentive programs in which employers are paid part of the wages of young workers by the government. In Germany the firm of Krupp trains apprentices, some of them high-school dropouts, in training facilities like vocational schools, housed in a compound set off from the plant. Apprentices are virtually guaranteed jobs as lathe operators and the like. The German government gives tax cuts or subsidies to firms that take on apprentices whether they need them or not.

Unions outside West Germany sometimes criticize these programs; minors learn trades at a fraction of the minimum salary, and they often develop a loyalty to employers that undermines trade-union solidarity. In France, the government pays 90 percent of the minimum wage if young people agree to undergo job training. In Britain, the Labour government has been subsidizing companies that accept sixteen- to eighteen-year-olds for up to six months of training; the British program differs from traditional apprenticeship, however, which is usually run and financed by the firms themselves, and it provides no guarantee of permanence.[42]

Ironically, some Common Market countries show one unfilled job opening for every three persons registered as unemployed. Many overqualified young people, hoping for social mobility, decline to take on uninteresting, repetitive, and even grimy jobs that offer little hope for responsibility. "The level of training has risen but the demand for manpower has not followed," says Roland Tavitian, a Common Market specialist in social affairs. Educated young people rarely receive vocational guidance, and they shun manual labor. Graduates of British provincial universities face bleak prospects. In France, a special program has been launched to upgrade and dignify manual labor, but the hope of success is dim since, according to most expectations, manual labor can be upgraded only when the pay goes up, too.[43]

The cross-national differences, then, are less striking than the parallels to our demographic, structural, and cultural problems. Here and abroad, women, youth, and minorities pose a similar challenge. Unskilled labor must contend with automation, yet there is still a place for the menial work that many in the indigenous population disdain. And job vacancies coexist with drastic unemployment, indicating not only a gap between available skills and available jobs, but a gulf between career expectations and the realities of the working world.

In effect, what we have been pleased to call the American dream of success through hard work is the modern dream of a much-publicized "postindustrial" order that has not been realized quite so completely as its academic prophets have proclaimed. In dealing with our own high unemployment rates, we would do well to focus less on our changing demographic patterns, which

117

show striking parallels to those in Western Europe, and more on changing our incentives.

THE PHILLIPS CURVE MYSTIQUE

Economists have contributed to the current confusion in economic theory and government policy. One example is the frequent invocation of the "Phillips curve" depiction of the inflation-unemployment tradeoff, with its aura of quantitative precision. The "tradeoff" refers to the degree of unemployment that will prevent inflation, and the level of employment at which inflationary pressures begin. Although the original Phillips curve research studied the relationship between unemployment levels and wage increases, it is often, and often erroneously, taken to represent the relationship between unemployment levels and price increases, too, because wages are the largest component of costs, and increased costs (if productivity does not change) push prices up. Thus, when no more slack labor (unemployment) exists, wages and prices (of which wages are the major component or determinant) will go up. Conversely, unemployment should bring with it a lowering of wages, costs, and prices.

The concept is credited to Alban William Phillips, who studied the long-term (1861–1957) relationship between the rates of change in wages and unemployment rates. Phillips had expected a straight-line relationship between the two factors but found that a curve fitted the data better. "The curve showed that zero wage change occurred at a positive level of unemployment; that wages increased at an increasing rate as unemployment fell below this level; and that the rate of increase became very large as unemployment approached zero. However, unemployment above the zero wage change level caused little downward change in wages, and the rate of fall in wages was relatively small even as unemployment became very large. . . . Phillips noted, but did not stress, the aspect of the curve that was to become famous—the portion showing the tradeoff that must apparently occur between reducing inflation (as measured by downward change in wages) and reducing unemployment."[44]

118

It is this aspect of Phillips's research that has become relevant to policy analysis, for economists have been suggesting an increasingly expensive tradeoff between unemployment and inflation—that is, that increasing levels of joblessness are required to keep inflation down. By now the man-in-the-street echoes the term "Phillips curve" as if it presented a fixed guide to policy, even though economists are not agreed, or even clear, on the issue.

Some, like George L. Perry of the Brookings Institute, have blamed the worsening tradeoff on the increasing proportion of women and decreasing proportion of prime-age men (twenty-five to sixty-four) in the work force. If these groups could more readily be substituted for each other, Perry maintains, "these structural shifts might not have worsened the unemployment-inflation tradeoff. Actually, however, both women and young people tend to suffer much higher unemployment rates than men in the prime-age group—and the ratio of unemployment rates among women and young workers to rates among prime-age men has in fact been worsening markedly."[45]

The argument fails to confront a paradox: if women and teenagers do not displace men but simply augment the supply of labor, the effect should be *de*flationary. And if they do displace men, their unemployment rates should decline while rates for men increase, while their generally lower wages should have a deflationary impact.

Leonard Silk, drawing on a report by Jay Forrester of MIT, admits that rising joblessness among women and young people "has not been clearly explained," but relates it to urban trends and higher job skill requirements. According to Forrester, low-income people were drawn to cities by low-cost housing at a time when job opportunities in cities were vanishing. As poor people flowed into cities and jobs flowed out of them, the cities became "social traps" of decaying housing, joblessness, and recipients of welfare. The trend continued until lack of job opportunities was so extreme that further inflow was discouraged. Silk concludes that "the structural change in both the composition of the labor force and the nature of central cities appears to be worsening the Phillips curve—the tradeoff between unemployment and inflation."[46]

This explanation also leaves some questions unanswered. There is no comparative analysis of what the poor worked at before they came to the city, lured by that low-cost housing. Though the lack of jobs might impel a move out of the city, the possibility that public subsidies may deter such a move is not discussed. There is an important difference, moreover, between unemployment among poor minorities and among women and teenagers. They stem from different causes and entail different degrees of hardship.

Whether the statistics on unemployment actually conform to a Phillips curve is also moot. Silk, in his review of the theory, observed "the wide scatter to the plots."[47] Yet Phillips curves continue to be drawn selectively from an array of points so scattered that the outliers, or exceptions, outnumber the points on the curve.

Policymakers seem to have been making claims for the theory that A. William Phillips himself had the modesty to forgo. His research has been widely disseminated and cited,[48] incorporated into textbooks, and popularized. It was discussed in the 1969 *Economic Report of the President*. Yet Phillips stressed the *reverse* of a simple tradeoff. Examining wages and unemployment levels, he found a downward rigidity (the much observed "stickiness") of wage levels. This is why increased unemployment, unless of course the increase was dramatic and of long duration, would not bring wages down—that is, would not reduce inflation. Although the principle is valid, there are limits to the possibility of decreasing inflation by increasing unemployment.

Moreover, Phillips became increasingly aware of the problems entailed in "estimating the relationship he considered necessary for policy design and of the fact that the necessary techniques were beyond his grasp. His intellectual integrity was such that he felt he could not continue to 'profess' in an area in which he felt he had no further contribution to make." He moved to different areas of research.[49]

The concept of the Phillips curve has by now been developed and modified so that we have short- and long-term tradeoffs, "expectations-adjusted" tradeoffs, and the like.[50] Yet its major problem remains. It supposedly depicts a relationship so complex that it can hardly be described, much less analyzed, in terms of a correlation or of single-factor analysis. A correlation does not tell us which of the two variables has causal priority. It ignores intervening variables—the many contributing factors to inflation. It does not deal with the possibility that other causal factors may be affecting both inflation and unemployment. The astronomic increase in energy costs, and the strangling effect of interest rates, are among the most prominent of these factors.

At one time, unemployment did lead to greater competition for available jobs, a process that lowered wages and thus reduced unemployment. But today, a variety of politicoeconomic arrangements—from union wage contracts to minimum wages and public subsidies—keep wages from falling and contribute an upward bias to prices. The more discretionary unemployment of women and teenagers, entailing less hardship, also has a lesser impact on curtailing demand, the source of deflation. These subgroup differences are masked by the overall contours of the Phillips curve.

Given the security and stability of various government transfers, as well as union resistance to wage competition, increased unemployment no longer leads to the need, or even the possibility, of a worker offering himself at a lower wage. Wages at prevailing high levels become sticky. Even with unemployment rates of 7 percent, unions until recently achieved wage increases in excess of productivity increases, as well as cost-of-living raises, negating the erstwhile basic validity of the Phillips curve. Only in 1980–81 have we again seen a powerful Phillips curve effect as the combined threats of recession and renewed feelings of job insecurity have led to milder wage settlements and even some wage cuts. The Phillips curve effect becomes visible when heavy unemployment hits the married male head of family, for it is at this point that consumer demand is significantly reduced.

The impact of unions also demonstrates the complex interplay of unemployment and inflation. Their wage increases are of course translated into higher prices, but these increases also have exacted the sacrifice of jobs. Unions support the host of government policies, from minimum wages to generous unemployment benefits, that act as disincentives to hiring and to working and thus restrict the supply of labor. Second, they have systematically endorsed higher wages at the expense of a smaller labor pool. Unemployment is often the tradeoff of higher wages for that smaller pool.

This preference has been shown in the unions' discriminatory resistance to the training and hiring of minorities in the construction industry; their opposition to public works that might compete with their jobs; their hostility to CETA workers. Only lately, as the ailing automobile, steel, and housing industries have forced widespread layoffs, have the large unions finally recognized the elasticity of demand for labor and made wage concessions. Trading off these increases for greater job security, the unions protect the source of their dues—their members.

It might be feasible to fight inflation with unemployment if the unemployed had to compete by offering their labor at competitively lower rates, bringing down production costs. But even that is not the solution. It is efficiency of employment that keeps inflation down, and neither fuller employment, as the Italian experience suggests, nor more unemployment, as the United States patterns demonstrate, will have the same effect. If you pay employees for doing nothing and give them buying power, you are encouraging inflation. Productivity is a link between wage and price changes. If it increases, wage increases will not necessarily be inflationary; if productivity falls, as it did in the 1970s, wage increases are bound to be inflationary. In any case, so long as productivity is not under control, one cannot precisely equate wage and price increases as many Phillips curve analysts do.

Inflation alone, then, in and of itself, cannot cure or reduce unemployment. Nor is it the price of, or *necessary* "tradeoff" for, full employment. Indeed, it may serve to increase unemployment, as the recessions produced by the Fed's high-interest, inflation-producing policies testify.

But, neither does unemployment in and of itself cure or reduce inflation. It is not the *necessary* "tradeoff" for achieving price stability; in fact, it may aggravate inflation as subsidies maintain demand for an ever-smaller product supply. A direct linkage of inverse movements of these two factors can be made to occur, but only if other directly related and influencing factors are dealt with in that equation. This is why both traditional conservative and liberal solutions to inflation and unemployment—tolerating high unemployment to stem inflation, or hoping to reduce unemployment simply through government spending—are decreasingly effective. At high enough levels they may finally work, as we have seen in the United States, United Kingdom, and Western Europe—but only when jobless rates have cut through discretionary unemployment to inflict the hardship that once defined joblessness.

THE MYTH OF FULL EMPLOYMENT—
OR, THE FREEDOM NOT TO WORK

To be sure, a job for everyone who needs and wants it must be a priority in our society. Unemployment that cripples breadwinners as the price for lowering inflation is not a policy to be tolerated.

Nevertheless, it should be apparent that full employment is impossible in a democracy that gives job seekers the option and even incentive to turn down job opportunities that fail to meet their requirements. The system first provides them with the freedom not to work, then incorporates them into the statistics denoting "the unemployed."

We might achieve full employment were this not the case. If unemployed people feared hunger, illness, or lack of clothing and shelter, as they did before our social programs were introduced to mitigate the periodic hardships of free enterprise, then the incentive to accept work would be greater. Adam Smith envisioned the impulse of workers as the major incentive to work, and the competitive spirit as the driving force to fill jobs and fill them well. If every member of society really had this happily selfish motivation, then the nation might operate closer to maximal efficiency.

With the expansion of so many transfer programs, we have in effect undermined the basis for the success of our system, which rests on a high degree of self-motivation to work as well as you can for a maximal return on your own capital—your labor together with your native qualities and acquired knowledge. Under Adam Smith's assumptions, government would intervene only in the case of a major disruption such as war, monopoly, environmental pollution, or depression. Instead, what should have been an emergency mechanism has become a structural feature of our political economy. With each recession, our unemployment rates become and remain higher.[51]

These figures have been misconstrued. Union leaders and politicians proclaim the need for vast expenditures, tax cuts, government programs, and extended periods of compensation .to deal with a problem that may be more apparent than real, to reduce what may be, because of its nature and consistency, a largely irreducible unemployment rate. The calls for augmented government spending, speedier money growth, stimulative fiscal policy, and vast job-creating programs are not only excessive but counterproductive. They accelerate inflation and ultimately create economic disruptions leading to recession and sharper unemployment. They engage in overkill just when a moderate course is called for.

This is not to claim that we have full employment for all, or that, under our system, we can ever have it. We may need some unemployment to cope with changes, to have a reservoir upon which to draw for new possibilities, to avoid wild wage demands, to prevent runaway inflation. Just as we cannot operate our plant at 100 percent capacity, we should not have 100 percent use of our labor force.

However, the need for a flexible reserve pool of labor does not necessarily relegate a segment of our population to permanent misery. A large pool of secondary earners, temps, and part-time workers already fulfills our need for flexibility. In the secondary sector of the much-disputed "dual labor economy," many young and not-so-young men, even in dead-end jobs, are not exploited, but have, as some of our recent research indicates, a "preindustrial" mentality. They do not seek work careers, nor do they want full participation in our economy. For personal, sometimes creative reasons, they seek a freedom and flexibility that complement the need of some employers to use labor when necessary to cope with the less predictable aspects of the market.[52]

Real problems of unemployment do exist for young people, especially blacks, black adults, and to some extent women. Young people suffer from their lack of training, tenuous reliability, and the effects of minimum-wage requirements at a time when they generally have few skills to contribute. (In fact, they often cost an employer the time of others just to get them to the point where they are productive.) It is hard for them to find first jobs except during the peaks of boom growth, at which point just about anybody who can breathe is recruited. What do we do with this reservoir of energy and talent the rest of the time? Young people, frustrated by lack of employment, are not just a wasted resource, but a potentially divisive force in society. Young blacks, often with less preparation and training to enter the business world, are even harder to place.

What is true for the young is, unfortunately, also true for many mature unemployed blacks. Few have been prepared for the desirable employment they would wish. They are burdened with the remnants of prejudice that further limit their opportunities, and, in turn, incentives. Finally, women, except for those willing to accept the traditional roles of secretary or clerk, for which they are always in great demand, still cannot attain positions that they are qualified to fill in numbers sufficient to absorb their growing availability.

TARGETS FOR PLANNING

The unemployment that these groups suffer must be dealt with constructively and decisively, if we are to fulfill our obligations to them and improve the performance and quality of our economic life. But to deal with this vital problem, we need a sharply focused approach, not a massive general attack that ultimately destroys more than it resolves.

1. **We must target sectors of the unemployed, rather than try to deal with the entire spectrum of the jobless.** The way to deal with youth unemployment, for example, is neither to inflate starting wages nor stimulate the entire economy to so strong a boom that the last marginal worker, the least skilled, productive, and reliable, is employed; the resultant increases in wages, prices, and government spending will merely add to inflationary pressures without adding significantly to total production. The answer to youth unemployment can only be *targeted* specific employment—a Job Corps, a permanent draft, a government-sponsored apprenticeship program.

2. **Minimum-wage policy should be modified to take into account different segments of the jobless.** Given the limited skills and needs of this age group, minimum-wage requirements

might well be modified to stimulate employment. A 1981 survey by Data Black Opinion Polls found that 37 percent of black Americans supported the idea that a lower minimum wage for teenagers would benefit the black community, the group in which teenage joblessness is most heavily concentrated.[53]

3. We need a peacetime draft and a system of universal national service to recruit and train young people. We have been systematically neglecting universal military service as a means of solving the problem of unemployed youth. Instead, we waste ruinous amounts of funds to tease a professional army into service, recruiting an underqualified military force motivated by mercenary considerations barely tempered by patriotic commitment. The results are disappointment on all sides and an enormous dropout ratio.

A draft, by contrast, would span the entire age spectrum and a broader range of ability. At small expense, it would create career options, provide training and employment for young people with little work experience or value to employers, youngsters who are still unstable, yet whose moves in and out of work contribute disproportionately to our unemployment figures and the emotional alarm that these statistics generate. A draft would reduce both these figures and the political drama surrounding them, and at the same time establish a disciplined work force. Once government drafts youth, as it did during the Vietnam years, unemployment drops quickly enough to that magical 4 percent level.

4. As an alternative and supplement to military service, we need an American Service Corps that would siphon off the jobless, rootless, and alienated, providing alternatives to military careers for untrained young people. Beyond that, some unemployment must be accepted for this highly amorphous group. Many of our best employees and executives found it difficult in their initial years to enter the job market. Between the ages of sixteen and twenty I myself had at least twenty different jobs, from busboy and waiter to office boy, shipping clerk, furrier, and sales clerk. I even collected unemployment compensation for merely loafing between jobs. Few people really aspire at an early age to the rigidity of a nine-to-five job. Youth is a time for self-discovery, change, and a certain amount of freedom and irresponsibility that permit the search for self-knowledge and adventure that eventually leads to maturity, independence, and the assumption of consistent daily commitment and responsibility.

5. **The amount and duration of unemployment benefits should be related to the length of time employed** so that they do not serve as disincentives to work and do provide fair and proportional compensation to those who have worked longer. The training and benefit policies of Germany and Japan should be adapted to our economy. Their practice of tagging unemployment benefits to the duration of time employed is far superior to our own. It avoids the built-in incentive of the American system that encourages workers to take jobs for the minimum of time in order to collect the unvarying amount of benefits, so that a worker with six months experience can receive as much as someone who has worked for twenty years without a break. Germany's subsidies of workers willing to travel or accept lower-paying jobs also provide positive incentives because they foster a return to work.[54]

6. **To provide alternatives to subsidized unemployment, we should create private-sector jobs, using incentives like tax credits and subsidies for training programs to induce employers to provide these jobs.** These programs should be established in predefined areas of high-priority social need (see chapter 12). Germany's apprenticeship programs could provide a model for our own job-training and employment programs, which often train people without insuring positions for them, or put them in jobs with little productive potential.

7. **We should use public funds to maintain employment rather than subsidize layoffs.** The Japanese government, which uses public funds to help employers prevent layoffs, shows its grasp of supply-side economics, maintaining demand through jobs, not transfers, and spending no more, and possibly less, than it would on unemployment programs. At the same time it maintains ongoing production and hence supply.

By contrast, our own programs have long exaggerated the tension between inflation and unemployment. The harsh alternative the Reagan adminstration has chosen, to cut back on *both* subsidies *and* jobs without providing an imaginative or innovative alternative, has only backfired. It has forced even greater benefit payouts and larger deficits, all shoring up the demand side, but not enough to sustain the investment confidence to a degree that would radically pull us out of recession. To paraphrase Mark Twain, the difference between the right government action and the almost-right government action is as the difference between lightning and the lightning bug. One has impact. The other merely flickers without force.

NOTES

1. Lekachman, *Age of Keynes,* 68, 84, 86, 90.

2. Ibid., 88–91.

3. Samuelson, *Economics,* 10th ed., 333–335.

4. Dornbusch and Fischer, *Macroeconomics,* 390, for the neoclassical perspective.

5. Lekachman, *Age of Keynes,* 171, 175.

6. Faulkner, *American Economic History,* 713–18; Samuelson, *Economics,* 11th ed., 240.

7. *Economic Report of the President,* 1979, Washington, D.C., U.S. Government Printing Office, 1979, 217, 218.

8. Ibid., 1, 9, 10.

9. Ibid., 106, 108.

10. "The Truth About Unemployment," *Forbes* 119, February 15, 1977, 97, in *Saving America's Cities,* Evelyn Geller, ed., New York, H. W. Wilson, 1979, 5.

11. See Seth King, "Making Labor Statistics Make Sense," *New York Times,* May 24, 1982, A16.

12. "Women Entering Job Force at Extraordinary Pace," *New York Times,* September 12, 1976, 1; Philip Cagan, *Persistent Inflation:* 207; *Statistical Abstract,* 1979, Table 644, 392.

13. *Economic Report of the President,* 1979, 217.

14. Cagan, *Persistent Inflation,* 206–207.

15. Ibid., 212; Michael L. Wachter, "The Nature of the Unemployment Problem," *Challenge,* May–June 1978, 35.

16. Cagan, *Persistent Inflation,* 212–213.

17. William Robbens, "Data on Jobs Show Variety of Ills in U.S.," *New York Times,* January 11, 1982, A1, D10; *Economic Report of the President,* 1979, 217.

18. John Herbers, "Changes in Society Holding Black Youth in Seamless Web," *New York Times,* March 11, 1979, Sec. 1, 44.

19. Ibid., citing U.S. Labor Department study by Orley Ashenfelter.

20. "310,000 Auto Workers Eligible for Jobless Pay Due to Imports," *New York Times,* August 15, 1980, D2.

21. Thomas J. Hailstones and Frank V. Mastrianna, *Contemporary Economic Problems and Issues,* 5th ed., Cincinnati, South-Western Publishing Co., 14.

22. "The Structure of the Labor Market for Young Men," in *Unemployment and Inflation: Institutional and Structuralist Views, A Reader in Labor Economics,* Michael J. Prior, ed., White Plains, New York, M. E. Sharpe, Inc., 1979, 186–88.

23. Cagan, *Persistent Inflation,* 208.

24. Ibid., reports from unemployment agencies, news reports, personal inquiries; Robert D. Hershey, Jr., "Employment Rates Show U.S. Economy Retaining Strength," *New York Times,* February 7, 1981, 1.

25. Philip Shabecoff, "Uncounted Jobless: No Work, No Hope," *New York Times,* May 18, 1980, Sec. 4, 4. See chapter 3.

26. *Statistical Abstract,* 1979, Table 645, 392.

27. Herbers, "Black Youth in Jobless Web," 44.

28. "Jobs Scarce for Unskilled Applicants," *New York Times,* February 8, 1982.

29. *U.S. Economic Performance in a Global Perspective,* Office of Economic Research, New York Stock Exchange, February 1981, 44, 46.

30. Steve Lohr, "Japanese Earned Labor Harmony," *New York Times,* February 13, 1982, 31.

31. D. Prakash Sethi, "Behind the Facade of Lifetime Job Security," *New York Times,* June 5, 1977, Sec. 3, 5.

32. Saul J. Blaustein and Isabel Craig, *An International Review of Unemployment Insurance Schemes,* Kalamazoo, Mich., The W. E. Upjohn Institute for Employment Research, 1977, 37–75; *U.S. Economic Performance,* 51.

33. Clyde H. Farnsworth, "Motivation a Factor in Europe Job Crisis," *New York Times,* December 15, 1976, A13.

34. Blaustein and Craig, *International Review,* 37–75.

35. "Bonn to Pay Unemployed Who Move to Distant Jobs," *New York Times,* November 11, 1976, 3.

36. Stephen Marston's studies indicate that the American unemployment insurance system may add between 0.2 and 0.4 percentage points to the U.S. unemployment rates. Cited by Roger Kaufman, "Why the U.S. Rate is High," in Michael J. Piore, ed., *Unemployment and Inflation,* 160. See also Cagan, *Persistent Inflation,* 209.

37. Kaufman, "Why the U.S. Rate is High," in Piore, ed., *Unemployment,* 160–64.

38. Clyde H. Farnsworth, "Joblessness Among Youth Is Raising Worry in Europe," *New York Times,* December 13, 1976, 1, 10; Paul Lewis, "Leaders Voice a Growing Concern Over Unemployment Among the Young," *New York Times,* May 8, 1977, 16; Jonathan Kandell, "Problem of Youth Joblessness Grips West Europe," *New York Times,* January 4, 1978, 25, 27.

39. Farnsworth, "Joblessness Among Youth Is Raising Worry in Europe," 10.

40. Ibid.

41. Kandell, "Problem of Youth Joblessness," 27.

42. Clyde H. Farnsworth, "Europeans Creating Jobs for Idle Youth," *New York Times,* December 14, 1976, 13.

43. Farnsworth, "Motivation," A13.

44. Kevin Lancaster, "A. William Phillips," *International Encyclopedia of the Social Sciences,* vol. 18: *Biographical Supplement,* Davis L. Sills, ed., New York: Free Press, 1979, 634.

45. George L. Perry, "Changing Labor Markets and Inflation," *Brookings Papers on Economic Activity,* 1970, no. 3, 441–43, in Leonard Silk, ed., *Contemporary Economics: Principles and Issues,* 2d ed., New York: McGraw-Hill, 1979, 320–21.

46. Silk, ed., *Contemporary Economics,* 322.

47. Ibid.

48. Anthony M. Santomero and John Seater, "The Inflation-Unemployment Tradeoff: A Critique of the Literature," *Journal of Economic Literature* 16 (1978), 499–544.

49. Lancaster, "Phillips," 634.

50. Dornbusch and Fischer, *Macroeconomics,* 429–435, 503–507.

51. Robbens, "Data on Jobs Show Variety Of Ills," A1.

52. Charles F. Sobel, "Marginal Workers in Industrial Society," in Piore, ed., *Unemployment and Inflation,* 172–75.

53. "37% of Blacks Found in Favor of Lower Wage Floor," *New York Times,* June 17, 1981, A18.

54. In 1981 and 1982 the state of Ohio, under a CETA grant, paid job hunters mileage and a salary to find work elsewhere, in or out of the state. Although most workers in the program found jobs, the program raised controversy among unions, critics who charged that Ohio was exporting its unemployment problem, and those who did not find placement. See Wayne King, "Northerners who Follow Dream of Jobs in Texas Find Work Scarce and Welfare Skimpy in Reality," *New York Times,* June 14, 1982, A16. Typically, the headline is more alarmist than the story.

7

Our Past and Future Wars

We have been compelled to create a permanent armaments industry of vast proportions. . . . We annually spend on military security more than the net income of all United States corporations. . . .

This conjunction of an immense military establishment and a large arms industry is new in the American experience. . . . We recognize the imperative need for this development. Yet we must not fail to comprehend its grave implications. Our toil, resources, and livelihood are all involved; so is the very structure of our society.

In the councils of government we must guard against *the acquisition of unwarranted influence,* whether sought or unsought, by the military-industrial complex. The potential for the disastrous rise of misplaced power exists and will persist.

We must never let the weight of this combination endanger our liberties or democratic processes. . . . [emphasis added]

> Dwight D. Eisenhower, Farewell to the Nation Address, January 17, 1961

THE POOR MAN'S MARXISM AND OUR RACE TO CATASTROPHE

In George Orwell's *1984,* contending totalitarian powers maintained their economic "health" through ceaseless warring, producing a constant demand for military weapons that were endlessly consumed. We have adopted essentially the same policy since World War II, defending it in the name of fighting possible wars, of averting wars, of maintaining peace, and, most outlandishly, of sustaining full employment. We stop just short of actually saying that the government should build airplanes and armaments, then dump them in the ocean to create jobs and generate or maintain economic activity. The assumption seems to be that creating a new supply of doctors would be less useful in generating jobs and activity.

It is ironic that this Marxist logic, which sees defense spending as the only way for capitalism to sustain itself, should have trickled down—from our own political leaders, no less—to become the unconsidered view of the man on the street. "It's a helluva thing to say," says a utility worker, "but our economy needs a war. Defense spending should be increased to make jobs for people."[1]

These illusions persist even though the devastating *peacetime* consequences of war (not to mention its blind waste of natural resources and human blood) are economic commonplaces. American wars have swollen our government debt and inspired the colossal inflationary strategies of printing money. Our paper dollars—greenbacks—were introduced during the Civil War. Inflation has invariably accompanied wartime spending, and since World War II especially, each succeeding conflict has pushed us on to higher levels of inflation.[2]

In peacetime, defense spending fires inflation by consuming precious resources, capital, manpower, and genius that could be put to more constructive use. It is not the quantity of these resources drained from the civilian sector that is so important as their strategic nature. The brilliant scientists and scarce materials preempted by defense represent the margin of difference that could propel our peacetime economy to new levels of prosperity.

Why, then, does our romance with the defense program persist? Because industry loves it. Such an activity, in which the consumer—and the sole *legitimate* consumer—is the government, competes with no one. It does not infringe upon anyone else's product or service. Its products are quickly obsolescent and hence regenerate themselves at fantastic expense. It creates huge profits because the government, as the buyer, does not really care what it pays, and blithely goes along with enormous cost overruns.

Unions love it because it creates new jobs without threatening existing occupations or interfering with featherbedding or induced inefficiency. Senators, congressmen, presidents—politicians at all levels—love it because it is a visible program that helps business, labor, and communities. It makes them givers, sponsors, philanthropists, even creators, with immediate tangible material results that contrast with the deferred benefits of other capital programs, like new medical schools, that would ultimately provide equal benefits in construction and job creation while producing infinitely greater social goods. Congressmen compete strenuously for military contracts and bases that bring Pentagon money—jobs and income—to constituents. Is there a president's wife or child, or a congressman, who is not vulnerable to the threat of cancer or heart disease—at least as vulnerable as to an attack by the U.S.S.R.? Yet the government throws billions at the potential Russian threat while squeezing out measly sums for research against cancer and heart disease. It is ironic that the first major political figure to warn us of the peril of the military-industrial complex to our political system and our liberties—President Eisenhower—was also the major American military figure of the twentieth century.

Any economy must face the classic choice between guns and butter, between military and civilian goods. As our elementary economics textbooks never fail to stress, such resource allocations permit a variety of choices, each choice entailing some opportunity cost. But that cost is not merely a tradeoff of goods. Just as an economy operating at capacity is strained toward inflation, *any* combination of factors uses resources that would not just be available for other uses, but would be cheaper. Military purchases constantly bid up the price of capital, and labor, and of consumer goods. The more goods allocated to one sector, the higher the prices in the other. The rosy view that we can have both more guns and more butter with a higher "production possibility" boundary[3] confuses variable capital (labor) with limited natural resources in predicting the consequences of expansion. And it ignores the inflationary pressures that must result from the need for added imports.

Our post–World War II history illustrates this dilemma. The cold-war hysteria, Korea, and Vietnam have all inspired military escalation. The nuclear industry and the proliferation of small- and large-scale weapons it has spawned inspire competition in overkill across the world and heighten the threat from abroad, only to escalate our fears, our building of warheads, our deployment of resources from the civilian sector, and our inflationary pressures.

The nuclear fallout—it's in the rain
The inflation fallout—it's in the pain
*   in the drain—of buying power, of the*
value of our currency.

As we accelerate our nuclear weapons arsenal, do we ever remember what nuclear explosives do?

As we feed inflation, do we ever remember what it does—for instance in Germany in 1923—and what it ultimately produces—for instance, in Germany in 1939?

Do we remember the danger and horror of nuclear weapons and the prospect of a nuclear holocaust? Or the prospect of relentless inflation?

The reality is so terrible that we think it can't be real.

We are running a race between understanding, perception, and action on the one hand, and catastrophe on the other.

VIETNAM: WAR IS PEACE

The defense of military spending in the name of economic stability is only another case of the cross-eyed logic that transplants Depression thinking into periods of relative prosperity. America entered World War II with substantial unemployment of resources and gradually moved to full employment of available resources. To critics of the New Deal, in fact, it was the war, and not the recovery program, that brought us out of the Depression. But that argument ignores not only the economic equivalents of wartime spending, but the different ways of financing wars.

It is sometimes said (by Samuelson, for example), that "in World War II and the Vietnam years, our economy was plagued by problems connected with too high a general money demand, leading to price increases and shortages."[4] But World War II and Vietnam were different in psychology, economic circumstance, government policy, and effects. It is true that our resources are limited in that we cannot do everything at once. We could not have guns *and* butter, Vietnam *and* homes at the seashore at the same time.

Yet it was not really the supply side—a sudden shortage of resources—that was at issue in the case of Vietnam. Rather it was that for the first time we fought a war, and an extensive one in terms of production and manpower, without fully mobilizing ourselves toward that end or forgoing part of our immediate discretionary, and even necessary, wants, as we did in World War II. This is what brought and accelerated the problems of inflation and shortages.

In World War II, heavy wartime production was accompanied by rationing, price controls, luxury taxes, conservation campaigns (even to saving bacon grease in coffee tins), sacrifice, the accumulation of savings. But Vietnam was to be a painless war. No political effort was made to enlist a consensus in its favor. Citizens were never asked to sacrifice. The explosion in grants, the war on poverty, the sudden flowering of college and university subsidies and fellowships and scholarships, all served as diversionary efforts for the poor and the middle class—until the poor were reminded that their sons were fighting the war, and college youth became subject to the draft. (Then came the campus antiwar movements.) Whereas in World War II the military and defense sectors used an enormous reserve army of unemployed, during Vietnam millions of college youth were exempted from the draft—*and* the labor force.

The price of World War II was exacted in curtailed consumer

demand; the Vietnam war generated a vast demand for additional goods and services to fight the war, but without a commensurate ability to pay. Consumer demand had to be met with imports for consumption, which increased from $14.7 billion in 1960, to $21.3 billion in 1965, to $39.8 billion in 1970, to $55.3 billion by 1972—or from $80 to $265 per capita—over a 300 percent increase. Correspondingly, our balance of payments surplus declined from $4.9 billion at the beginning of the decade to $.6 billion in 1969 then became a $6.4 billion *deficit* by 1972.[5]

The Vietnam War cost $676 billion at a time when the U.S. had little direct economic interest in the area, not even in oil. Its rationale was the cold-war strategy of sponsoring governments to undercut the development of Soviet-type economies.[6]

THE PENTAGON YEARS

Vietnam was an episode in the escalation of military spending that has continued since World War II. Military budgets show no decline in absolute terms after the Vietnam agreements of early 1973, despite the constant promise of the budget dividends that were to result from cessation of the war. As Seymour Melman puts it, "U.S. military planning is geared to wider perspectives within which Vietnam is one event in a continuing program." Military spending declined as a percentage of an increasing federal budget but has constantly increased in *absolute* terms, except for a slight drop in the postwar year of 1973. (And why not? Military spending *should* go down in times of peace.) Since that "low" of $74.5 billion, it increased to $114.5 billion in 1979.[7]

All of our wars have been inflationary, but there is a difference in this period. All earlier wartime inflations were followed by periods of price decline, so that no *long-term* inflationary trend occurred in the entire period between the American Revolution and World War II. But there has been no such postwar reversal since World War II,[8] either after minor wars or in peace. We are in the grip of an endless inflationary spiral that has persisted for four decades. Though it may have worsened in the 1960s and 1970s, the uptrend has lasted much longer.

Defense spending fires inflation first by draining resources that might be put to better use. The $3.8 billion spent on the B-51 bomber in research, development, and initial production could have financed about 700 medium-sized industrial enterprises. Had Carter not canceled the contract for this costly and unnecessary weapon, the bill would have come to over $20 billion.

Second, military products constitute a unique type of good. They are not useful in an economic sense. They go neither for consumption to raise anyone's standard of living nor for further production. To be sure, they provide jobs, activities, and profits for the military, for the civilian bureaucracy that supports it, and for the defense industries that service it. But the effect is just like that of transfer payments. By increasing consumption *without increasing the supply of goods and services* to be consumed, they can produce prosperity only "on the second round," that is, only when the added buying power has generated increased civilian production (or investment) to satisfy it. When that increased production is not forthcoming, and when civilian needs compete unsuccessfully with military goods, the result can only be inflation. Meanwhile the presumed benefit of a war economy—full employment—has been conspicuously absent.

The most tragic effect of defense spending has fallen on the federal budget. Well before the Reagan step-up, defense took an enormous chunk of the federal budget. In 1976 defense spending came to almost 30 percent of all federal spending, including transfer payments, and to two-thirds of the federal purchases of goods and services. This at a time when defense spending had dropped from the highs of the Vietnam years.

The Reagan budgets have been more ominous: The $195.4 billion in 1982 was only the prelude to a five-year plan aimed at reaching $364 billion by 1987, for a total of $1.64 *trillion* over five years. According to Elmer B. Staats, the former comptroller general of the United States, defense spending will absorb 30 percent of the goods-producing gross national product, as against 6 percent in 1981.[9]

Our economic theorists tell us, and with good reason, that capitalism does not need a war economy in order to survive. Depression can be averted through fiscal and monetary policy, that is, tax cuts and government (deficit) spending; and any macroeconomist knows that missiles and warheads are not needed for job creation and multiplier spending effects. We can achieve the same end by

> *building new factories, better roads, and schools, cleaning up our rivers, and providing minimum income supplements for our aged and handicapped. Aside from the primary and secondary money spending, we also get the lasting benefits of clean rivers, productive schools and plants, and higher living standards. In terms of economic mechanics and social priorities, you should be able to realize which of the following should win hands down: (1) a manned bomber squadron that never even leaves its base, or (2) a hospital for the alleviation of suffering and prolongation of life.[10]*

How is it, then, that this hoped-for conversion hasn't taken place? Why does this marvel of the modern mixed economy remain in the realm of speculation?

Largely because so many individuals and firms have a stake in the present military establishment: the Department of Defense, its military bases, its civilian employees in all sectors here and abroad, and the business firms under contractual obligations, not to mention those in covert operations, which don't figure in official statistics. Defense production in 1979 constituted only about 5 percent of our gross national product.[11] Yet it employs a strategic portion of our labor force, research talents, and capital assets. In 1977, about 4 million worked in defense-related industries, and another 3 million were military and civilian employees for the defense establishment under the federal government—a total of 7 million. These in turn generate another 7 million supporting jobs, according to Melman's estimate, to yield a figure of 14.2 million, or 14 percent of the labor force with a stake in the defense sector.[12]

The military and industrial sectors are closely tied by links of mutual dependence, reward, and control. The federal government contracts with about 20,000 companies and 100,000 subcontractors. Moreover, every major industrial group has some stake in sales to the Pentagon. The top 100 military-serving firms read like a *Who's Who* of American industry. Though firms not exclusively tied to defense may derive only 10 percent of their sales from government, these sales make an important marginal difference in profitability. The defense sector may carry much of the overhead, since the government often provides capital for construction and equipment. Similarly, workers in defense-related industries may account for only 15 percent of all union workers, but they wield considerable leverage. If one-third of these workers were unemployed, they would bring our unemployment statistics to unbearable levels.[13]

SOCIALISM WRIT SMALL

Although critics like John Kenneth Galbraith assert, not without cause, that the private defense sector wields important influence on the Pentagon and on public opinion, that influence is hardly unilateral. The relationship between the public and private defense sectors is unique in our capitalist structure. This structure of control may be called "socialism writ small," since the defense establishment makes the state's control greater than it is in some socialist countries.[14]

The state may not own, but it does control, the military-industrial firms. Over 55,000 government personnel work on allocating contracts and policing compliance with government specifications. In one firm, 210 Pentagon employees were situated in residence to monitor this close relationship. Thus the top management is really in government itself. Within the government, salaries for this segment are relatively higher, job for job—factors that spur loyalty and disincentive to change.[15]

As a result, the military industry is oriented to cost- and subsidy-maximization, and to protecting its industrial base, rather than to making profits as a reward for risk-taking. The competitive commercial firm, which cannot increase profits merely by raising prices, must try to cut costs, improve productivity, and gear its research and engineering to the ends of cost-efficiency. Otherwise customers will not buy the product or will replace it with a substitute.[16]

The military industry operates by a different dynamic. Its consumer is guaranteed once the contract is settled, since the government usually buys what it orders, even if the costs run three or four times the original estimate. Risk is minimized, profits assured. Moreover, large contracts are generally chosen by negotiation with one selected firm rather than by competition. When competition exists, it is not for costs but for "competence" or ability to meet Pentagon requirements—to collaborate, to design changes, to write manuals. Thus, says one firm, "proposals are our most important product."[17]

Since the Pentagon often provides buildings, laboratories, and staff to help subsidize compliance, the normal self-correcting mechanisms of the profit-maximizing firm do not operate. Risk is underwritten, markets guaranteed, cost-efficiency subordinated to regulation. Cost accounting and cost-efficiency estimates are discouraged in favor of historical costing, which is based on past prices, for price-bidding rather than on engineering design. Historical costing, which contains a built-in escalator for increasing costs, ignores the possibility that engineering improvements and greater productivity may cut costs. This method of accounting justifies higher prices. Firms become oriented to maximizing government subsidies to such a degree that cost-oriented engineers may be discouraged or even dismissed.[18]

Small wonder, then, that administrative overhead costs are about twice as high in many of these large companies serving the military as in corporations serving the private sector exclusively. Cost overruns are part of business as usual. Higher costs mean more empire building: facilities, employees, cash flow, and cost base for figuring profits. They justify inflated Pentagon budget requests. Companies fabricate inspections to meet specifications, then come out with defective products. Lockheed's CF, estimated at $29 million a plane, came out at $62 million and had major breakdowns; the cost overruns on Litton's ships and submarines required a settlement of about $1 billion to the firm; Grumman's F-14 had over forty-three major deficiencies and a larger number of minor deficiencies.[19] Grumman, apparently, could not even build efficiently or reliably the civilian "Flxble" bus sold to cities, which are subject to much lower tolerances and much less stringent demands for reliability.

Given the size, strategic location, and orientation of the military-industrial complex, the conversion from a war economy that seems so theoretically appealing in reality, poses only practical threats and terrors of mass unemployment just like those raised by technological change. Unions resist antimilitarist efforts, with only a few notable exceptions (for instance, the UAW); witness union support of the SST. The closing of the Brooklyn Navy Yard some years ago met with much organized resistance and few successful efforts to find constructive work programs for the displaced employees. The history of defense cutbacks shows that the shock of displacement has seldom been buffered by income support or retraining.[20] Little has been done to coopt the predictable opposition to conversion on the part of these vested interests.

Resistance to conversion may be even stronger among professionals and managers than at the level of production work. Blue-collar workers could be retrained for other occupations. Engineers, however, would have to change the mind-set that has discouraged cost-efficiency estimates, while managers would need flexibility for conversion to competitive and risky civilian work. How many houses would Boeing have to sell to equal the profits from one airplane? A Grumman executive has cautioned that the company is not "mass-consumer" oriented.[21] But that is hardly the problem. The Grumman buses for New York City proved a fiasco, breaking down almost as soon as they were in operation. They highlighted a problem that with military contracts simply is not visible to the public eye. Considering how simple it is to produce buses, compared to sophisticated military equipment, it is hardly surprising that defense companies prefer to stay where they are neither visible nor held accountable for their mistakes.

DÉTENTE: PROFITS ÜBER ALLES

Economic considerations dominate international as well as domestic political behavior. Hardly a day goes by that the president, or some member of his cabinet or Congress, or a member of the Chiefs of Staff, does not warn that we can be destroyed through the overwhelming Soviet military and nuclear superiority. Controversy may exist on whether we still enjoy military parity or mutually destructive retaliatory power, but not over the assumption that Soviet military and economic strength threatens our way of life, even our survival.

Nevertheless, we do absolutely nothing to frustrate the advance of the economic machine that threatens our demise. On the contrary. To maximize domestic corporate revenues and profits, we encourage the very trade and export that help lubricate that engine. Wherever the Russian technological system is weaker or weakest, as in advanced computer know-how and equipment, we readily supply the products of our far superior scientific research, the development of which rests on our free exchange of ideas and on our economic incentives. We supply the most scientifically and technologically advanced products that our vast capital investments and collective human and natural resources can produce to strengthen our major adversary, all for the sake of larger corporate profits.

When Russian agricultural output lags, we step in and supply just what our competitor needs to surpass or destroy us. We supply the food that Russia desperately requires to maintain its system without disrupting its economy or its productivity. Thus the machinery presumably moving inexorably to overwhelm us, as both Soviet leaders and ours proclaim, is not even momentarily detoured. The continued export of wheat, even as technological transfer has been cut back, attests to the supremacy of these interests.

Nor is the issue the humanitarian one of saving millions from starvation. We export the agricultural products they need so much to give our farmers greater profits. Again, economic motives outweigh political considerations. We merely help the Soviets avoid shifting much of their labor force from manufacturing, engineering, and defense to farming. In November 1981 the Reagan administration, over Defense Secretary Caspar W. Weinberger's initial objections, permitted the ailing International Harvester to sell technological expertise to the U.S.S.R. Weinberger declined to block the transfer because the Department of State and Commerce approved the sale.[22]

The banks' attitude toward Polish bank debt also shows that "commerce comes before communism." While we deplore military domination on international telecasts, our government does all it can, at the taxpayers' expense, to shore up Poland's shaky economy.

In fiscal 1982 our foreign arms sales were at $25 to $30 billion, more than double 1981's spending. We have forgotten our earlier concern about sales to unstable countries, violators of human rights, and potential developers of nuclear weapons.[23]

To an impartial observer from Mars, it might seem amusing that we act as the ultimate reservoir to fill the most desperate needs of our so-called major enemy; that we appear as saviors to our opponents, wherever and whenever they are bottlenecked or suffer shortages; that we consciously and continually smooth the way for their potential military superiority. We not only supply the critical needs of the Soviet but are encouraged by our leaders to do so; and we do it, worse yet, on a most-favored-nation basis, with such major concessions as extended cheap credit and privileged low-cost shipping rates, so that these needs may be met as cheaply, efficiently, and expeditiously as possible. How explain our apparently insane, self-defeating, ultimately self-destructive behavior?

The answer is overwhelmingly simple. Leaders of our defense industry testify before congressional committees; advise the executive; court politicians with plane rides and other favors; and constantly bombard and "educate" the public on the need to increase our "defense" (or offense) budget, in order to maintain at least military parity.[24]

To justify that argument, the Russians must really increase their military productivity and output each year. So we act as emergency supplier of any technology or product whose absence might jeopardize that forward march. To justify allocating ever more of our precious resources for military use, we must ensure that the only competition that matters stays precisely in step with our own accelerated effort. Only then can we generate the fear required to inspire the effort and sacrifice necessary to sustain this vast and ever-increasing burden.

There is no question but that if the Russians slowed their own effort, we also would have to wind down—unless, of course, some other specter, like the Chinese, could replace the Russians and serve the same role in the defense argument. Perhaps this accounts as much as anything for the fact that, despite détente, a realistic arms- or nuclear-limitation agreement with the U.S.S.R. cannot, or will not, be achieved. President Reagan's delaying tactics make that all the more apparent.

And the problem is not political. Were it political, we would stop trading, stop supplying Russia what it needs most. We would do all we could; we might even possibly institute a blockade to impede Russia's functioning. Carter's grain embargo after the Afghanistan crisis kept the U.S.S.R. smarting for over a year. The problem is exclusively economic. If the U.S.S.R. had to retrench militarily to avoid insurrection by its starving citizens, we would have problems. The enormous defense-industry-generated revenues, profits, jobs, activity, military promotions and advancement, kickbacks, and other lucrative amenities, even the large corporate political contributions, would all come to a sudden halt.

The interplay of our military and civilian trade objectives is illustrated by our treatment of the 1971 balance-of-trade crisis. By then, our heavy wartime spending, lagging productivity, increasing imports, and foreign travel had combined to produce our first balance-of-payments deficit ($2.3 billion) since 1893, and a foreign-exchange crisis. In response, Nixon abandoned the gold standard, devalued the dollar, taxed imports and foreign securities, and mobilized the government to improve our poor competitive standing in the world market. Alarmed federal officials announced moves to spur and pool civilian research and development. A bill to provide seed money for new high-technology enterprises was submitted to Congress in 1972.[25]

By 1973 the White House had dropped the subject of productivity. Administration officials, recovering from their initial panic, looked for "alternatives for making large sales overseas which they, the state managers themselves, could initiate and operate. They soon discovered major opportunities. First, the Department of Defense came through with a major plan for enlarging world sales of armaments from the United States, increasing such exports from $925 million in 1970 to $3.8 billion per year in 1973." By 1978 U.S. military sales and aid to foreign governments reached $13.5 billion; the 1970–78 total was $72.9 billion.[26]

145

The relevance of this policy to our trade deficit was explicit. In June 1973, the government announced that arms sales were a good way to solve the balance-of-payments problem. The *New York Times* for June 8, 1973, indicated that "another reason, stressed less, is that with the decline in arms for the Vietnam war, American producers need new markets. This had led to increased pressure from American manufacturers on the Administration to adopt a more liberal attitude." Government officials used the balance-of-payments problem, which they had helped to create, to justify maintaining the industrial base of the military-industrial complex, the base of much of their own power.[27]

No less timely was the Great American Grain Robbery of 1972. While the administration tried to get Japan to slow its penetration of American markets and accelerate our exports to Japan, negotiations were undertaken with the U.S.S.R. for large sales of agricultural produce. Engineered by Secretary of Agriculture Earl Butz, who had close ties with the enormous grain-exporting firms, the 1972 wheat deal was arranged to sell $1 billion worth of wheat through low-interest credit and at highly subsidized per-bushel prices. In the name of détente, Butz cheered a deal that gave exporters, who had bought wheat at extremely low prices (grain was about $1.27 a bushel at the time of the arrangement, which fixed sales at $1.67 a bushel), subsidies of up to 46¢ a bushel as the price of grain soared to $2.10 after the announcement was made. Finally, the Office of Management and Budget protested and demanded suspension of the subsidy.[28]

The only ones who benefited from the transaction were the Russians, the six grain exporters involved, and several U.S. negotiators who were given high-level jobs with two of the grain exporters before the ink was dry on the contract. Meanwhile, taxpayers paid about $131.6 million for the deal, while our grain reserve, which had functioned to stabilize world grain prices, was depleted. As prices of domestic grain went up, livestock prices soared with them.

As Theodore Lowi stresses in this analysis of USDA operations, the Department of Agriculture can operate as its own Department of State. It is striking that the separate political operations converged to enhance our "preparedness" while feeding our enemy, to use détente and defense as partners, protecting specific interests at the expense of the public. Economics dictates. Economics determines our political behavior.

REAGAN: THROWING MONEY AT DEFENSE

The entire Reagan economic program exaggerates the pattern of more guns, less butter. Reagan and his officers, we are advised, do not shrink from this description. They vaunt it as the necessary response to the threat of communist aggression in the world. I do not take issue with the reality of that threat. But if they believe it is real, they should act accordingly by introducing policies and legislation that will manifest that concern, and not merely throw ever greater numbers of dollars at the problem through the military-industrial complex.

Notwithstanding the endless and indiscriminate funding of defense and military "preparedness," we are far *less* prepared today to fight a war—much less win it—than at any time since just before World War II, and not for lack of "parity." We were impotent against an almost primitive enemy in Vietnam. We were unable to activate our forces or deliver the equipment supposedly readily available to us in Germany during the 1973 Egyptian-Israeli war. We were totally inept in the abortive Iranian "rescue" mission, in which a good part of our invading forces was destroyed before ever meeting the enemy. We spend billions on defense and are far less safe today than five years ago. And five years from now we will feel even less safe.

Today we have no ready standing prepared army. We can destroy the Russians and the world and ourselves along with them many times over. But that power paralyzes us. We cannot instantly defend ourselves or our closest allies. In an age of ever more sophisticated and complex weaponry, ill-prepared enlistees, many of whom industry will not accept for the most menial tasks, are entrusted with the most expensive and destructive equipment in the history of man. Tragically—it hurts to say it, but it must be said—our forces are made up predominantly of misfits who are rejects from the private sector and whose average IQ was constantly declining—despite recategorizations to conceal the trend[29]—

until Congress in 1980 required that the proportion of enlistees with below-average mental aptitudes be limited to 25 percent in each service. In February 1982, the Pentagon was able to assert proudly that test scores showed new recruits to be "a cut above the average." One would hope so, when the Pentagon in 1981 programmed over $1 billion for recruitment, including $5,000 enlistment bonuses.[30]

The voluntary army suffers also from its high turnover rate. Some 30 percent of new recruits fail to complete their first term of enlistment, and the army suffers a turnover rate of 25 percent. One result is a lack of the cohesion that members need to fight together as buddies and sustain morale.[31]

Buying and building ever more expensive sophisticated equipment will not repair the military balance. It will only permit our forces to blow themselves up, and others with them, faster and more expensively than they did in the Iranian episode. Our great strategy consists of building more gigantic even if outmoded bombers; constructing little railroad-carried MX missiles with fake silos; and "demothing" giant antique battleships, or promoting whatever ultimate alternative Reagan can persuade Congress to accept. What an approach!

We do not at this juncture require a tremendous step-up of defense expenditures, but rather the efficiency and dedication to deal with the economic and moral equivalent of war that currently confronts us. If he were more stubborn in correcting what he has termed a hemorrhaging budget, Reagan would also avoid the political hemorrhage that results from the apparently cruel policy of dramatically increasing defense spending while implementing colossal tax cutbacks and cutting social programs, affecting many needy people, to the bone.

TARGETS FOR PLANNING

1. **Let us upgrade the quantity, quality, and dedication of our military manpower.** Most military analysts agree that we already have the nuclear firing power to destroy the Russians a hundred times or more. They can do about the same to us. What we

don't have are the personnel to assure the proper use of the arsenal we possess. Let us concentrate on that first and immediately.

We can do this without money, but with some sacrifice. "Ask not what your country can do for you, ask what you can do for your country." It is time that we, Reagan, the country, implemented the actions implied in that statement.

2. Each young person should serve his country for two years as a means of paying for, and demonstrating his or her appreciation for, citizenship in this remarkable country. There is no war on now. Young people are not being asked to give their lives in a worthless cause, as many suggested they were in Vietnam, in a war to which the country was really never totally committed. They are not even asked to fight for a worthy cause, as were so many in World War II for the $21 a month that drafted buck privates were paid. Each of us owes something to his country. Just as we must accept taxes, we must accept the tax of a portion of our time. In this way we would ensure our own security and preparedness; and we would improve through our actions— our contributions during this period of service—the nature and quality of our society and our lives. That period may be for military or civilian service.

3. A draft should be implemented immediately as a replacement for the recruitment of voluntary mercenaries. The pay structure of the military draftees should demonstrate that theirs is an act of sacrifice and patriotism, as well as a period of learning and constructive contribution. In contrast to the ever more exorbitant and almost totally inept voluntary army we now have, we would have the benefit of being served by all our youth, the very best as well as those not so blessed, without privileged exemptions. In due course we would have a readily available, fully defensive military force. Like the Israelis, who many military experts believe have the best trained and best prepared army at a low cost because to serve is a patriotic privilege as well as a duty, we would be militarily superior and secure. Our present posture is marked by a strident, never-ending, urgent call for ever increasing funds, ever increasing weaponry, ever increasing demands for higher pay and higher pensions in order to attract superior volunteers—who are nevertheless not forthcoming—and all to produce an ever less effective military and defense capability vis-à-vis our potential Russian adversary.

Such a Reagan program would substantially reduce our military budget. For in this period of sterile voluntarism, military payroll and pension costs have exploded. In 1978 our Department of Defense personnel numbered 3.04 million, hardly less than the 3.4 million of wartime 1972. Active-duty military personnel constituted 67.8 percent of that number—barely down from the 68.2 percent of 1972. Federal defense-related agencies, when we include the armed forces, employed 62.1 percent of all federal personnel. The Reagan budget for 1983 calls for $65.3 billion in personnel and pension expenses in a total budget of $216 billion.[32]

Given the present inadequate incentive structure, military personnel can retire with hefty pensions while young, while their skills are still needed. We recruit for "careers" short-term volunteers eager for the initial bonus, while our dropping of GI Bill benefits has reduced the incentive to remain. Our services are locked into complex weapons systems that permit little flexibility on the battlefield. Our armed forces remain too small, particularly in terms of skilled workers, for their technology.[33]

If we could cut back on this effort to build a mercenary army, we would have a far superior defense capability and presence without having to increase our already burdensome, and almost totally ineffective, defense spending. It would be great for the country. It would be great for the military. It would be great for young people, teaching many of them discipline and sacrifice at an age and at a time when, much to the detriment of youth and us all, a kind of anything-goes anarchism and selfish "me"-ism prevail in society. We may have had enough of total permissiveness and Dr. Spock. Our children could use a few responsibilities and the recognition that it is worthwhile in life to be guided by certain universal values.

4. Beyond that, we must turn our energies to constructive peacetime production by channeling the profit motive, for in a capitalistic, free-enterprise, profit-fueled society, profits come before all else. "Profits über alles." Profits are essential to

create the incentives to accumulate and risk capital, to create jobs for enhanced productivity, to inspire the dedication and commitment of our most creative and energetic workers and managers.

Given that profits are the catalyst and the rationale for our politically self-destructive behavior, and that they also work to produce our economic and political superiority, we can hardly advocate their elimination. It would be like asking us to stop breathing because the air is polluted. The resistance, moreover, would be far too great. Entrenched interests would rebel.

Without an ideological mandate and a plan for transition, the coalition of military professionals, managers and technicians, engineers and blue-collar workers, unionized and nonunionized civilians on military bases, in the Pentagon, and in private industry, will defend its perquisites and security. Despite the practical benefits, conversion to a civilian economy is not politically feasible. Congressmen still are judged by the military contracts they bring their constituents. Defense spending may be as wasteful as transfer payments or other make-work projects, but it carries the halo of national security. And eliminating its immense activity, jobs, and profits, its strategic contribution to the GNP, would jeopardize the foundations of our economic system.

The answer can only be to design government incentives that will substitute equally profitable and, ideally, more profitable, areas of activity that do meet society's long-term needs: the rebuilding of our deteriorating infrastructure, energy production, food production, clean air and water production, new medical facilities and cures. Favored enterprises would substitute their profits for those of the military-industrial area, and seduce leading capitalists into reallocating their energies and society's always limited resources toward meeting vital goals and providing creative outlets for the greatest number of human beings. Such an evolution would require government leadership and policies firmly committed to dramatic reconstruction within the framework of a society geared to maximum profit.

Government can effect such change by pressing the right button, in this case profits. It can motivate change by making those areas that are most beneficial to society the most profitable as well. It has always been able to do so in the case of defense, with the development of new aircraft by Boeing or McDonnell Douglas, or new nuclear submarines by General Dynamics, or new spaceships by Grumman, or the atom bomb by the Manhattan Project, or the crash program that combined education and the profit incentive of space projects to overtake and surpass *Sputnik* despite the immense Soviet head start. Through planned programs and the introduction of targeted incentives to achieve them, government can create solutions to pressing social problems.

In this kind of race, to solve world problems rather than to produce ever more frightening mutually destructive capacity, everyone can benefit. Even the U.S.S.R.

NOTES

1. *Washington Evening Star,* August 14, 1972, quoted in Seymour Melman, *The Permanent War Economy: American Capitalism in Decline,* New York, Simon and Schuster, 1974, 25.

2. Samuelson, *Economics,* 11th ed., 256.

3. An invariable component of the introductory undergraduate economics course. See for example, Lepsey and Steiner, *Microeconomics,* 8, 10.

4. Samuelson, *Economics,* 11th ed., 22.

5. *Statistical Abstract,* 1979, 100th ed., Tables 1506 and 1507, 860.

6. Melman, *War Economy,* 66, 264–65. This figure includes direct military outlays and military aid to client governments, interest on the national debt, and veterans' payments. The direct U.S. military cost is given at $150 billion.

7. Quote from Melman, *War Economy,* 18; *Statistical Abstract,* 1979, 100th ed., Table 428, 257.

8. Lipsey and Steiner, *Macroeconomics,* 203; Samuelson, *Economics,* 11th ed., 256.

9. Quoted in Leonard Silk, "Military Costs vs. Inflation," *New York Times,* May 7, 1982, D2.

10. Samuelson, *Economics,* 11th ed., 767.

11. *Statistical Abstract,* 1979, 100th ed., Table 587, 364.

12. *Statistical Abstract,* Table 600, 372; Melman, *War Economy,* 227.

13. Melman, *War Economy,* 257, 258, 324, 41.

14. John Kenneth Galbraith, *The New Industrial State,* New York, New American Library, 1978, 1978, xii, 2.

15. Melman, *War Economy,* 51, 53, 61.

16. Ibid., 234, 44, 28–29, 33–35.

17. Ibid., 34, 38; *Statistical Abstract,* 1979, 100th ed., Table 587, 370, on Department of Defense-advertised vs. negotiated military procurement.

18. Melman, *War Economy,* 57, 41, 27–28.

19. Ibid., 31–33, 44, 48, 51, 36.

20. Ibid., 51, 239, 236.

21. Ibid., 51, 41, 242–43.

22. "Harvester's Plant Technology Approved for Sale to Russians," *New York Times,* December 1, 1981, 24.

23. "They Can't Eat Bullets" (Editorial), *New York Times,* February 16, 1982, Sec. 4, F16.

24. Galbraith, *New Industrial State,* xii–xiii, 297–301.

25. *Statistical Abstract,* 1979, 100th ed., Table 1491, 847, Table 1507, 860; Melman, *War Economy,* 107–09; Heilbroner and Thurow, *The Economic Problem,* 617, 619, 624, 525; Samuelson, *Economics,* 10th ed., 654.

26. Melman, *War Economy,* 108–109; *Statistical Abstract,* Table 594, 368.

27. Quoted in Melman, *War Economy,* 269–70.

28. Lowi, *End of Liberalism,* pp. 87, 149–161.

29. Juan Cameron, "It's Time to Bite the Bullet on the Draft," *Fortune* 101, April 7, 1980, 52–56.

30. Cynthia A. Roberts, "We Must Reinstate the Draft," *New York Times,* February 25, 1982, A31.

31. Ibid.; Senator Gary Hart, "What's Wrong with the Military?" *New York Times Magazine,* February 14, 1982, 16.

32. *Statistical Abstract,* 1979, 100th ed., Table 601, 372, Table 603, 373; Richard Halloran, "Criticism Rises on Reagan's Plan for 5-Year Growth of the Military," *New York Times,* March 22, 1982, A1.

33. "Bigger Bucks for Security But How Much and for What?" *New York Times,* March 22, 1982, Sec. 4; Roberts, "Reinstate the Draft," A31; Hart, "What's Wrong with the Military?" 16, 19, 40.

8

Our Star-Spangled Bankers

*Banking establishments are more
dangerous than standing armies.*

Thomas Jefferson, 1799

I have always been impressed with the altruistic and dedicated
zeal with which our commercial banks fight inflation by promptly
raising their prices—the interest rates that they charge for their
product. Any observer must marvel at their audacity in raising the
prime rates, even, at times, in the face of sluggish loan demand,
and as a consequence raising costs and the inflation rate.

Theoretically, high interest rates were supposed to put a brake
on demand, which in turn reduced employment and buying power. These mechanisms served as an automatic gyroscope that produced a new, noninflationary equilibrium. In reality, the demand
for money has become essentially inelastic and its price irrelevant.
Business passes the cost of credit on to the borrower, selling money at prices that become fashionable, hence acceptable. The federal
government, being itself in debt, hardly concerns itself with the

cost of money. Like all debtors, it benefits from inflation, and, unlike state and local governments, it puts no ceiling on the interest it allows itself to pay creditors. Consumers, in turn, have protected themselves against inflation by buying more and buying now. In 1980, installment debt stood at 22.5 percent of disposable income. [1]

The federal government, of course, finances much of the cost of high interest rates paid by both individuals and businesses through tax policies that favor borrowing. Since interest rates are deducted from taxes at prevailing corporate tax rates, the government ultimately absorbs about half of any increase in interest costs. In effect, it subsidizes the banks' errors, operating costs, and profits.

Not all this inflationary credit can be blamed on demand. The overhead of the banking system has risen. Built into it are an impressive array of high costs: branches on almost every corner; highly paid officers with luxurious executive dining rooms; ill-considered business and real-estate loans; and equally ill-fated loans to foreign and developing countries. Banks remain viable by maintaining and encouraging high interest rates, begging the increased costs of doing business (not the least of which are the rising rates they pay depositors).

The process bears a suspicious resemblance to the rounds of wage and price increases, and with the same destabilizing consequences. High interest rates contribute immediately to inflation by raising the cost of doing business and hence prices. Interest rates must then move up to provide a return over and above the prevailing inflation rate, because of both increased costs and the expectations of lenders who demand a higher inflation premium. As these expectations become epidemic, more and more people acquire a stake in inflation, knowing that their debts will be repaid in cheaper dollars. A network of vested interests evolves that amasses great wealth, thanks to inflation. These interests exert their influence to keep inflation going while the middle class is stretched on the rack.

To the public at large, the costs of high interest rates have become increasingly intolerable. They have raised the price of money not only to private borrowers but to government. The mere difference between what in any event would be a historically high 10 percent interest rate and the prevailing 15 percent rate on government bonds in 1981, translates, on a debt of $700 billion, into an increment of $35 billion a year. This amount equals the entire budget cut that was worked out so laboriously by Congress in 1981. The bulk of the present trillion-dollar debt was incurred at far lower interest rates. Yet, since it is refinanced increasingly with short-term obligations, the deficit is compounded at rates that threaten our best budget-cutting efforts and throw the government into disarray, as the Reagan administration discovered to its chagrin.

In the private sector, high interest rates produce an inflationary spiral and fan the anxieties of the business groups that watch the inflation indices so apprehensively. An analyst quoted in the *New York Times* on February 26, 1980, pointed out that each percentage point increase in the cost of home mortgage loans drives up the CPI by 0.8 percent.[2] Such an increase in turn drives up government spending on payments like Social Security that are tied by law to the CPI, as well as the CPI-adjusted wages of several million unionized workers. Public subsidies further accelerate the spiral, increasing the need for funds, the cost of debt financing, and the deficit. Continuing price increases in turn encourage a "buy now" mentality—the opposite of their presumed effect.

This vicious cycle repeats itself until a crash occurs when credit costs become so onerous that demand is abruptly halted; business, buckling under the burden of these costs, can no longer sustain them the moment that demand for goods and services drops off. The result is a series of bankruptcies that cripples the economy.

Higher interest rates are thus self-defeating in the fight against inflation. They undermine business endeavor not only because of their costs, but also because the associated volatility of interest rates destroys predictability, which is an absolute prerequisite to business planning. It is impossible to run a business or plan an investment or the purchase of a home when interest rates gyrate from day to day, and when credit policies are changed almost as often as bedsheets.

In the international arena, high interest rates push up the relative value of the dollar. This "defense" of the dollar raises export prices, damages our competitive standing in the foreign markets, and produces a balance of payments deficit. Eventually it results in domestic unemployment as our exports decline and imports increase after inflation has already wrought its damage. Moreover, high rates lead to greater volatility in the foreign exchange markets. Attracting foreign deposits, they add to our reserves and our monetary base, producing a larger potential money supply—the reverse of the Fed's presumed goal.

High interest rates have also threatened the survival of savings institutions. Encouraged by the government, these agencies have issued long-term mortgages bearing rates far lower than the levels that must currently be paid to attract deposits. The resulting transfer of investment to higher-yielding money market funds has meant that, barring some other bail-out provision—the "all-savers" certificates of 1981, whose sale has been limited to fifteen months, won't solve the long-term problem—savings and loan associations will be forced to sell mortgages at enormous losses. Ultimately the government, through its various deposit-guarantee agencies, will have to make up these deficits, a situation that will lead to more government borrowing and further enlargement of the money supply.

Perhaps the most widely asserted advantage of a high-interest-rate strategy, one in tune with the current administration's survival-of-the-fittest philosophy, is the system's purported neutrality in the marketplace. But, one may not unreasonably ask, what is impartial about hardships differently experienced? Many small businesses, innovative and entrepreneurial in spirit, form the hope for America's thrust for productivity and job creation. But they are unable to bid for capital as freely as mammoth, technologically less enterprising corporations. By contrast, federal, state, and local governments, the borrowers of last resort, are hardly, or at least not invariably, the most efficient users of capital. Yet there is no price so high that it can dissuade the federal government from borrowing.

There is, however, an obverse to this gloomy scenario. If higher interest rates contribute to inflation, then lower rates must contribute immediately to *dis*inflation. If the estimate that a one-point rise in home mortgage loan rates produces an 0.8 percentage point rise in the CPI is even roughly accurate, then each point's reduction in the mortgage loan rate must reduce the CPI by an equivalent amount. Instead of a higher CPI triggering automatic wage and transfer-payment increases, only to raise prices further, we could see an abrupt halt to, or even reversal of, this cycle. According to Bernard Goldsmith, president of Bastian Industries, each percentage-point drop in the prime rate (which was running at 19 percent when he spoke in February 1981) would raise his company's after-tax profits by eight cents a share. High loan rates choke off this profit potential, aborting the ultimate source of reinvestment and destroying the incentive to modernize, improve, and augment the supply-side components of our economy that are so essential to obstructing inflation.

EXPENSIVE EASY MONEY: THE BANKER'S NIRVANA

A policy of halting inflation and stimulating much-needed productivity and growth should focus strongly on lowering interest rates. Yet inflation seems, ironically, to be inflamed by the very agency designated to control it, the Federal Reserve Board, which adamantly persists in high-interest-rate policies supported by the banks, despite overwhelming evidence to the futility of these efforts. Each rise in interest rates has generally been followed by a rise in the CPI; and the worst inflationary increases have coincided with parallel escalations of the prime, discount, and federal-funds rates. Between 1977 and 1980, the inflation rate more than tripled. It was running at 5 percent when President Carter took office in 1977; by 1980 it reached 18 percent. By early 1981 the prime rate—the cost of money that banks charge their premier customers—reached 21.5 percent. By then, a drop to an outrageous and still historically high 17 percent was considered a major accomplishment.

The easing of inflation has hardly affected this usury. In the first quarter of 1983, the inflation rate was only 0.4 percent. Yet the prime rate that banks offered only their very-blue-chip clients was 10.5 percent, a real interest rate charge of 10.1 percent and an all-time record interest rate for the United States. Some have argued that the high rate was a necessary protection against the potential inflation threatened by the Fed's tolerance of rapid monetary growth. Even if they were correct, however, their argument would not justify real short-term interest rates of 10 percent for the very short thirty-, sixty-, and ninety-day periods during which no such risk prevailed. More plausibly, banks needed to subsidize their mismanagement, their poorly collateralized energy loans, their uncollateralized foreign loans. Indirectly (or directly), they were taxing American industry and the American consumer who was paying 18–21 percent for his loans. Thus the banks held back what might have been dramatic growth for the economy and for American exports in order to camouflage and survive the consequences of their own bankrupt policies.

The discount and federal funds rates, by means of which the Federal Reserve Board controls reserves and the money supply, have only followed suit. In 1977, the discount rate, which the Fed charges member banks who borrow reserves in order to expand loans, was only 5.75 to 6 percent. In early 1978 it was raised to 6.5, 7, and, by November, what was at that time an extreme 8.5 percent. Commenting on this upward creep on May 22, 1978, a *New York Times* editorial warned that "short-term interest rates are the tail that can wag the entire economy. They are already so high—above 7 percent—that they threaten to hobble economic growth. Monetary policy is one tool for retarding inflation, but only one, and historically there is reason to fear the Fed's zeal." Since then, the discount rate has virtually tripled at times. In 1981 it went to 17 and 18 percent, if the surcharge was included; and that once alarming 7 percent seemed to belong to a bygone age.[5]

A similar climb has marked the federal funds rate, the rate at which commercial banks lend excess reserves to each other overnight; this rate is determined by the Fed through its open market activities as it increases or cuts back the banks' reserves. In summer 1977, it ranged from 5.38 to 5.63 percent. By April 1980 it had reached over 20 percent, and in 1981 it came close to that level.

The extended period of record-high prime and bond interest rates, the then depressed Dow Jones average, the howling of Main

Street businessmen, of consumers, of labor leaders, testify to the failure of this insistent high-interest policy, a vicious cycle in which the only gainers are the banks. Yet the Fed, created at least in part to control them, seems in some respects to be playing into their hands. Sporadically, some outsiders—Congressmen Neal, Reuss, and Proxmire among them—have challenged these policies. Within the economic community, some dissenters on the Federal Reserve Board have at times criticized its tight money policies.

Whether the Fed really can more easily control the money supply than interest rates is moot. Its October 1979 shift to an effort to control money supply growth has hardly met with success. It seems easier to peg interest rates through open-market sales and purchases than to control the money supply, which depends on several factors outside the Fed's control. The forms in which individuals and corporations hold their liquid money have been rapidly changing, as the explosive growth of money market funds attests. In any case, Keynesians and monetary theorists of the Friedman school split on this issue consistently.

It is more commonly agreed that the Fed cannot control both the money supply and interest rates at the same time. If interest rates are set at, say, 5 percent, the Fed must let the money supply grow to whatever point it must so that the demand for money at that price is satisfied. If it targets money supply growth at 7 percent, it must let interest rates fluctuate—rise and fall where they may until the demand for money is aligned with the money supply. If demand exceeds supply, the interest rates will be forced up. This, in fact, has been the Fed's argument for high interest rates since its "historic" shift of October 1979, in which it announced that it would concentrate on controlling money growth rather than interest rates.

What's wrong with the picture?

First, the market assumptions of this equilibrium model make little sense in the political environment of money supply determination. Theoretically, tight money (or slow growth) and high interest rates imply a shortage of money. And an oversupply of money should mean low interest rates. Yet the assumption that high interest rates are synonymous with (that is, result from, and produce) tight money is no longer valid. The massive accumulation of credit funds for the Conoco takeover in 1981 made this abundantly clear. We have simultaneously had both high interest rates and great availability of money for some time. The Fed has not slowed the growth of money so much as it has raised its cost and the cost of many goods and services that hinge on the cost of money—the costs of carrying inventory, of financing machinery, plant and equipment, of accounts receivable, as well as the carrying costs of housing and merchandise purchased on credit. Meanwhile, the supply of money has kept flowing and has been readily available, not choked off as it was in earlier periods of high interest rates.

There are several reasons for this unhappy turn of affairs. In some respects, Federal Reserve policies dovetail with the interests of the banks. In other respects, the American commercial banking system effectively obstructs the Fed's intentions and destroys its ability to influence the American economy constructively. The government itself under Nixon, Carter, and Reagan has put pressure on the Fed to expand the availability of money. But whenever its harsh measures begin to take effect, and become politically threatening, the Federal Reserve reverses itself and negates actions that it has undertaken, or implements policies that undercut the effectiveness of its own efforts.

There has seldom been a sustained effort to check money supply growth. Growth of the money supply has consistently exceeded the Fed's targets. As has become apparent since 1975, when Congress demanded that the Federal Reserve announce its targets for monetary growth, it has missed its goals for M1 and M2 as often as it has attained them, despite the fact that it sets extremely broad ranges for itself allowing two to three points' difference. Sometimes it has allowed the money supply to grow without offering resistance; sometimes the expansion has taken place after the administration has publicly or privately exerted pressure on the Fed. The Nixon 1972 strategies are one classic if controversial case (see chapter 7). In the fall of 1977, also, the Fed, then chaired by Arthur Burns, decided to "acquiesce" in the rapid monetary expansion that had taken place in the preceding year and a half; the new target rates that it set only camouflaged the tolerance of added monetary stimulus. For, while the Fed adhered to certain of its targets and lowered others, it calculated growth from successively higher starting points, offsetting its own moves. Once it tampers with the base levels of the monetary supply the Fed can claim to have achieved almost any target.

Since its policy shift of October 1979, when the Federal Reserve announced that it would concentrate on the money supply rather than interest rates, interest rates have gone even higher. Yet, in view of the limited number of strategies that it uses—its focus on open market activities and the discount rate, and its shuttling between setting high interest rates and pumping reserves into the system (a pattern followed in 1980 and again in 1981)—it has produced little significant change. Not only interest rates but the money supply are more volatile than ever.

In February 1980, for example, Paul Volcker announced a planned decrease in the M growth rate. A month later, when the money supply and bank loans were both reported up, a business writer intoned piously, "The latest rise in the money supply may force the Federal Reserve to push up interest rates despite its desire not to do so." At the same time it was announced that the Federal Open Market Committee, which sets monetary policy, had decided (on March 7) to "allow" the Federal Funds rate to rise as high as 18 percent "to help slow monetary growth." If high interests are the *strategy* used, it hardly matters whether they are pegged at a high level of "allowed" to rise to it.

In other ways, too, the Fed has adopted contradictory policies over the long term. It has allowed the monetary or reserve base to grow. As price inflation of the 1970s quickened, Samuelson has observed, the Fed also quickened the growth rates of reserves and of the other money aggregates.[4] It has scaled down the legal reserve requirements for demand deposits to about 12 percent. This reduction may be a necessity, perhaps, for the banks, what with the high interest they must now pay on longer term deposits and the interest on demand deposits in NOW and ATS accounts, but it is potentially inflationary. The legal required-reserve ratio for time deposits, which is always much lower than the reserve requirement for checking accounts, is down from 5 percent (as of 1972) to 2.5 percent for deposits held between 180 days and 4 years, and 1 percent for deposits held 4 years or more.[5] And the Fed, as it provides loans at its discount window, permits banks to add to their reserve base with borrowed money, giving them a further line of credit with a guaranteed high profit markup.

Perhaps the worst inflationary touch is the fact that the federal funds and discount rates, both controlled by the Fed,[6] are below market interest rates, and thus hardly discourage borrowing. The spread between these rates and the prime shows the flaw in monetary policy. Not only has the prime rate gone up with the discount (some say the discount rate only tamely follows the prime); but the spread has often increased as well. In March 1980, there was no less than a 6 percent spread between the prime and the discount rate, as against only 2.25 percentage points in 1979. On October 16, 1981, when the discount (excluding a surcharge for large borrowers) was 14 percent and the federal funds rate was 16.38 percent, the prime rate was 18 percent. In both cases, the banks were able to use borrowed reserves—with a significant multiplier effect on effective lending power—to augment their profits.

The spread between the federal and discount rates themselves is also significant. In March 1980, even after tight credit controls were announced by the Carter administration, the spread between the discount and the federal funds rate was 2.73 percentage points, as against only .31 in 1979. In October 1981, the spread was again 2.38 percentage points. Banks will naturally turn to the discount window wherever possible to increase their profit markups.

The policy of generally keeping the discount and federal-funds rates below market interest is intended to smooth out seasonal and emergency needs. Yet, as Daniel Hamberg points out, it also gives member banks the incentive

to use the borrowing mechanism for profit, especially during periods of monetary restraint, high money market interest rates, and strong customer demand for loans. That this is not entirely idle speculation is suggested by the behavior of member-bank borrowing. . . . Member banks have made good use of the discount window in times of high and rising interest rates, and in general the more so the greater the gap be-

tween the federal-funds rate and the discount rate. Care must be taken against inferring too much from this ratio, for other forces are at work. . . . But, at the least, the evidence suggests that the banks may not be averse to occasional abuse of the borrowing "privilege."[7]

Even higher rates will do little to check this demand, for there is little incentive for banks to keep their own borrowing costs down—that is, to reduce the interest they pay to their depositors (or to the Fed)—if they can immediately pass these costs on to their own debtors by increasing the prime. The incentive, in fact, operates in reverse. The more banks pay for money, for deposits and reserves, the more they can justify the higher charges on all the money they lend out, claiming "increased costs of doing business" (the perennial bank refrain), including significant amounts available to them at much lower rates. When the prime was 18 percent (as in October 1981), they were still able to borrow from the Fed window at the 14 percent discount rate for a profit of 4 percent on easy money.

Banks are indifferent to high interest costs for other reasons too. Because banks can *create* credit, each source of funds provides a marginal increment in profit by expanding the lending power of the bank. With an 18 percent prime rate in October 1981, banks still had cost-free checking-account deposits with ample profit potential. On top of that they could pull in surplus funds at less than 6 percent for passbook savings, with a 13 percentage point spread between what they paid for funds and what they charged for loans. The six-month savings certificates, which paid 14.05 percent, provided them close to a 4 percentage point spread. On top of that, banks could borrow from the Fed window at 14 percent for a profit of 4 percentage points on each dollar of easy money from which nothing had to be withheld in reserves—since these are already borrowed reserves. When the banking system as a whole is considered, each added billion dollars in borrowed reserves (assuming a 12 percent reserve requirement) generates a potential lending power of well over $8 billion. Thus the effective yield on these borrowed reserves comes to at least 20 percentage points. On CDs the potential is almost as high.

Furthermore, new banking regulations now permit banks to

pay whatever rate of interest they need in order to attract deposits. In addition, changes in the financial markets (for example, the rise of money market funds) and in state usury laws merely raise the cost of money to borrowers without necessarily making it less available. Here lies the ultimate fallacy of the high-interest tight-money theory.

Until recently, interest rates were high because money—that is, money for loans—was essentially rationed, limited in supply, so that the cost of those funds that were available was bid up by demand. Under the Fed's Regulation Q, a ceiling was placed on what banks could pay depositors. Whenever the Federal Reserve forced interest rates up, the banks continued to extend loans to business to their utmost ability. That, after all, is the way they function and maximize profits. But as rates rose to levels beyond what banks could legally pay to savers, banks were automatically limited in the supply of funds they could provide to their potential borrowers. Not only was the inflow of new funds limited. The disintermediation that resulted as depositors shifted to other liquid assets with competing rates decreased their deposits and banks' available reserves, forcing an automatic slowing of loans and monetary growth that in turn checked economic growth. The result was what was often referred to as a credit crunch.

Today this situation no longer obtains. The former regulator of money availability from banks—the automatic rationer—has effectively been dismantled. In 1978 the banks, along with other groups, argued against the legal limits on the amount paid for small savings deposits, contending that they were discriminatory both to small savers and themselves. The result was the virtual elimination of the ceiling on the interest that could be paid to savers, since small-savers certificates now offered yields equal to six-month Treasuries. The new regulations created thereby the limitless availability of funds to banks, albeit at ever-escalating rates. In 1980, legislation was passed to phase out Regulation Q altogether over six years,[8] improving the banks' position vis-à-vis nonbank competition. The result was that in 1980 and 1981 the banks generated the highest prime rates in U.S. economic history, while hardly slowing the money supply, or limiting the funds available for borrowing, or slowing inflation at all.[9] Funds paid to depositors are now built into the ever-increasing cost of doing business, further raising the prime. Whatever benefit depositors gain from the higher interest rates they receive is washed out by the effect of these rates on prices, on business bankruptcies, on jobs lost. Having gotten around the limits on demand deposits with NOW accounts and automatic transfers that add to their costs, having obtained license to offer rates on six-month deposits that compete with Treasury yields, they must raise their prices to maintain the same spreads between payouts and income, and augment their profits. In the process, the banks, along with the money funds, also cancel out some of the supply-side effects of savings, which are presumably deflationary because they withdraw funds from consumption. For higher interest payments to savers are inflationary in that they increase the credit expenses and costs of the supply side—investor-businesses—so there is no net gain.

At present, the Federal Reserve collaborates to push up the cost of money as a way of "rationing" loans, perhaps misgauging the elasticity of demand for credit, without effectively rationing the amount of loan dollars available. Yet in many cases loans cannot be delayed, often precisely because of the high cost of borrowing. They are essential to paying off previous commitments, including the principal of prior loans or the ever-increasing costs on these loans. In the case of takeovers, the view obtains that the "opportunity" must be captured immediately, almost without regard for the interest-cost penalty. As a consequence and paradoxically, high interest rates increase the demand for money, since they force borrowers to borrow further merely to service their high-interest payments. Hence the recent serious escalation of corporate debt, both short- and long-term, especially in 1981.[10] At a prime rate of 21 percent, a borrower, in less than four years, must pay in interest alone a sum equivalent to the total principal that he has borrowed.

The elimination of the laws limiting the maximum that banks could pay to attract funds has completely undermined and made inoperable the single logical rationale that the Fed had for raising interest rates as a means of slowing money growth and credit availability. What made this formula work was the impenetrable upper limit that banks could not exceed in order to attract funds.

Under those circumstances, raising the rates high enough brought an abrupt end to credit availability and effected the result that is now being debated—that the cost of business, at some appropriately high level, finally limits borrowing.

Consequently, the Fed's strategy of pushing interest rates up rather than resorting to other methods such as increasing the reserve requirement or limiting availability at the discount window no longer makes sense. Like indexing, this strategy merely accelerates the inflationary process by which these rates enter the production, inventory, and consumer cost stream. Like a value-added tax, the cost of money is tacked on at each stage of production, finally raising the cost of carrying inventory and forcing prices ever upward.

With this outmoded approach the Fed is continuing to fight the last war without ever divining that a seemingly equitable and relatively undramatic change has made a major difference in the structure and functioning of the money system. It has pursued a battle plan that has generated damage and self-destruction more than progress. Given the basic structural change, new, or at least different, weapons are required this time around, and the Fed's failure, whether deliberate or unintentional, to recognize this fact has wrought inestimable harm.

The growth of the money market funds themselves highlights the fallacies of this strategy. During 1981, assets in the money funds grew at an average $2.2 billion a week, continuing at almost that pace even after the introduction of All Savers' certificates, to reach $166.04 billion as of October 21, 1981, and $200 billion by June 1982. By providing higher yields precisely because they were not required to set aside "sterile" cash reserves, as banks must, the money funds had been draining enormous amounts of deposits from our traditional financial institutions: the commercial banks, the savings banks, the savings-and-loan and life-insurance companies. In the process the money funds were already threatening serious and irreparable damage to these institutions which, perfect or not, are the foundations on which is built the financial structure of our economy. Although some of those funds come back to the banks in the form of CDs (certificates of deposit), even the interim outflow of money rapidly raises the costs to the banking system, creating a shocklike disequilibrium that many of these institutions may not be strong enough to adjust to or survive. Moreover, at the very least, the yield differential lifts the entire interest cost curve to a higher level for all—for the banks, savings and loans, insurance companies, and government, without producing any compensating benefits, such as inducing investors to take the longer term supply-side debt and equity risks.

The viability of investment in productive equipment and facilities on which supply-side economics and, indeed, a healthy economy and noninflationary growth depend rests on significant rate differentials—specifically, high long-term rates and lower short-term rates. The yield differential was long a constant pattern in the financial and capital markets, as compensation for the larger risks incurred in longer-term debt. But with real interest rates up and money market fund yields often at 16 or 17 percent, as against only 15 and 16 percent for double- and triple-A rated corporate bonds, this distinction and the potential for long-term investment were undermined. Who is likely to invest in long-term debt or equity securities when the highest yield, and hence greatest investment incentive, is provided by the short-term, presumably safe, and liquid money funds?

The first thing you learn at any business school is that the basic investment decision—to buy or build new plants and equipment—is determined by the expected return on capital. The most important factor determining that expected return is the cost of capital, debt as well as equity, both of which are determined by the prevailing rate of interest. When interest rates are high the cost of capital is high, with the consequent expectation that the return on investment will be poor to nil. High interest rates discourage investment. Very high interest rates, like those prevailing in recent periods, obliterate new investment. If we hope to stimulate the new productive investments supply-side economics demands, we must force interest rates down.

The obvious solution, in a noninflationary context, would be to put the money funds into competitive parity with the banks by imposing reserve requirements on them that parallel those imposed on the banks. This would preserve the banks from unfair competition while checking the expansion of credit. Yet protection for the banks has taken the opposite form: easing the restraints on banks so that they can compete better with the money funds by eliminating interest ceilings promising still higher payments on deposits. In this manner, it has only reinforced the inflationary process and the movement of savings to ever-shorter maturities that are undermining our economy.

THE FED: CAPTIVE OF THE BANKS?

Why, despite this dismal track record, has the Federal Reserve been allowed systematically to exacerbate the problem it is intended to solve? It requires no conspiracy theory to provide an answer. Like Smith's invisible hand, a harmony of interests with the banks is built into the structure, functions, and traditions of the Federal Reserve System. Conceived in the wake of the bank panic of 1907, the system was established in 1913 essentially as "a cooperative enterprise among bankers for the purpose of increasing the security of banks and providing them with a reservoir of resources." It has also assumed other functions, the most important being its operation as a central national bank to help control the nation's money supply and credit conditions. It determines reserve requirements for its member banks, issues Federal Reserve notes (currency), acts as the government's fiscal agent, and makes loans to its member banks.

Its structure embodies a number of "unusual public-private elements," as the Commission on Money and Credit has called it. It is a private corporation whose stockholders are member banks, yet it functions as a public agency. An extremely profitable agency by virtue of its legal privilege to hold reserves without interest cost, it pays annual dividends to its member banks. Yet its profits are limited: above a certain level, they revert to the Treasury. The seven members of the Federal Reserve Board are appointed by the president, yet their official allegiance is to Congress and not the executive branch. Their paychecks do not come from the government, yet the board members are not considered private citizens. Even their allegiance to Congress must be limited, for Congress can exercise few sanctions over them. Since Congress provides no appropriations, the Federal Reserve is not dependent on it for budgetary allocations.

The twelve-member Federal Open Market Committee, whose open-market sales and purchases of government securities are central to the control of the money supply, is even more independent. It consists of the members of the Federal Reserve Board plus five of the twelve presidents of the regional reserve banks, the latter chosen by member commercial banks. This committee, which has been called the most powerful group of private citizens in America,[11] has five members who are not appointed by the president or approved by the Senate, yet who exercise policymaking power as government officials.

Also independent of public sanction are those who are appointed to the boards of the system's twelve regional or district banks. Six of each district board's nine members are elected by member commercial banks of the district. Three, including the chairman and deputy chairman, are appointed by the Federal Reserve Board. The chairman must be "a person of tested banking experience," and three members must be bankers. Another three must be businessmen. Thus, by representation or by vote, the banking community controls the membership of the regional reserve banks.

The potential for conflict of interest is impressive. The Fed's leaders come from the banking community, have been trained in, and have probably taught in, its schools. Their daily interactions are with bankers, and they generally expect to return to careers in the banking community. On the basis of their schooling, experience, and orientation, they have come to think in terms of the needs of the banking community—their stockholders and probable future employers or benefactors.

How do they retain their independence of the government and the banking community whom they both serve and regulate? Paul Samuelson puts it this way:

> *The Federal Reserve . . . is a* public *agency. It is directly responsible to Congress; and whenever any conflict arises between its making a profit and the public interest, it acts according to the public interest without question. . . . The Reserve authorities—the regional and*

*Washington officials—never think of their stockholders, the member
commercial banks, as dictators of their actions. Rather, they act as a
public body.*[12]

Yet the events of recent years cast doubt on this analysis. The
Fed shuns congressional as well as executive control. Since an ac-
cord of 1951 was signed by the Treasury Department and the Fed,
pressure from the Treasury and the president is at least officially
constrained. In practice it sometimes bends to informal pressure,
as often as not shuttling between resistance and capitulation—to
wit, Volcker's 1981 debate with the Treasury Secretary Donald
Regan on whether looser money was needed, what fiscal policy
should be followed, and even whether the monetary growth targets had been achieved. (The answer depended on which definition of the money supply was adopted.)

In effect, the Federal Reserve exercises public power with private control—its rewards and sanctions come largely from the
banking community. No institutional controls exist to ensure performance in the public interest. Its members may be men and
women of impeccable integrity; but a system of power cannot be
based on the *assumption* of altruism. If the leaders of the Federal
Reserve were less reverentially regarded as statesmen and seen as
bankers or businessmen, their statements, policies, and perspectives might become more comprehensible—especially their resistance toward any monetary strategy except one that results in
generally raising interest rates.

It is its strategies that require versatility and effectiveness, not
the Fed's goals. Certainly the problems of debt and short-term liquidity have reached crisis proportions. In 1979, when our GNP
was $2.5 trillion, total short- and long-term debt stood at $4.3
trillion, with most of it in the private sector. Corporate debt accounted for 1.4 trillion, mortgages 1.3 trillion, and consumer
debt $400 billion. (The federal debt accounted for $900 billion,
and state and local government debt $300 billion.)[13]

Short-term debt is even more alarming. Where short-term debt
in 1962 came to 33 percent of total corporate debt outstanding,
that ratio in 1977 was 40 percent. By the second quarter of 1981
it came to 46 percent, almost half of all outstanding debt.[14] The

current ratio also declined dramatically. In the auto industry, the ratio of cash and short-term investments to current liabilities dropped from 98 percent to 15 percent between the early 1960s and 1982. In steel, the drop was from 112 percent to 19 percent; in chemicals, from 81 percent to 14 percent; and in nonferrous metals, from 97 percent to 25 percent, according to a Bank of New York study.[15] Henry Kauffman of Salomon Brothers and Milton Hudson of Morgan Guaranty Trust have also pointed to the dangerous level of interest costs. Interest expense alone comes to nearly 45 percent of net pretax profits, as against 14 percent in the 1960s. Where corporations had a pretax income of almost $8 for each $1 of interest in 1965, and $4 in 1977, they had only $2.39 in the second quarter of 1981.[16]

Though easy money is inflationary, expensive easy money is not only inflationary but crippling. Many of these corporations may not survive a depression. At the same time, interest rates come to have a ratchet effect. Even in the 1982–83 recession, they barely dropped below the double-digit level.[17]

It may be that the stubborn adherence to expensive easy credit will finally check the inflationary spiral. But at what expense? What level of interest rates must finally be attained to slow business activity enough to halt inflation? How long will it take, and what concomitant damage will this policy produce? The *procyclical* policies thus adopted (and some hold that these strategies are deliberately procyclical) may hasten the cyclical process; but by exaggerating it they threaten also to exaggerate its dislocations.

The Reagan administration has shown little imagination in monetary policy. The spring of 1981 under Reagan repeated the pattern of the spring of 1980 under Carter; and with few of the attempted remedies, such as the requirement of reserves on money funds or some form of selective credit controls, that would have had a decided impact in bringing down the devastating high interest rates. We have seen the same guesswork and imperfections in open market strategies, and the consequent volatility of the federal-funds rate. After a brief honeymoon endorsement of the Fed's high interest policies, the Reagan administration put the same pressure on the Fed for more money under highly inflationary circumstances, so that the Treasury can finance an increasing deficit brought about by the $750 billion in forgone revenues that were given away with the 1981 tax cuts. [18]

Obviously, if the government needs money the Federal Reserve and Treasury must supply it. Thus, inflation is given a double boost with the "printing" of money to finance the government debt. To increase the money supply, the Fed buys government securities with a check that not only creates money *ex nihilo* but augments reserves with all their multiplier effect on credit creation. As it buys up securities with new money, it permits the banks to expand their loans at even higher rates. After the government has crowded out private capital, the private sector can return to borrow from the banks at the higher rates they have helped to produce. Who gains in this process? The banks, who have more reserves from which to make loans at higher yields; the Treasury, which obtains the funds it needs; and the Federal Reserve, which can collect interest on the Treasury bills it has purchased with the high-powered money it has created. There must be a better way.

TARGETS FOR PLANNING

Two principles are critical to devising a more effective monetary policy. The first is to move more directly, efficiently, and promptly toward our monetary objectives. If easy money and high interest are both inflationary, we must move toward tighter money and lower interest. We cannot afford to shuttle from one policy to its opposite as the Fed has by raising its rates, then pumping reserves into the system (as it did between August and November 1981) after it has done its damage, all the while trumpeting its commitment to tight money. If high rates checked inflation or even suggested that they might discourage it, Israel, as well as Brazil, Argentina, and other "banana republics," would have the lowest inflation rates in the world rather than the highest.

The second principle is to focus on more precisely targeted goals that favor certain sectors of the economy more than others. In this manner, undesirable side effects can be controlled and kept from destroying worthwhile or strategic enterprises along with lower priorities on our national agenda. Even more, credit policies can be planned as they are in Japan, with a view to their contribution to an overall economic design.

1. We must institute selective credit controls that limit lending power and the money supply without raising interest rates. "We have in the past," writes I. W. Burnham, board chairman of Drexel Burnham Lambert in the *New York Times* (September 20, 1980), "had easy money and low interest rates for relatively long periods without inflation, and we can have these conditions again if we enforce a few rules to restrain would-be borrowers. Credit restraint by the government through the Federal Reserve doesn't impair our freedom. It just restrains the banks from falling all over themselves to lend Du Pont $6 billion for a takeover, or from increasing a mortgage from $15,000 to $100,000 on the same house. It restrains a worker from buying a second car if he hasn't got one third of the cash available for a down payment."

2. If the objective is really to tighten money, we must use the direct approach of truly controlling the amount of credit. The first strategy should be to increase bank reserve requirements. Some economists contend that such measures are undesirable because they are *too* effective. Raising borrowing costs may be less painful in the short run, and the banks surely prefer it. Yet this method has not achieved the desired result. In the face of ever higher interest rates, the banks still have money to lend, and they lend it. Borrowers still borrow it and pay the going rate, to the delight of the banks. And, given the escalating cost of "sterile" (noninterest bearing) reserves, reserve requirements keep declining. This is no way to rationalize the money supply. If money must be rationed, it should be rationed even if it hurts. As in most cases in life, there is no cure without pain.

3. Given the uneasy state of the credit markets, reserve requirements must be extended immediately to the money funds. Since investors use them much like savings accounts, for very short-term storage, as call money that is expected to be instantly available, a run on the money funds could ruin the credibility of the entire financial structure. That threat is just as real today as it was for the banks in 1932, when many banks did experience such a panic. This eventuality could easily occur with a sudden drop in short-term interest rates, or at the first hint that even the smallest fund could not immediately meet its cash obligations upon demand. A panic could result, too, if word spread that a money fund was holding the equivalent of a Penn Central's, or a Lockheed's, or a Chrysler's commercial paper just as the investment community became aware that such a firm was declaring bankruptcy. Many funds do invest in some equivalent firm, although the fact may not be apparent. It was certainly not apparent in the case of Penn Central, which Goldman, Sachs was placing in large volume with sophisticated institutional clients almost up to the moment of its bankruptcy.

The money funds must take these risks in order consistently to produce yields higher than those available from Treasuries or from the premier banks. It must be recognized that, in a kind of self-fulfilling prophecy, the colossal rates that so many corporations must now pay for their commercial paper greatly increase the probability of more Penn Centrals. The potential acceleration of bankruptcies and defaulted commercial paper could itself trigger a panic run on the money funds.

Only a Federal Reserve requirement on money funds on the order of perhaps 20 percent can ensure against such a hazard. It would reduce the frenzied competition between the banks and the money funds as well, and eliminate the unfair and unwise competitive advantage of the funds over the banks, which has generated their present inflationary interest-rate war, the destructive competition between banks and money funds.

4. **To achieve more predictable results in credit control the Fed should tie what banks as lenders can do more precisely to what the Fed does, particularly to its interest-rate policy, the area in which banks have the greatest vested interest in inflation.** If, for example, the Fed charges 14 percent at its discount window, the prime rate should be tied definitively to the discount rate—fixed, for example, at no more than one percentage point above the discount, at 15 percent. The prime is sometimes called a meaningless rate because of the variety of lending rates; yet it is an important benchmark for the cost of money. Similarly, the federal-funds rate for overnight loans of surplus reserves can be precisely tied to the discount, for example, at no

more than $\frac{3}{4}$ or 1 percentage point above it. By reducing the spread between these rates, and, in turn, between these rates and the prime, and inhibiting the banks from maximizing their profits with these highly leveraged borrowed reserves, the Fed would significantly reduce the banks' inflationary borrowing. Moreover, in this manner the Fed could immediately achieve the exact interest-rate level it desired, producing that result more efficiently, and eliminating the volatility and uncertainty that inhere in the present imprecise policy.

5. The Federal Reserve Board should reinstate interest-rate ceilings on deposits in all banks. Banks care as little about what they pay depositors as they do about what they pay the Federal Reserve, so long as they can pass along their costs in their loans. Since high interest costs don't deter banks, low payouts must be used as a deterrent to bank depositors, in order that the money supply be held down. Interest-rate ceilings would not necessarily encourage consumption to the detriment of savings. Savers would simply move their funds into other short-term or long-term interest instruments.

6. The makers of monetary policy should exercise their discretionary use of tax surcharges and credits more vigorously. If loan demand is elastic, it can be controlled, provided a surtax is added to interest, thus making a 4 percent rate a 5 or 6 percent rate. Although such a tax seems inflationary because it increases borrowers' costs, the Fed would be improving upon the present situation if it did no more than take from the commercial banks the highly profitable privilege of constantly raising their prices. The Fed could always remove the surtax immediately when it was no longer needed, rather than wait for ever-changing and arbitrary formulas implemented by commercial banks that move interest rates up quickly but down at a snail's pace.

The strategies of the Federal Reserve must be versatile enough, flexible enough, and *targeted* enough to check credit creation at the source. Given several alternatives for controlling the demand for money during excessively expansionary or boom periods, the Fed could limit the money supply, encouraging stricter allocations; and/or it could couple such control with policies that at the same time kept interest rates from becoming a significant input into inflation. Having direct impact on the prime rate and the availability of funds, it would not have to tinker, adjust, and attempt to fine-tune interest rates every hour of each day. It would give a clear signal—more than that, a precise guideline—to the banks and the economic community, indicating clearly what it wished to implement immediately and what it hoped to achieve vis-à-vis credit, interest rates, and counterinflationary, or counterdeflationary measures.

TARGETED CREDIT: MESHING MONETARY AND ECONOMIC POLICY

7. Targeted credit controls should mesh monetary policy with economic planning. Targeted surcharges can be used more generally to fulfill a hierarchy of preidentified social needs while discouraging activities or areas of production that may as well be delayed or even canceled. In these cases, the change would operate through the demand side of the equation rather than the supply side, to which control of the money supply is directed. By discouraging inflation-producing loans and encouraging loans that met worthwhile demands of the economy, surcharge policy would keep the price of housing and other essentials low.

8. The discretionary surcharge should be used to tax different industries differently and discourage borrowing for counterproductive or poorly timed purposes. A 4 or 5 percent surcharge, for example, could effectively inhibit commodity speculation or even inventory accumulation. Since inventories are often built up in anticipation of higher prices, thereby raising prices in themselves, they should be discouraged during inflationary periods. Gold and silver speculation drives up the costs of jewelry, photographic film, dental treatment, and electronic components, raising both producer and consumer prices. Similar surcharges on borrowing for counterproductive or poorly timed purposes might also hold for consumer loans in a highly expansive period. Even the interest-rate increases on consumer credit cards instituted in 1980 failed to create this disincentive: at present, they in fact encourage heavy borrowing by placing a lower interest rate on borrowing above a given credit line. The Fed can significantly influence the banking system to reduce extension of nondesirable or less desirable loans, such as those for leveraged buyouts or loans to foreign governments, which counteract and obstruct its objectives.

9. **At the same time, the Fed can forgo a surcharge, or even use the proceeds of its surcharges as subsidies, in the case of activities that meet some identified social objective or need: middle-income housing, new domestic energy drilling, the building of such new capital equipment as oil refineries, pollution-inhibiting machinery, or productivity improvements.** Commercial banks would really have no incentive to raise their rates (indeed, they would not be permitted to do so above prescribed limits), and would make only loans that seemed promising and safe.

Since the purpose of high interest rates imposed by the Fed is presumably to discourage borrowing and to slow business activity, it seems altogether valid to apply these strategies discriminatingly, through targeted credit controls that mesh monetary with planned economic policy. With this selective approach, the Fed would not itself be contributing to inflation through the imposition of high interest rates on all, willy nilly, irrespective of their importance to the nation. It would also eliminate the constant backing and filling that occurs when the Fed discovers that it has produced one of the adverse and only too predictable consequences of its policies, such as depression in the housing and construction industries, and unnecessarily high unemployment.

10. **One effective way to fight inflation is to increase productivity through capital investment.** One would expect, then, that encouraging such investment would be a linchpin of any plan to fight inflation through the extension of low interest rates. At the same time, selective credit controls would pinpoint, then restrain or eliminate, certain borrowers by careful direction rather than through the market mechanism. The huge bank loans generated by Du Pont, Seagram, and Mobil as they battled in the Conoco takeover had the effect of startlingly (if temporarily) increasing the money supply. Takeovers thus present a cardinal illustration of inflationary borrowing to which selective controls could be applied.

11. **Credit controls should also be used to discourage the purchase of third and fourth homes and condominium units, speculative inventory loans, loans for currency speculation, and borrowing for stock and commodity purchases.** These and other nonproductive or temporarily less urgent activities should be discouraged. One method would be to establish high interest rates geared specifically to funds borrowed for those purposes. Another would be to ration borrowed funds used for these purposes, in the way that funds for the margining of common stocks are rationed. Margin requirements for stock purchases are now about 50 percent, but for commodities they range as low as 5 percent.

12. **Interest rates themselves can be subjected to such targeting.** If it is determined, for example, that maintaining the strength of the dollar is a goal worth pursuing, monetary policymakers should offer high interest rates only for deposits from overseas, imposing a selective credit approach at home. On the domestic scene, the Fed would not deal with interest rates, but center on the money supply and specifically on reserve requirements. In this manner it would avoid the additional inflation imposed on the domestic economy by high interest rates intended to achieve the external objective of defending the dollar. Alternatively, if a weaker American dollar is desired to increase our exports and improve our international trade position, then lower rates should be paid to overseas depositors.

13. **The Federal Reserve should systematically analyze bank loan portfolios to determine their usefulness or desirability in light of the Fed's goals, as well as their quality and soundness.** Such asset analysis could reduce the extension of many loans, with two positive results. First, it would contract loan demand, thus reducing interest pressure in interest rates. Second, it would diminish the size and nature of these loans, which are sure to produce problems for the banking system—and even require that the Fed print money to avoid the banking disasters that might occur.

14. **Bank loans to foreign countries may be treated in a similar manner.** Banks often reach out and make overseas loans to marginal developing countries for the sake of an extra half-

point of income, or because they can negotiate a large loan quickly and easily, regardless of whether or not it benefits the U.S. economy and the best interests of its citizens. Under our free-enterprise system, which encourages each business entity to seek to maximize its volume of revenues and profits, such efforts on the part of the banks may be necessary in order to compete and survive. Yet it need not be assumed that banks will promote the best interests of the domestic economy. To impel banks to behave in a manner consistent with the best interests of society as a whole, incentives should be designed that produce such a result. Where our domestic interests require the reduction of bank lending, especially to reduce the currency and balance-of-payments problem (since many loans abroad are spent abroad and depress the value of the dollar), the government might introduce a heavier tax on earnings derived from such a source.

Since such loans are really matters of foreign policy, perhaps they should be made directly only by the government itself or by a new governmental bank. In the last analysis, if and when loans to foreign governments threaten default (as, for example, a loan to Poland), the government will undoubtedly substitute itself as the lender. Since it accepts the ultimate risk, it might well acknowledge its responsibility formally—removing this potentially counterproductive activity from the banking system and making it a function of federal monetary and/or fiscal policy.

It would not be the first time the government stepped in the market to designate priorities. Indeed, choices are set forth by the Reagan administration in its budget messages. Choices are also evident in its tax legislation: this is intended to foster capital spending and jobs, to favor rehabilitation over new construction, and to create a tilt toward selected industries such as oil and gas and defense. No one has ever assumed that banking and money creation could be a function of an unregulated market system. The continuous market operations of the Federal Reserve illustrate far more massive government intervention than the most grandiose state-sponsored project. And to the degree that they do not, they represent the most extraordinary case of monopolistic special privilege ever granted to a private institution—the creation of our money.

If implemented, selective credit controls would require only a brief period of time until their impact has been made; then they could be promptly rescinded, with the Fed reverting to a laissez-faire policy. These measures, irrespective of their ideological cast, would convey clearly the administration's intent to cope with inflationary or deflationary surges. At the very least, selective credit controls can be used as an adjunct to a moderate-interest-rate policy. As a supplemental weapon in the Fed's armory, they would reduce the pressure of prevailing monetary policy, which forces interest rates to sky-high levels. Together, these strategies would enhance our chances of holding back the inflationary tides.

In short, the effort to destroy borrowing power for nonproductive, nondesirable purposes should take a direct shape. We do not need the shotgun approach that now prevails and that discourages, in one fell swoop, both the most useful and desirable loans and the loans that are detrimental to our societal goals. To kill inflation, a rifle is surely more effective than a shotgun; for a shotgun kills all, the good and the bad, with equal indiscrimination. "Equal" is, in fact, an understatement. The effect is *not* equal, for speculators and gamblers are always more willing to pay the higher interest than are responsible business borrowers. High interest rates, in effect, move funds from the more efficient and desirable segments of the productive society to the less effective, counterproductive, speculative segments.

A shotgun approach implies not management but irresponsibility and negligence, or worse. Perhaps this is why, in the face of the Federal Reserve's constant and relentless effort to stem inflation through such ineffectual means, we have experienced for such extended periods nothing but disastrous results and the worst of all possible worlds, stagflation.

NOTES

1. Clyde H. Farnsworth, "Credit and Credit Controls Are Studied," *New York Times*, March 10, 1980, D1.

2. The mortgage component of the CPI was at this writing under review.

3. *Statistical Abstract,* 1981, 102d ed., Table 874, 522.

4. Samuelson, *Economics,* 11th ed., 281.

5. *Statistical Abstract,* 1979, 100th ed., Table 854, 527.

6. The federal funds rate is not directly fixed by the Fed, but the Fed determines the federal funds rate through its purchases and sales of Treasuries in the open market.

7. Daniel Hamberg, *The U.S. Monetary System: Money, Banking, and Financial Markets,* Boston, Little, Brown, 1981, 359.

8. Mary G. Grandstaff, "New Savings Certificates Help District Banks Resist Disintermediation," *Federal Reserve Bank of Dallas Voice,* November 1978, 24–26; "The Depository Institutions Deregulation and Monetary Control Act of 1980," *Federal Reserve Bulletin,* June 1980, reprinted in Hamberg, *The U.S. Monetary System,* 483–92.

9. For a brief period in 1980, the Fed did try credit controls, but those were so immediately effective that the Board, fearing a recession, promptly rescinded them. See chapter 12.

10. Leonard Silk, "Private Debt: Hidden Pitfalls," *New York Times,* October 28, 1981, D2; Edward P. Foldessy, "Companies Facing Severe Problems Because of Rising Short-Term Debt," *Wall Street Journal,* October 26, 1981, 29.

11. Quoted in Samuelson, *Economics,* 11th ed., 276.

12. Ibid.

13. Hamberg, *U.S. Monetary System,* 8.

14. Foldessy, "Companies Facing Severe Problems," 29.

15. Quoted in Silk, "Private Debt," D2.

16. Foldessy, "Companies Facing Severe Problems," 29.

17. Ibid.

18. Leonard Silk, "Private Debt: Hidden Pitfalls," D2.

Part Three

NATIONAL ECONOMIC PLANNING: A NEW FRONTIER

9

New Beginnings?
Reaganomics in Review

Reagan was swept to victory on the shards of broken promises. In 1976 Carter, too, had promised a balanced budget, and an end to inflation and nagging unemployment. He stressed the need for long-range planning. And, addressing the country's post-Watergate suspicion of public power, he opted for less, and less centralized, government.

Four years later, the budget carried a $60 billion deficit. At $577 billion, it was over a third more than its $364-billion level when he took office. The economy was in a recession. Unemployment was still at 7.8 percent and rising. The GNP showed an actual drop, not merely slower growth. Investment was down by 12 percent and productivity was declining. Inflation was running at about 12.6 percent.[1]

In the face of this cancerous growth of costs and prices, the budget had to be cut to the bone to restore the economy's resilience. But Carter, like his predecessors, was willing to do everything but go through the requisite surgery.

Carter never faced the problem of fighting inflation. An incomes policy—wage and price control—was too controversial; and a fiscal policy—increasing taxes or cutting down spending—was politically inconvenient. And the money supply was never restricted. Instead, interest rates were allowed to mount, rising to staggering heights and increasing inflation, before that measure had its effect and produced a recession.

By 1980, the government was in disrepute. Just as the public had rebelled against private industry in the 1930s, demanding that the private sector be curbed and the government be strengthened, it now blamed the government for double-digit inflation, high interest rates and unemployment, stunted industrial growth, and crushing taxes. The public demanded that the government be curbed.

THE ECONOMIC EQUIVALENT OF WAR

Our destiny is not our fate, it is our choice.

Ronald Reagan, address to AFL-CIO,
March 30, 1981

From the start, President Reagan's mandate was defined as a minor revolution, the parallel of what Roosevelt had achieved in his first hundred days. We face an economic Dunkirk, said Reagan's advisers, and they urged him to declare a national emergency, then follow up with concrete action "to really shock the American people." Accepting his mantle, Reagan announced, "We are confronted with an economic affliction of great proportions," and promised, "We are going to act beginning today." His program would revive industry, bring government within its means, lighten the tax burden. "These will be our first priorities, and on this principle there will be no compromise."[2]

If anything has characterized Reagan's tenure, it is determination—sometimes stubborn, usually controversial, but always vigorous and certain of direction. He showed this vigor when he quipped on the surgeon's table, "I hope you're all Republicans," and he maintained it throughout his first year. In his first State of the Union message, too, he stuck to his supply-side approach, refusing tax increases even in the face of a ballooning deficit.

That vigor may have been forced on him, in a sense, as he tried to capitalize on public confidence, to capture his opponents by surprise and act before reaction could be organized. But it entailed more. As the *New York Times* put it, many "who might have shouted angrily about the Nixon cuts are not shouting now. They recognize the nation's economic straits. They want to be economic good citizens." They might differ on the details of his program, but they did not question its dimensions, a change in national direction, or, as the *New York Times* called it, the "economic equivalent of war."[3]

Thus Democrats joined Republicans in March 1981 in unanimously supporting $36.4 billion in budget cuts—more than Reagan had recommended—and the tax cuts which were the major features of his economic policy. When his cancellation of the planned increase in dairy price supports went through, even representatives of farm interests were resigned, expressing hope that other groups would acquiesce in the same manner.

Reagan's leadership operates best in winning this kind of cooperation among conflicting interest groups. The presidency is, as a thoughtful Public Agenda Foundation report has put it, "the cockpit for conflicting pressures that have grown increasingly numerous in recent years. There is no reason to assume that the good of the country will automatically be realized today by the interplay of these conflicting interests. On the contrary, there is every reason to believe it will not. To represent the common good calls for strong moral leadership at the top—someone who, in the trite but true phrase, is capable of being the President of all the people."[4] Congressmen are constrained by their constituencies. Lobbyists, recipients of federal aid, and public bureaucrats can hardly be expected to pursue some overarching vision in the face of threats to their life styles or their jobs. But they can rally around true leaders who persuade citizens to transcend competing claims *that may all be legitimate* but cannot all be acted upon at once.

Carter had the opportunity to exercise that option time after time and always missed it. The fall of Iran presented the perfect occasion for mobilizing Americans to accept a gasoline tax, conservation efforts, virtually any energy program he wanted. Yet having had the *vision* (an energy program was his great ambition as president), Carter could not act at the strategic moment. By contrast, despite his mistakes, Reagan's popularity long remained strong, even among those who expected to be unemployed.[5]

THE BOTTOM LINE

How does Reagan's approach stack up? Will his stimulative tax cuts ever reduce those deficits to any significant degree? Can we eliminate inflation without courting the effects of Margaret Thatcher's 1981 budget and tax program—what Michael Foote, the British labor leader, called a "monstrous deflation," a "catastrophe of the first order for the British economy and the British people"?

And which strategies may fumble this chess game whose details and outcome will color our political lives and our life styles for years to come? Which actions are logically consistent, and which suggest potential contradictions and counterproductive measures? Might other steps move us more certainly and directly toward the same goals?

First, Reagan's defined goals, to check inflation and revitalize our economy through a program of budget cuts, tax cuts, restrictive monetary policy, and regulatory reform, are laudable. His paramount order of business has been to make substantial, meaningful budget cuts for several critical purposes: (1) to ease the ever-increasing tax burden that has hindered investment and effort; (2) to reduce the government's demands on the credit markets and encourage private investment—the "supply-side"—at lower interest rates; and (3) to reduce the government's intrusive influence both as spender and as regulator, to unleash free markets and the enterprise and creativity that will allow the private sector to replace government as the dominant force in economic growth. Freud characterized government as one of the three endeavors predestined to yield unsatisfactory results (the other two being psychiatry and education). If government is indeed predestined to yield unsatisfactory results, reducing its role certainly belongs on the Reagan agenda.

Almost magically, practically no one, irrespective of political affiliation, challenged the urgency to reverse the direction that has led to stagflation and a lower standard of living. Citizens have come to realize that government cannot create wealth. A country—consumers plus the government as public consumer—can only spend the sum of what the country produces. If the government spends more than it takes in, creating a deficit, the public must compensate by spending less and saving more, to provide the funds that the government borrows. Otherwise, inflation makes the necessary adjustment. Inflation is the penalty imposed on an economy that spends, or consumes, more than its members produce. So, too, redistribution programs that confiscate wealth, either directly through taxation or indirectly through inflation and the printing of money, only reduce the incentive to save and invest and hence the total national product.

It is this threshold perception that Americans finally attained in the 1980 election. They expressed it in their endorsement of Reagan's promises to adopt sound budget policy, sound tax policy, and sound money.

In the light of these principles, Reagan swiftly moved against a number of favored programs. One of the most dramatic was his cancellation in March 1981 of the scheduled increases in dairy price supports. Reagan staffers felt it would set the right tone of austerity if the administration cancelled the April increase. The cancellation, however, was a one-shot affair, a symbolic gesture eliminating only one automatically scheduled increase that did not tamper with the principle of routine semiannual price increases in dairy products. In most respects—sugar, wheat, even dairy foods—agricultural products have retained, regained, or increased their privileged price supports, despite Reagan's proposal that they be cut in half from $1.8 billion in 1980–81 to $890 million in 1981–82.[6]

Unemployment insurance is finally being made rational. In line with its 1981 reforms, the Labor Department will no longer grant automatic extended unemployment benefits, but will target these extensions at areas of high unemployment. (In the 1982 recession, they had to be reinstituted—another example of the boomerang effect produced by the internal contradictions of Reagan's policy.) According to its planned reforms, those unemployed for three months may have to take jobs that do not match their usual occupations or wages; "suitable work" will be any job a person can handle that pays at least the minimum wage. And, in an end to one systematic abuse of the system, former military service personnel can receive unemployment benefits only when they are unemployed through no fault of their own, not if they leave the armed forces voluntarily! These measures, which seem fair and long overdue, should save the government about $1.4 billion.

Reagan has established the "workfare" requirement that he instituted in California and that has been tried and adopted elsewhere. The twenty-hour-a-week requirement was expected to affect up to 800,000 of the 3 million adults receiving AFDC (see chapter 5). In 1981 he also cut from $14,000 to $11,000 the top wage that a four-member family could earn and still be eligible for food stamps. Some abuses, such as student eligibility, were eliminated earlier, and today the program grows with the unemployment rate. However, since the average food stamp family in 1980 had an annual income of $3,900 and almost 90 percent of its families earn less than $7,450, the poverty level for a family of four, the 1981 cutbacks still left eligible the vast proportion of families now receiving food stamps.[7]

It has been said that cutting back such benefits for the working poor will reduce their work incentive and put them on welfare. Yet that dilemma is built into any benefit program as it affects those just above the boundary line. Policymakers constantly must make tradeoffs between minimal living standards, work disincentives, and cost. Liberals have suddenly become aware of work disincentives at a time when workfare is reducing them, particularly when they argue that cutbacks in programs for working families will make it rational for them to go on welfare.

The student loan program was also due for an overhaul. These outlays have soared since 1978, when income ceilings for the loans were abolished. Children from affluent families could purchase cars with these loans or put money into high-yielding money market funds with no interest to pay for years.

More questionable, possibly, is Reagan's elimination of legal aid to the poor; certainly more questionable is his curtailment of the CETA (Comprehensive Employment and Training Act) and WIN (Work Incentive) job programs. CETA may have been misused to provide jobs for middle-class students, or to replace locally funded with federally funded positions to save city money. But these abuses may suggest the need for correction, not elimination.

Ronald Reagan himself recalls that his family's economic survival during the critical Great Depression of the 1930s was possible only because his father was provided work by the WPA when no private-industry job was available. Yet in 1982–83, when unemployment and its attendant pain and ignominy reached the highest levels since that depression, President Reagan would not consider or recommend any similar, publicly supported, constructive work projects or training opportunities. In light of his own experience, Reagan's inconsistency and lack of empathy are bewildering.

It is inconsistent to require workfare on the one hand, then cut the public works that should provide it, especially when welfare could provide some of the criteria for legitimate CETA programs. As a positive alternative to welfare, CETA should be expanded into a national job creation program (see chapter 12). The same reservations hold for WIN, which is targeted at welfare recipients.

By focusing his cuts on the mere $12 billion of programs aimed at the poor—barely 6 percent of a $218-billion safety net, Reagan in 1981 did not leave himself very much to work with. He left intact aid to the elderly, to veterans, to politically powerful populations who are not necessarily poor and who constitute our major budget problem. In large measure, he has merely shifted funds—and the deficit spending record along with them, from social spending to defense.

NEEDED: A NO-INFLATION MYTH

In view of these questions, one may ask how dedicated Reagan is to his professed goals. His strategy has not really been one of supply-side economics, stressing saving and capital investment, and a noninflationary budget. He has been ranting about runaway spending even while doing it himself.

When politicians really set their sights on a goal, they pursue it with such zeal that they will enlist the most creative semantics to glamorize and validate their objectives. When in the 1960s Kennedy sought to increase spending in a period of declining economic activity, he used the creative concept of the full-employment budget based on the "potential" or "full-employment" GNP, a concept that had been introduced in the 1940s by the Committee for Economic Development. The full-employment GNP was based on the question: What could have been produced had the economy been operating at full-employment levels? Correspondingly, the full-employment budget was based on the question: How much would, should, and could be spent if the economy were operating at full-employment levels? The hope was that the level of spending would create the desired salutary economic environment to bring about full employment, and would even reduce the budget by lowering government benefit obligations.

The principle was, "Don't balance the budget over each year, or even over each business cycle. Instead, set the budget so that it can be financed by the tax revenues that would be generated by full-employment economy." Johnson glorified the concept with the term "fiscal dividend"—budget surpluses that would be generated by a booming economy—and Nixon adopted it as well. By now the approach is enshrined in our economics textbooks, which explain how a "full-employment budget surplus" can really coexist with "an *actual* budget *deficit.*"[8]

Whatever the validity of the theory, it was one of the all-time stupendous acts of political and economic genius to justify with complete ease of conscience—indeed with a sense of genuine obligation—the efficacy and even righteousness of deficit spending as the ultimate means of solving the problems of our economy. This is political economics in the raw, stripped of all pretension, naked for all to see in the real-world everyday modus operandi. Once we refine the semantics of the program to make it acceptable, we gain consensus, legislative cooperation, enactment, and action.

Political semantics explains why we have a "defense" budget. It is so much easier to identify with the necessity of defense than with the necessity of offense. Political semantics can move mountains and perhaps save, or destroy, economies and societies.

Accordingly, if Reagan had truly wanted a reduced and ultimately balanced budget he should first have created the proper semantic frame. The full-employment budget was invented to smooth the political way for ever-recurring and ever-increasing deficit budgets; Reagan could have introduced a new myth, the "noninflationary budget," based on the assumption that we would experience zero inflation, just as the mythical full-employment budget envisions zero (or approximately 4 percent) unemployment. Instead, he designed a budget that accepts, and thereby encourages, continued inflation.

A mythical—or, more charitably, hypothetical—no-inflation budget would start out by specifying what the government would have to spend—that is, what its budget would be—if we had no inflation. A budget would then be designed on the basis of this assumption. This might prove self-fulfilling and reduce or eliminate inflation. At the least, it would check the tremendous opposition to the budget cuts that has been mounted by special-interest groups resisting an austerity that will ultimately benefit them as well as others.

To specify the difference between this noninflationary budget and the Reagan-Stockman proposals: The Reagan administration seemed tacitly to be questioning its own confidence in harnessing inflation in its 1981 budget projections, even before the reality of a $100-billion deficit upset its targets. For, when Reagan's reductions were compared with what spending levels would be if programs continued unchanged, it turned out that the 1982 spending cuts, though affecting over 200 programs totalling $8.6 billion, did not scrape more than the tip of the iceberg. Moreover, the fiscal 1982 budget of $659.3 billion was *up* 6.1 percent from the 1981 fiscal year ending September 30. The percentage may not have been large, but it was still higher than a Carter budget that Reagan considered completely unjustifiable but felt it was too late to correct. It hardly corrected, and in fact perpetuated, a budget already charged with producing a "hemorrhaging" economy. Finally, Mr. Reagan acknowledged that his $48 billion in "savings" included, in some cases, merely the omission of some spending increases that had been proposed by Mr. Carter.[9]

Nor were the long-range projections more encouraging. From fiscal 1981 to fiscal 1986, the *planned* budget outlays increased from $665.2 billion in fiscal 1981 to $912 billion in 1986—up 37 percent. This was an increase of over one-third, even after the substantial "cuts" of $48.2 billion in 1982, $81.2 billion in

1984, and $102.7 billion in 1986 were taken into account. The cuts were not really cuts at all but shavings from even larger expected increases! By 1982, Reagan's request for 1983 raised the budget to $757.6 billion and the deficit to an *optimistic* $91 billion, $107.2 billion when off-budget entities are included. [10]

This approach embodies indexation with a vengeance—indexation to permit an ever-growing budget and probably continued deficits. For cuts requiring tough political action in the face of opposition are never as certain as budget increases, which are built in by virtue of "uncontrollable" increases that are indexed and inevitable.

Can this be all? Is this kind of puny tinkering the centerpiece of Reagan's grand design to "stop runaway inflation" and "revitalize the economy"? From the very beginning, the outlays were what Steven Rattner, an economics reporter for the *New York Times,* called "a flood not yet stemmed." Early on, Michael Evans, a Washington consultant, saw that "the failure to come to grips with either of the two overwhelming issues—namely indexation and entitlements"—challenged Reagan's commitment to sweeping cuts. "His nickel-and-dime approach is unlikely to have the desired effect of bringing government spending to heel." Between entitlements and increased defense spending, the budget by 1985 will be $1,013 billion and the deficit, according to the Conference Board, $233 billion. [11] Ronald Reagan has become the biggest spender of them all; he is piling up deficits greater than all previous presidents combined.

Indexation merely disguises unwillingness to accept discipline. Wherever Milton Friedman had advocated and encouraged it—for example, in Brazil and Israel—it has impeded decisive actions needed to halt inflation, and in fact has increased inflation. It is not merely no solution; it is counterproductive, however politically attractive it may be, because it simply introduces math games that adjust everybody's "monopoly" paper money *ad infinitum* instead of imposing the required but recognizably unpopular political and economic austerity actions.

Of course, the Reagan administration has been justifiably eager to discredit the charge of being cold or socially irresponsible. So it has stressed the "safety net" that will remain under the neediest

Americans through continuing Social Security, unemployment, veterans', and welfare benefits. But in a noninflationary economy each of these programs *would* in fact cost the government less. In fact, Reagan was far less ambitious than even Carter, who in January 1979 proposed ten substantial changes in Social Security to bring costs down, and in January 1981 proposed linking Social Security benefits to a less exaggerated measure of inflation than the CPI.

It has become blatantly clear that the administration's budget goals are unthinkable if they ignore the built-in distortions that puff up such mammoth programs as Social Security and veterans' benefits, whose indexed increases exceed even the cost-of-living index. If Reagan could not deal with these matters at the height of his popularity and with the vast political consensus behind him, he can hardly reverse the trend and initiate the promised New Beginning.

THE LORELEI LURE OF THE LAFFERITES

The boldest feature of Reagan's administration has been the theoretical underpinning of supply-side economics. This approach departs from both traditional conservatism, which would fight inflation with high interest rates and the tolerance of widespread unemployment, and traditional liberalism, which accepts deficit spending and inflation as the price of full employment, or endorses wage and price controls to control inflation.

Supply-side theory combines Adam Smith's classical liberalism and its reliance on the market with a macroeconomic theory that is essentially a restatement of Say's law that supply creates its own demand. This notion is construed to challenge the Keynesian notion that demand creates its own supply. Its main policy consequence is the tax cut, modeled after John Kennedy's cuts of the early 1960s. In presumed contrast to Keynesianism, now called demand-side economics, Reagonomics holds that this tax-cutting program, together with reduced government spending and regulation, will increase the supply of goods and services, lower their prices, and ameliorate and eventually eliminate inflation. The supply-side tax cut theory also contrasts with the conservative tenet that high taxes will scotch demand and cure inflation by stressing growth as the major strategy for revitalization. One reduces inflation most effectively not by checking demand but by increasing supply: the supply of labor, the supply of goods, and the supply of services.

How will a tax cut and reduced government spending accomplish these ends? The answer is supplied by the Laffer curve and the process it illustrates. High tax *rates,* paradoxically, can result in low tax *revenues,* and low rates in high revenues because of the way they work on expectations and the incentives to work and invest. Tax cuts increase revenues by this dynamic:

1. Tax cuts will increase the incentive to work. Marginal tax rates are now so high that workers are discouraged from more productive labor, feeling their higher earnings will not only be taxed away but will put them into a higher bracket. More work means that more goods and services will be put on the market.

2. Lower taxes will fortify the motive to save, reducing consumption and providing funds for investment.

3. Investment will also be encouraged for three reasons: First, a lower tax means a larger after-tax profit and makes investment more attractive. Second, increased savings, which provide investment funds, will lower interest rates, increasing both the probability and the level of profit. Finally, cuts in public spending and debt will take pressure off the capital markets.

4. Supply-side incentives will also act as self-fulfilling prophecies. Men and women do not simply repeat their past behavior, but change it in terms of their expectations about the future. The belief that inflationary rises will be reversed can itself work powerfully against the "expectational inflation" that has trapped prices in an upward spiral.

Union labor, once its fear of inflationary pressures has been allayed, will moderate its wage demands. The unemployed and unemployable will gradually enter the work force, partly because budget cuts will reduce transfer payments and hence the disincentive to work, and also because investments spurred by a tax cut will provide more jobs.

Of the two types of expansionary policy, public spending and tax cuts, government spending is seen as inherently inflationary because it bids up the price of goods and money. By competing for funds, government boxes out industry for available capital, or at least raises the cost so much as to discourage productive investment. Tax cuts, by contrast, are not inflationary because they do not increase aggregate demand but simply shift funds and spending power from the public to the private sector. Although that shift increases the disposable income of individuals, it also decreases the disposable income of government, of its beneficiaries (that is, recipients of transfer payments), and of its debtors—the potential buyers of the government bonds that would otherwise have to be issued to cover the deficit. Spending cuts stem the inflationary tide that might result from cutting taxes. If every dollar spent by business or consumers is balanced by a $1 decrease in government spending, increases in private-sector demand will not provoke inflationary pressure.

Not all supply-siders are that concerned with government spending or even deficits, which they see as the effect of what the late Arthur Okun called the "misery index," the sum of the indexes of inflation and unemployment. In October 1980 the misery index stood at almost 20, with inflation at 12 percent and unemployment at 7.6 percent.

The misery index shows how the two factors, unemployment and inflation, are not simply components of a tradeoff, but can be additive as well. A rising misery index pushes government spending up, since government outlays are sensitive both to unemployment, through unemployment and welfare benefits, and to inflation, through the indexing of many of its payouts.

The unexpected $36-billion increase in government spending from June to October 1980 demonstrates this point. Unemployment levels required the disposal of an extra $9.15 billion in unemployment benefits, food stamps, Medicaid, and the like. Declining economic conditions accounted for another $8.25 billion. Inflation triggered a $5.9-billion increase that included $1.2 billion for Social Security and other pension benefits, and $4.7 billion stemmed from rising fuel costs for the military, Medicare, and food assistance. Another $2.8 billion in outlays stemmed from rising interest rates. In sum, these figures account for 72 percent of the $36-billion rise in federal outlays.[12]

The answer to deficits, say supply-siders, is not frugality but a lowering of the misery index, of the sum of unemployment and inflation. Even though the Kemp-Roth tax cut will have cost the government $750 billion by 1986,[13] spending will also go down as inflation declines and as investment and employment expand to bring in revenues that equal or even exceed the tax cuts. Despite lower tax rates, the collective result will be higher tax income and fewer government outlays, since higher employment means more tax revenues and fewer government benefits.[14]

IS KEYNES DEAD?

You don't have to be a Democrat to question the supply-side scenario. What an idyllic program! It seems to provide the ultimate solution to all our economic problems. In one fell swoop it takes care of the need for increased savings, for greater capital investment, for government's need for more tax income and lesser cash outgo, and for a slowing in inflation without the unpleasant burden of austerity. Small wonder it's called the Laffer curve. If it worked we could all be happy forever "laffing," or at least smiling, our way through economic life. Small wonder that its critics include such solid conservatives as Alan Greenspan; Arthur F. Burns, former Federal Reserve chairman; Charles Schultz; Paul W. McCracken; and Herbert Stein, chairman of the Council of Economic Advisers under President Nixon; as well as Walter W. Heller, chairman of the Council of Economic Advisers under Kennedy and Johnson; William Nordhaus; and Lawrence Klein.

The main problem with supply-side theory is that if its assumptions don't work, we'll be propelled to new levels of inflation. Tax cuts, which are a stimulative fiscal policy, can exacerbate inflation and actually hurt growth by throwing so heavy a burden on monetary policy as to force up interest rates, checking business investment and consumer spending on housing, autos, and other durable goods. Wall Street financiers prefer the traditional strategy of spending cuts and a move toward a balanced budget. The bond market, especially, no longer responds to mere promises of a balanced budget four years hence, like those both Carter and Reagan have delivered.

In fact, each area of presumed impact can be questioned: work, savings, and investment—the triangle on which supply-side theory depends.

With respect to work, anyone familiar with the "backward-bending curve of labor" knows that any monetary work incentive—higher pay or lower taxes—has a variable effect. Some workers will work more; but others will work less, using the added income to "buy" more leisure, since they can attain the same after-tax goal with less work. Lafferites assume only one of these possible outcomes. Besides, many wage-earners, locked into a pattern of fixed hours, do not even have the option of significantly changing their hours. Research, says Walter Heller, has "not yet established even a sign of the work response"—that is, whether it is positive or negative as it bears on consumption or savings—"let alone its magnitude."[15]

Moreover, what evidence there is suggests that even if a 10 percent tax cut increases the number of hours worked (labor supply) by 1 or 2 percent, it will also raise demand five to ten times as much. We can hardly be sure that the added funds will go into savings. It depends on people's tendency to spend or to save the extra dollar. Ironically, the Democratic objection to the Kemp-Roth uniform, across-the-board tax cuts—that they give disproportionate benefits to the rich—is a strong argument for supply-side theory, since the wealthy save and invest proportionately more of their increased income. Ironically, the social inequity of the law underscores its economic validity.

Nor can tax cuts alone pass for tax reform. To increase savings through taxation you must change the system—shift from taxing income and savings to taxing consumption. Some congressmen have developed effective tax incentives to save: extended IRA benefits and exemptions, lower taxation of income earned from savings or from investment in initial capital-raising ventures. IRA incentives have already been passed into law. The negative incentive of a value-added or consumption tax, or, less directly, larger Keogh exemptions, would also check demand or reduce the government debt, which in turn would release funds to the capital markets.

Finally the smooth passage from savings to investment is a

moot issue. Keynesians disagree with the entire chain of supply-side logic, denying not only that tax cuts will necessarily increase savings, but that savings will in turn inevitably go into capital formation. Keynes, observing that tenuous relationship in the 1930s, when people saved far more than businessmen felt confident to invest, called this imbalance "leakage." If savings exceed investment spending, the result can be unemployment of people and disuse of resources.

Not all savings and investments are productive, in any case. Gold purchases are not. Company takeovers are not. Moreover, tax benefits for certain kinds of savings—larger interest and dividend exclusions, tax credits for investments in stocks and bonds, deductions for housing down payments, nest eggs—will not necessarily *increase* savings. They may just *shift* savings from those that are not tax sheltered, such as life insurance and real estate, to those that are.

Tax incentives require an equally critical eye. Supply-siders stress accelerated depreciation, which allows you to deduct a greater part of your cost per year. The faster the depreciation, the more income is sheltered and the more funds you have for plant and equipment. But accelerated depreciation is a weaker investment stimulus than the direct-investment tax credit. For with the tax credit, the investor can subtract from his tax bill part of every dollar spent on new machinery.

Supply-siders also hope to augment productivity and investment by relaxing safety and environmental regulations and quality controls, in order to cut down production costs and hence prices. Whether we can afford the social costs of such deregulation is questionable.

THE KENNEDY PRECEDENT

As precedent for the strategy, supply-siders like to invoke the 1964 Kennedy tax cut, which they say paid for itself by expanding the economy's productive capacity and bringing in more revenues. But the cut is both misapplied in the 1980s and misdiagnosed as a supply-side strategy.

It is true that Kennedy used supply-side initiative to preserve price stability while promoting vigorous expansion. But the tax cuts were not among them. Kennedy's strategies consisted of two important, precisely targeted innovations.

The first was the 1961 investment tax credit and the easing of depreciation guidelines. The former, especially, pulled the country out of the doldrums. In his January 1962 *Economic Report of the President,* Kennedy epitomized supply-side logic, saying the credit would "stimulate investment in capacity expansion and modernization, contribute to the growth of our productivity and output, and increase the competitiveness of American exports in world markets."

His second innovation was the "monetary twist," which reduced long-term interest rates to make funds available for investment, but kept short-term rates high to keep funds from flowing abroad. It is a supreme example of targeted incentives that respect the logic of the margin.

Although inflation in 1960 was running at only 1.2 percent, Kennedy developed his wage-price guidelines as precautions, to keep his stimulative measures from expanding wage and price inflation. The wage guidelines urged unions to limit their wage demands to productivity gains, even if their industry had improved more rapidly than the nation at large. Price guideposts asked businessmen to maintain existing prices if productivity matched the national average; to raise prices if they did less well; to lower them if efficiency was above average. The guideposts were a compromise, dividing the gains of enhanced productivity between labor and capital, but retaining the existing division of income between them.[16]

By using supply-side initiatives to keep prices stable while promoting expansion, Kennedy anticipated and sought to prevent inflation with a comprehensive program of fiscal, monetary, and incomes policies. But no part of it involved a tax cut.

The tax cut came later, in a shift to *demand*-side economics, when the economy didn't seem to be expanding enough. Since it was still running well below its potential output, Kennedy prescribed raising aggregate demand with a $12-billion tax cut in a $600-billion economy. According to Walter Heller, who was Kennedy's chief economic adviser, the cuts succeeded "not by miraculously invoking new supplies of work effort and savings, but by stimulating demand for goods and services in a slack economy and thereby putting idle workers and excess inventory capacity back to work."[17] Both the supply-side investment credit and the demand-side tax cut were antidepression strategies, not anti-inflation strategies.

In pushing a tax cut despite a budget deficit, however small (it was $4.8 billion in 1963, on outlays of $111.3 billion), Kennedy had to engage in a program of justification. He denied that a deficit *per se* produced inflation, and that a surplus prevented it. Walter Heller had not only convinced him that some fiscal stimulus was needed to lead the economy out of depression, but had developed the corollary of the "fiscal drag." According to this notion, an expanding economy generates tax revenues that balance the budget and even produce a surplus—but *before* the economy is operating at satisfactory levels of output and employment. These revenues put a fiscal drag on the economy because they remove money from it that the government doesn't put back in. Kennedy then urged the paradox that deficits occurred because of too much, rather than too little, taxation. Taxation was an economic impediment, and in 1963 it threatened the three-year recovery.[18]

Two forms of fiscal stimulus could increase aggregate demand: higher social spending or a tax cut. A tax cut reduced the government's proportion of the GNP, but it could have the same effect as public spending on national income and employment, so long as the level of public spending remained the same when it went into effect. The liberal Galbraith, like Keynes, stressed public spending, while the Council of Economic Advisers preferred a tax cut as more politically appealing. However, the two strategies were functional equivalents, with the same budgetary impact.

What Kennedy was propounding, then, was hardly supply-side economics but pure demand-oriented Keynesianism. And so does "supply-side" economics in large measure support Keynesianism through its emphasis on investment demand, except that it endorses the private-sector version, or "commercial Keynesianism."[19]

Not that the tax cut worked the magic, even in the past, that the Lafferites claim for it. Together with the cyclical recovery then under way, the stimulus did generate enough revenues to balance the budget briefly in 1965, just before the Vietnam War escalated. But, says Heller, neither the tax cut's demand stimulus nor even the long-delayed supply stimulus produced enough revenues to "pay for itself." Having made such a claim and retracted it publicly, Heller winces when supply-siders quote him.

Then, too, as Edward Kennedy pointed out in a WNET interview in January 1982, these policies worked when both inflation, at less than 2 percent in 1960, and the deficit were low. They cannot simply be extrapolated to the 1980s.

Like Keynesian strategy, supply-side theory holds up in a depression, when there is slack in the economy, but it is hardly a cure for inflation. Whatever the case, the Vietnam War contaminated the results of Kennedy's experiment. Can it be that, with our renewed craze for defense spending, the parallel is complete?

Nothing is more needed today than a good supply-side strategy to stimulate investment. But the demand-oriented Kemp-Roth tax cut can at best do so only on the second round—as transfer payments do, and as defense spending does—and, even then, only in a slack economy in which it can spur increased production to satisfy that demand. Without these conditions, a tax cut is sure to be inflationary.

True supply-side strategies must be *targeted*, focused on production, not consumption. An across-the-board tax cut falls short of this criterion. Moreover, supply-side policies involve far more than taxes. Supply-side effects stem from government regulation—or deregulation; from tariffs, import quotas, and farm-price supports; from subsidies to the merchant marine; from synfuels or low-income housing or research; from unemployment insurance and welfare; from spending on defense.

Reagan's break with tradition has forced a reconsideration of assumptions we have held too long. His efforts to reduce the government role and its often counterproductive regulations are steps in the right direction. And his decisiveness and enduring popularity generate an impression of leadership that has been strangely absent in past years. By inspiring confidence, he encourages action in the private sector. This is no mean accomplishment, and its leverage should not be underestimated if, indeed, he has the wisdom to use it properly.

Yet the inconsistencies in his program impede his achievement. To index automatic increases into the budget and then cut back on these built-in rises, rather than work *initially* from a noninflationary, *non*indexed (or less heavily indexed) budget, is to admit defeat from the start. As David Stockman has repeatedly insisted, this gradualism never worked and never could work.

Moreover, Reagan has relied too heavily on the Kemp-Roth-Laffer-inspired three-year tax cut to increase savings, investment, and hence employment and tax revenues. Supply-side economics does have merit, and can work at the right stage of the cycle, just as demand-side economics has validity—Keynes is not dead or even irrelevant—at another juncture in the cycle. And Reagan is correct; now is the time to implement it.

But supply-side economics is not what Reagan is trying via the diffuse, demand-oriented Kemp-Roth approach. To trigger a maximal increase in supply, one must design incentives that will *directly* increase savings and investment and reduce consumption, so that capital equipment can be produced with available productive facilities. Such policies might include:

1. Eliminating the tax on *all* labor to encourage and reward work and productivity;

2. Eliminating the capital gains tax on *productive* capital goods investments, while retaining and even increasing taxes on gains from such sterile investments as gold, silver, commodities, currency speculation, antiques, and even housing;

3. Taxing consumption with a new value-added tax both to raise revenues and discourage present consumption spending.

These steps, unlike the *un*targeted Reagan-Kemp-Roth supply-side strategy, would be designed specifically to meet the Reagan objectives. They would result in a substantial acceleration of supply, the buildup of productive capital goods, a corollary diminution of consumer demand, and thus a significant slowdown in the ultimate cost of goods produced and the prices charged for goods sold—the key to price stability and noninflationary growth. The present across-the-board tax cuts ensure neither the desired increase in savings nor the desired acceleration in capital investment. In fact, if they turn out, as they well may, to accelerate demand, they can prove counterproductive, increasing the budget deficit without accomplishing any of the hoped-for results, and ultimately exacerbating inflation.

In the end, however, even the most precisely targeted supply-side strategies miss the basic and irreparable fallacy in supply-side theory and Say's law; they neglect demand. Supply and demand have dialectical relationships, and demand cannot be assumed. The two sides of the equation also require different time frames.

Demand can always be created quickly, in fact instantly, almost by government edict, at the simplest level by government itself, through increased spending for defense, farm goods, or what have you. Not quite as immediately, the government can also make more dollars available to the consumer by cutting tax rates, thereby expanding demand for goods and services.

Supply, on the other hand, can be increased only over a period of time. The government may be in a position to create incentives for greater savings and investing. But it takes time, not to mention responsiveness on the part of businessmen (and of unions that may resist expanded productivity), to plan, design, and build new plant, machines, and equipment, and then to recruit, hire, and train the help required to generate an expansion in productivity and supply.

The nature of economics is that demand, where it is perceived to exist, will create supply. The "carrot," the promise of the profits that come from supplying the consumer his needs or desires— that is, his *demands*—is what makes economics, particularly capitalist economics, function. Say's law, that supply will create its own demand, is utter nonsense. Otherwise we would never have the present excess capacity in our steel mills, our auto factories, our construction industry. The Soviet economy often demonstrates the real-life fallacy of such thinking when its bureaucrats determine what supply of a given good will be produced/supplied, only to find that much of it lies on shelves with no takers, almost irrespective of price. Supply unequivocally does not create its own demand; if it did, someone could still supply buggy whips. In fact, buggy-whip factories and production were discontinued when there were no takers of the supply.

That being the case, we cannot hope for a successful supply-side program without demand, or at least a perceived imminent demand. More than that: we cannot simply plan, or hope, to generate greater production of supply-side goods—new plant, machinery, equipment—simply by drastically cutting or eliminating the demand for other, nonsupply-side—that is, consumer—goods. Although you can diminish or eliminate the demand for nonsupply-side goods, freeing the resources, manpower, and especially savings to make supply-side investments, you at the same time destroy the very incentive to invest. For when there is no perceived significant demand, no rational player will provide the supply facility, regardless of the abundance of savings available at however low an interest rate. As a matter of fact, the early 1930s saw little, if any, capital investment, except for government-sponsored public works—WPA projects, dams, roads—even with funds available at 1 percent interest or less. The absence of demand suggested to businessmen that it was pointless to waste themselves by investing in productive supply-side capital without promise of a return, when even existing capital was largely unused and generating losses if anything.

It is obvious that supply-side and demand-side must go hand in hand, must coexist, not substitute for each other. There are times when demand is excessive vis-à-vis supply, throwing prices out of balance or pushing them up without generating the needed supply rapidly enough. At such times government action should stress slowing demand by raising taxes, perhaps imposing value-added taxes that directly affect consumer demand while at the same time granting tax credits, accelerated depreciation allowances, favorable tax treatment of R & D (research and development) projects, even lower corporate taxes to accelerate capital formation and the supply-side activity that will meet demand and halt inflation. But neither supply-side nor demand-side emphasis alone can work. Stressing one or the other too much leads to a disruptive imbalance that is damaging and costly, in terms of unemployment, recession, hardship, to the entire economy. Like a ship's pilot, the government must steer the economy delicately in the ever-changing balance of its economic ebb and flow, not tilting too far, too drastically, or too abruptly, to one side or the other, between supply-side and demand-side economics, in order to ensure the smooth sailing of the economic ship of state.

NOTES

1. Jimmy Carter, news conference, November 15, 1976, quoted by Sam I. Nakagama, *Economic Perspectives,* 10, no. 25, Kidder Peabody, September 19, 1980, 1; *Budget of the United States Government,* Fiscal Year 1983, 9–62, 2–2; *Statistical Abstract,* 1981, 102d ed., Tables 700 and 701, 421; Table 671, 400.

2. "The Economic Equivalent of War," *New York Times* editorial, March 15, 1981, Sec. 4, E18.

3. Ibid.

4. "Moral Leadership in Government," Public Agenda Foundation, September 1976, 13, 29–30.

5. "Poll Finds Reagan's Economic Plan Raises Hopes," *New York Times,* January 19, 1982, A20.

6. "Federal Budget Scorecard," *New York Times,* June 2, 1981, Sec. 4, 4E; Seth S. King, "Harvest of Wheat Worries Farmers," *New York Times,* June 29, 1982, A14; "The Sour Politics of Sugar," *New York Times* editorial, June 22, 1982, A26.

7. "Food Stamps Program: How It Grew and How Reagan Wants to Cut It Back," by Steven V. Roberts, *New York Times,* April 4, 1981, 11; "GOP Solidarity Upholds Cuts in the Food Stamp Budget," March 20, 1981, A23.

8. Lipsey and Steiner, *Macroeconomics,* 95; Samuelson, *Economics,* 11th ed., 340, 341; Robert Lubar, "Making Democracy Less Inflation Prone," *New York Times,* September 21, 1980, B1. For a discussion of the full-employment deficit, see chapter 4.

9. Edward Cowan, "Reagan Delivers His Budget," *New York Times,* March 11, 1981, 1; "Budget Revision Highlights," *New York Times,* March 11, 1981, 1.

10. *Budget of the U.S. Government: Fiscal 1983,* 3–23, 9–3. Less optimistic projections see spending at $742 billion in fiscal 1982, $827 billion in 1983, $918 billion in 1984, and $1,013 billion in 1985. The Conference Board projects the deficits alone at $119 billion in fiscal 1982, $182 billion in 1983, $216 billion in 1984, and $233 billion in 1985, for a total of $750 billion—a

total deficit amounting, in just four years, to 75 percent of the $1-trillion total deficit accumulated in our entire history. The Congressional Budget Office had even higher projections. See Leonard Silk, "Grim Reality of the Budget," *New York Times,* April 28, 1982, D2.

11. Steven Rattner, "A Flood Not Yet Stemmed," *New York Times,* March 11, 1981, 1; Silk, "Grim Reality," D2. See also note 10.

12. Leonard Silk, "Growth as Way Out of Dunkirk," *New York Times,* December 12, 1980, D2.

13. Walter W. Heller, "Introduction," to Francis M. Bator and Richard Musgrave, *Economic Choices: Studies in Tax/Fiscal Policy,* Washington, D.C., Center for National Policy, 1982, 10.

14. William Baumol, "Supply-Side Theory Acquires New Respect Among Economists," *New York Times,* March 5, 1981, A1, D14.

15. Walter W. Heller, "Supply-Side Moves Assayed," *New York Times,* December 19, 1980, D2; see also Heller's "Kennedy's Supply-Side Economics," *Challenge,* May–June 1981, 14–18.

16. *Statistical Abstract,* 1979, 100th ed., table 780, 476; Lekachman, *Age of Keynes,* 264–65.

17. Heller, "Supply-Side Moves Assayed," D2; Heller, "Kennedy's Supply-Side Economics," 14–18.

18. Lekachman, *Age of Keynes,* 270, 272–74, 279–80, 285.

19. Ibid., 105, 273, 282, 287.

10

Incentive Planning:
The Visible Hand

Must the alternatives be bureaucratic totalitarianism or unplanned anarchy? That seems to be the dilemma confronting us as
Reagan's policies prove frustrating and futile. Expressing the public disaffection, he has checked the last half-century's increasing
government encroachment upon our economic activities and has
challenged traditions built up over decades. But he is limited
both politically and by a narrow social vision. Above all, he is
governed by a negative view of the state, and this fear of planning
conditions his policies.

The liberal view of the state as the panacea may have failed; but
the conservative image of the state as adversary, or of planning
and regulation as a crimp in the marvelous workings of the visible
hand, is just as untenable. There is a way out of this impasse. In
the chapters that follow I hope to show how we can forge a new
kind of public-private partnership.

One of the most perverse obstacles to bringing rationality into
our policies has been our semantic chauvinism, our confused fears
that planning will bring about the "socialist" state. Labels like
Socialism, Marxism, Communism, the Soviet Union, China,
"centrally planned economies" evoke nightmare visions. They are

misleading weapons in an economic cold war that persists while we do business as usual with totalitarian and fascist regimes, from the Soviet Union to Argentina, just as easily as with democracies. We cry out against a coup d'état, as we did with Cuba. Yet we fall back on our economic interests irrespective of ideology. We rail against Poland's martial law, but our taxes subsidize its deficits.

Only if we abandon the absolutist claims that our system alone, pure and uncompromised, is workable, can we begin successfully to monitor and modify our economic activities. Our ideal political evolution should be to integrate, as much as possible, the best adaptations of other systems with the best features of our own. Collectivist systems offer the benefits of health care, economic security, controlled but planned educational opportunities, long-range planning, and a spirit of cooperation. We offer greater freedom of choice, free market flexibility, and an emphasis on individuality and innovation.

The move toward convergence is already taking place. Our own history, of course, demonstrates that process as, from the nineteenth century on, the government has intervened increasingly to prevent some of the evils and abuses that would have to emerge in a system predicated so completely on the virtues of self-interest. Intervention was required to outlaw child labor, hazardous working conditions, destitution in old age, the ravages of cyclical unemployment, damage to the environment, and other deviations from the ideal image of a self-regulating system. The result has been a gradual evolution toward some of the goals of socialism. By today, many of the planks in the Socialist Party's 1928 platform have become law—progressive taxation, our Social Security system, public works, restrictions on child labor.[1] We have enforced minimal environmental, quality-of-life, and work standards. In many respects, we have achieved the ends without the form of socialism.

At the same time, the merits of laissez-faire and the profit motive have not been lost on communist countries. In the U.S.S.R., increased affluence and the ability to provide consumer goods beyond the bare and predictable necessities have modified central planning. When discretionary items fail to sell, planners know that they must cut back—that is, revert to market principles.

They have adopted such Western strategies as advertising. In trying to anticipate consumer wants they sometimes observe and then introduce products that are popular abroad. Wage differences reward skilled workers and professionals, while piece rates and incentive systems are often used to spur productivity. State planners may leave factory managers little leeway in deciding what to produce or how to combine the factors of production; yet the manager is expected to exceed the plan and "overproduce" the assigned item. Since 30 to 50 percent of his pay rests on bonuses tied directly to his "overfulfillment" of the plan, he has a great personal incentive to exceed the specified output. One ironic outcome has been skimping on design or quality or size for the sake of cost efficiency.

Success is also measured by the "profit" the manager can make for the enterprise. Although the planners set prices so that they cannot be manipulated to make profits, and though most earnings go back to the state, factory managers buy their inputs and sell their outputs. Their profits depend on their efficiency and sales—hence their sensitivity to consumer needs. Since part of the profits go for bonuses and other rewards, there is a direct incentive to run the plant efficiently.

Other parts of Eastern Europe, most notably Yugoslavia and Hungary, have gone even further in using market principles, though state control remains strong. And China, finding that it cannot create jobs quickly enough for its unemployed youth, is retreating on the promise of state-guaranteed full employment and urging private-sector activity. In Dahan, China, students are learning principles of American management in a U.S. Department of Commerce program that Chinese leaders hope will do for China what learning about management has done for Japan.[2] China has even introduced the concept of profits to encourage greater productivity.

It hardly matters what one calls an economic system. What matters, what defines it, is the way the system acts to distribute its resources, its wealth, its productivity, under what conditions, with what rights to retain one's earnings and to determine whom one really works for—whether for the state, one's self, or others.

Since we do make value judgments and create policies and laws to reflect them, we not only tolerate but insist upon government intervention. Noninvolvement on the part of the state is an asset only when the economy functions well and meets the needs of society.

PLANNING WITHOUT BUREAUCRACY

Planning is simply the intelligent hand behind the invisible hand. It is essential in any society that must implement legislation to move it in the direction of its goals. For the government to act, legislate, and impose its values, it *must* define goals and objectives and it *must* plan to carry them out. Ignoring this imperative threatens the emergence of the very totalitarian government that those who fear planning wish to avoid. The outcome for a society or a business that fails to plan is inevitably crisis and disaster. In such emergencies, total command by government becomes probable and even essential.

It is neither regulation nor planning *per se* that threatens freedom, but hierarchical direction from a single central authority. The liberal state seeks to preserve competition as the basis of coordination and to create conditions "under which the knowledge and initiative of individuals are given the best scope so that they can plan most successfully."[3] But preserving competition does not preclude state intervention or even state-operated enterprises. It does not ignore the need for either quality controls or social service, *even if* their establishment and enforcement serve to lower productivity. Free enterprise is defined not by profit but by competition under fair rules that affect all players equally, without the granting of monopolistic privilege.

Nevertheless, we want to avoid the communist premise that the cure for all social ills is a government takeover of the economy. This approach is not only deceptive and hence disillusioning— witness the unrest in the U.S.S.R. and Poland—but stultifying. By eliminating economic and political freedom, it achieves its ends through coercion rather than through positive incentives. By claiming to know each appropriate product and price, and directing each individual's education, job, salary, and residence, it produces a slavelike incapacity for self-expression and imaginative behavior that cancel out whatever material good it may achieve.

How then can we design a political system that can plan and implement social goals while ensuring a minimum of governmental intervention? The answer, it seems to me, is to limit *direct* government involvement and to avoid the establishment of any new federal positions, offices, or bureaucracies, except where no alternative is possible. Through targeted incentives, democratic planning can mesh our goals, our values, with our material interests so that what is socially desirable becomes economically attractive, too. This planned capitalism surpasses Marxism because it provides direction yet sparks individual effort, preserves the profit motive, and permits initiative and innovation.

Bureaucracies tend to produce all-inclusive plans and structures that are either too controlling or too unmanageable (see chapter 2). They also acquire a stake in their own existence that threatens to override the purpose for which they were created. The government's role should be that of policeman, creating and maintaining stability. But if government becomes one of the prime service operations of the economy, distributing wealth, creating jobs, building housing and aircraft, and consuming goods, it becomes an active participant and a competitor for our resources. At that point, it can no longer act as policeman, taking the necessary steps that economic conditions demand, since in effect it must act against itself. Its cumbersome programs lose the flexibility to adapt to change; it exaggerates crises in order to maintain itself; it competes with the public for the allocation of the economic vote. It becomes an interest group itself.

Another drawback to bureaucracy is the lack of real accountability in its incentive system, which, lacking the criterion of profitability, has no bottom line. Its main goals become eventually to ensure its own existence and security for its job holders, and to expand its promotions, management positions, and power. This tendency to convert means into ends is inherent in bureaucratic structure, but it becomes especially apparent in public bureaucracies because the lack of a profit motive removes the ultimate and deadly sanction of the private sector—economy or bankruptcy.

Few enterprises function well without sanctions against those who fail to perform. Yet bureaucracies are notoriously bad at insisting on productivity, on measurable performance and *results,* and at checking or dismissing ineffective employees. Their salary systems reward mediocrity, support the poorly motivated, and discourage the incentive to innovate.

Even their criteria of effectiveness reverse those of profit-making enterprises. Budget surpluses are rewarded in private industry, but public agencies that find themselves with a surplus at the end of the year must scramble to use it up. This widespread pattern is hardly due to sheer selfishness. It stems from the fact that frugality and budgetary efficiency are not rewarded. Good management does not provide a reserve against future needs. Instead, a budget surplus in one year only means a smaller budget allocation in the next fiscal year. Underspending, in fact, provokes nothing less than scandal. In 1976, when government spending fell short of its mark, planners were faulted for having overestimated their needs and having contributed, through underspending, to the poor performance of the economy. When public opinion only reinforces the natural temptation to inflate the budget, overspending becomes an imperative. The bureaucrat exaggerates his needs, then spends arbitrarily to protect himself from criticism.

The alternative to bureaucratic planning, in which the government's visible hand is laid upon every unfolding decision and detail, is to define our goals and design incentives to encourage the private sector and individual self-interest to fulfill them. Incentives work better than directives because they are based on voluntary decision. An individual can choose whether or not to respond to them, decide whether the reward is worth a change in behavior and business practice.

Government incentives, whether they are tax or direct incentives, have the virtue of being quantitatively measurable both in cost and in result. They are visible without being necessarily intrusive. Best of all, direct, tangible incentives can be designed to achieve their objectives without requiring bureaucratic structures. Incentives, once granted, may also be difficult to retract; but they are much easier to do away with than are established bureaucracies.

Incentives also provide the element of *leverage.* Where it might take $10 billion annually to implement a new government program, including the establishment of its bureaucratic infrastructure, the same end could be achieved by strategically injecting $2 or $3 billion into certain sectors of the private economy.

Had the government ever chosen to set up a *department* for capital investment, who knows how many people might now be employees or consultants and contractors; how much it would have spent; how far it would have spread; and with what (if any) measurable result? With the more direct, visible, and measurable investment tax credit, private industry has increased its capital investment each year by many billions of dollars, achieving far more, faster and cheaper, than could have been achieved by an agency, with colossal budgets, overhead, paperwork, and inevitable procedural blocks.

This is true despite what I am sure were many imperfections, loopholes, and instances of waste, negligence, and fraud. There were fewer costs and violations than there would have been had the government sought to do the job itself.

Finally, it must be recognized that if taxation really approximates the results of communism or socialism by confiscating the earnings on a company's production, it produces the same disincentives that make state controls so unattractive to us. Incentives, in the form of reduced taxes, rebates, and subsidies, support the superior productive drive of capitalism. If tax policy is not designed with incentives to achieve worthwhile social goals, then an unplanned and flawed tax policy will evolve.

Government incentives, far better than programs, achieve all those ends without touching our fundamental freedoms. They reduce the size and *direct* interference of government in our lives. The state need only define our goals and stimulate the free market to achieve them. It need not dominate; it need only use small, strategic, and timely inputs to trigger a move in the right direction.

A kind of planning is inherent in each unfolding action. If one chooses not to define a plan, that itself is a decision, a plan of the worst kind, planning by default. If we do not develop an energy plan, the OPEC plans for us. If we do not devise our long range plans, circumstances will. We see this threat in the present chaos stemming from political maneuvering, from our system of loans and subsidies, insurance, credits and price supports, food stamps, parity, and supply constraints. Tobacco must be supported by government, when the logical and socially constructive strategy would be to raise the tax, lower parity, and divert the land to health-producing crops. Monopoly pricing, the critical secret international negotiations of large oil companies, the production of inflation by banks—all show planning by default. Government intervenes in response to crisis and to large, organized pressure groups, using expedient, short-term criteria for arriving at its decisions. This is planning with no real evaluation of the input of the plan or its potential ramifications, because planning is still anathema in our society.

Our form of society demands responsiveness to these pressures and the votes they promise. Political leaders must satisfy their constituencies—lawyers, activists, businessmen, union representatives, nonprofit agencies. Responsiveness becomes more important than efficiency, indulgence more important than retrenchment. But if this is so, let us at least define, constantly update, and redefine a set of useful goals and build, even into our present subsidies, a design for achieving them. We can assist industry without uncritically adopting all of its demands and definitions of its needs. We can create meaningful public-sector employment instead of projects that are deliberately wasteful because organized groups resist any potentially competitive activity.

This is where President Reagan's deregulation falls amiss. He has adroitly maneuvered intraparty divisions to create a bipartisan supporting coalition; but he has failed to challenge entrenched interest groups. He owes too many favors to their representatives. Hence the tobacco subsidies, the restrictive import quotas. All this in the name of deregulation? Nor do his tax incentives have more than the narrowest economic goal. They may be intended to spur enterprise and to change the direction of economic activity; but they lack design or direction. Similarly, his cutbacks in social programs are mechanical, neither targeted at their defects nor geared to a positive alternative. And his "return" of power to the states does little but shift identical responsibilities (and taxes) from one level of government to another. Ironically, only the totally deplorable five-year defense buildup illustrates the goal orientation that should be part of government planning. If we are simply brought back to the days before the New Deal, we cannot learn from its lessons.

I am in favor of government intervention that is goal-oriented, realistic, and targeted. It should not try to solve all problems for all people for all time. But it should not, in the name of deregulation, simply relegate to the states and private industry all responsibility for social planning. The way to approach governmental policy, planning, and strategy is not by merely defining in advance the legitimate functions of government. Instead, the way to approach it is to define our needs and goals, then determine how public and private sectors can cooperate to meet them.

NOTES

1. Milton and Rose Friedman, *Free to Choose,* New York, Harcourt Brace Jovanovich, 1980, 311–12.

2. Christopher S. Wren, "China's Economic Shift Said To Need More Time," *New York Times,* December 1, 1981, D1, and "Chinese Study Capitalist Lessons," *New York Times,* June 27, 1982, Sec. 3, 8F.

3. Friedrich Hayek, *Road To Serfdom,* Chicago, University of Chicago Press, 1944, 35–37.

11

Growth or No Growth?
Beyond the Malthusian
Paradigm

Nowhere, perhaps, is the issue of government intervention so clearly highlighted as in the debate generated by our growth and productivity crisis. Historically, economic growth has been the solution to our problems. It has raised our standard of living as measured by gross national product—the dollar value of goods and services produced by working members of the economy. It has made the trickle-down theory a reality, providing employment, producing the surplus by which the rich could benefit themselves and others in the process, and reducing class conflict. Perhaps most important, it has been linked to our central values, our work ethic and our enduring faith in progress.

Today that advance has been checked. We are suffering the plague of slow growth. In 1980 our GNP growth rate, at 2.8 percent, was a full point lower than the 3.8 percent of the 1960s. Productivity growth was less than half of that of the 1960s, 1.2 percent as against 2.9 percent, and it actually declined between 1978 and 1980. Our share of free-world exports was 12 percent, down from 15 percent in 1970 and 18 percent in 1960. In terms of overall economic performance, we were sixth of eight major industrial nations, outranking only the economically plagued Italy and Great Britain.[1]

We may in fact be better off than we were ten years ago. But comparison with our past record gives us a sense of *relative* deprivation. As other countries raise their standards of living and increase productivity, they compete with our goods on the world market and even in our own domestic market, threatening the American Dream of constant growth and improvement.

Desperate for a slogan that will restore American confidence, economists and politicians have called for productivity and revitalization, invoking the values of the Protestant Ethic—industriousness and thrift. Productivity has become our new religion. Politicians are making it the pivot of our politicoeconomic reforms. Our economic gurus invoke it to solve our balance-of-payments problem: as one "therapy" for a chronic deficit, "our workers and industry can be urged to increase domestic technical productivity."[2] Businessmen promise that once we remove the regulations and standards that keep new drugs off the market, or that preserve our environment and natural resources, they can forge ahead to deliver us from stagnation.

At the same time, conservationists question growth models and call for less consumption. Traditional liberals, concerned more with the distribution of the national output than its growth, challenge the trickle-down theory as inadequate and perhaps irrelevant in a zero-sum society. Environmentalists demand regulation to check our reckless expansion, contending that a one-sided emphasis on productivity threatens the quality of life. Economists criticize the GNP as a measure of economic health, since it does not evaluate the national product apart from its dollar volume.

These conflicting interests force us to examine, one by one, the components of growth and productivity, to understand their dynamics as they contribute to economic growth and health, to assess the limits to growth. For the success of our policies, and of our politicoeconomic system itself, depends on the intelligence and honesty with which we use productivity as a genuine policy directive and not as a slogan. We must ask ourselves:

Can we have further growth?

Do we want more growth, at least as measured by the gross national product?

THE HUMAN BIOSPHERE

The major focus of this policy debate has been our dwindling resource base and problem of energy policy. At the outset of the Industrial Revolution, we seemed to face a world of endless abundance. But the world no longer puts a limitless cornucopia of resources at our disposal. It is often claimed that inflation is accelerating because we are running up against shortages of the natural resources needed for human consumption and industrial production. Our food supply is outpaced by population growth. Oil is running out. We are depleting natural gas, copper, silver, gold. We can no longer afford the carefree consumption of nonrenewable resources and must shift to an economy founded on a shrinking resource base and on renewable resources.

Nor can we any longer simply consume our way out of depression. Keynes's strategies called for demand management to take care of slack. But slack meant unemployment—unused labor resources. In that context, unused material resources could be seen as "wasted," just as unused manpower was wasted. Today this concept has become anachronistic as these materials are depleted.

Stark realities have forced us to rethink our assumptions about growth and productivity. A number of groups have renewed Doomsday predictions, visions of limits to growth, of a world dying down. Improved health and medical care have reduced the death rate and increased longevity, without being accompanied by a corresponding decrease in the birth rate. The result is a strain on our food resources. Someday we may be in ruthless competition for the resources on which our civilization has come to depend.

Coupled with that Malthusian vision is the related problem of environmental pollution. These twin concerns have fostered a political perspective that differs from traditional conservative and liberal traditions. Its adherents protest our single-minded focus on increased material goods, and they challenge an economy dependent on waste and endless consumption, on GNP growth, and on the technological quick fix when the damage has been done. Going beyond the desire for market control mechanisms, they demand disciplinary regulation and extensive zero-risk prohibition of dangerous products.[3]

Energy has become the prototype of the Doomsday vision. Not long ago you could stick a pipe in the ground and oil gushed out. Oil is still around, but now it requires a $40-million rig in the North Sea off the British Isles or a pipeline from Alaska. The declining productivity of capital is also showing up in other kinds of resource extraction and in food production. As a result, harder work cannot prevent lower productivity in such areas as oil production, mining, and farming. We have apparently skimmed the cream and are moving to less abundant, less rich, land or resource-bearing formations.

Much of our economic attrition has stemmed from these increased costs. Between 1970 and 1980, the price of oil multiplied twenty times, going from $2 to $40 a barrel. That increase represented about 1.5 percent of our GNP. From 1972 to 1979, while overall consumer prices went up 65 percent, the cost of gas and electricity increased by 132 percent and 73 percent respectively.[4]

Almost half our oil has been imported; though we have cut back on both imports and consumption, imported oil has provided the margin of energy needed for our economic growth and standard of living. Our payments to OPEC have been like an onerous and regressive government tax. Americans in the lowest income brackets have been hardest hit: the lowest tenth spend a proportionately larger 34.1 percent of their before-tax income for energy, as against 5.2 percent for the highest tenth.[5] Oil-based energy is crucial for low- and middle-income budgets. Its cost determines the cost of gasoline for cars, heat for homes, electricity for appliances. As these groups, who have the highest propensity to consume and thus tend to spend most of their income immediately, transfer funds to OPEC countries, demand for other domestic products is drained. The result is the worst of all combinations: higher prices, or inflation, along with an inevitable slowing of demand, growth, and employment—all the earmarks of recession.

Government fiscal and monetary policy have had little control over this situation because it is external. The external disruption of oil makes it virtually impossible to fine tune the internal domestic economy. Measures that would slow consumption and hence inflation, such as checking domestic demand with high interest rates, or encouraging savings through tax exemptions on interest, were inevitably overwhelmed by each succeeding OPEC increase, which forced consumption of the hoped-for savings and injected still another dose of inflation.

To a large degree, OPEC's success until recently in charging prices totally unrelated to cost has been made possible by our own tolerance, even our blessing. Our own lack of discipline kept us from reducing our dependence so as to force prices down and impel competition among the collaborators.

Yet, as events in 1980 and 1981 began to demonstrate, the "crisis" has been at least partly semantic. Faced with unexpected success of conservation efforts, oil producers here and abroad have suffered a sharp, if temporary, oil glut. Several OPEC countries sought to lower prices and finally did in 1983. The consensus on which their control of world production and prices depends has faltered and threatened to dissolve completely.

Our success in energy conservation provides another object lesson. According to the U.S. Geological Survey, the United States still has an amount of oil almost equal to all it has ever consumed. Over the last 120 years, in each 20-year period we consumed an amount of petroleum nearly as great as all that we had ever consumed before.[6] We cannot go on consuming recklessly, but we are not at the end of the road either. A combined conservation, exploration, and development program can stave off the threat of depletion of energy resources until we have invented replacements—preferably renewable replacements—that will match and even improve upon the often wasteful resources, oil included, to which we have become accustomed.

Doomsday prophets also understate the Third World's productive capacity. Witness China's stunning increase in wheat production—over 50 percent between 1977 and 1979; India's abundance of natural gas as a source of fertilizer; and the untapped hydroelectric power, the potential for irrigation, the promise of the fertilizers that India and China have just begun to use. Asia has made great strides in output per unit of land through biological technology, the use of better seeds and fertilizer, and the growth of two or three crops a year on the same land. Once the Third World has adopted new methods, it should challenge Western European and American supremacy in agriculture.

Malthusians fail to recognize our resilience, capacity for adjustment, and sheer technological inventiveness. Along with the agricultural revolutions and the current energy glut in the Western world, we have made advances in birth control. We have changed our eating habits away from expensive, nutritionally unessential, and ecologically wasteful heavy meats to such a degree that the beef industry is in decline. During the past two decades new industries have emerged and flourished, outcroppings of entrepreneurial daring, from semiconductors to cattle cloning and DNA research and development.

Growth, then, is still possible, essential, and desirable. But this does not mean that industry need be left to itself, unassisted *or* unregulated, to find its own solutions to our remaining energy problems, or that energy development should not be carefully monitored. The nuclear industry, which was developed with huge infusions of government aid, is resisting efforts at control in the name of national independence, peace (we won't have to go to war for oil), and, you guessed it, productivity and our standard of living. Yet its potential for accidents increases, its cost overruns exceed our wildest apprehensions, and its radioactive wastes pile up faster than our most ingenious efforts to control their transit and disposal. We now find ourselves in a situation where the courts and the Department of Transportation are battling over the rights of the nuclear industry to drive its wastes through city streets.

Thus the questions remain: How much do we want sheer economic growth and productivity? How much do we want to, or do we have to, give up their names? Must large-scale pollution be the price of economic growth? How are we to define growth? And why is regulation, rather than pollution, considered a threat to our growth and our well-being?

GNP, PRODUCTIVITY, AND THE QUALITY OF LIFE: BREATHING AIR INTO THE QUALITY OF THE STATISTICS

GNP is measured in dollars—in what consumers, government, and foreign buyers are willing to pay for the product. Such a measure appears on the surface valid. It is quantitative, statistical. It puts a uniform measure on the multiplicity of products that people buy.

At the same time, the GNP has widely acknowledged qualitative defects. It is neither perfect nor all-inclusive. It does not include the work of a housewife. Yet if she hired a cook, maid, laundress, and chauffeur to help her with all the chores she otherwise does alone, these services would be valued and added into the GNP. Similarly, the GNP gives only a "dollar" measure of the quality or social value of the output. It may value the services of a prostitute or bookmaker over those of a nurse or an ambulance driver, those of a napalm manufacturer over those of a producer of healing drugs.

Despite such imperfections, we have come to live with and depend on these statistics, and to make judgments and vital decisions based on them. We need relatively consistent, measurable information over time and at a reasonable cost. How many researchers would we have to hire, and at what price, to measure the value of each housewife's output?

Moreover, if we tried to measure the quality of output, we would open a Pandora's box of arguments about the values of each component, and we would lose the basis for even rough comparability. Depending on whose "value" we used, we would have so many different numbers from so many different preparers that, regardless of their merits, the statistics would prove functionally useless. For this reason, economists accept GNP as an approximation, an imperfect but useful measure.

Yet it is doubtful that we fully understand the potential economic and social cost of basing our decisions on the "value-less" statistic. We have not adequately focused on its distortions or on the consequences that may stem from interpretation and action based upon it. So many of the programs our leaders legislate, so much of what our citizenry agitates for, so much of our government budget and our life style, our standard of living, of what we believe it to be and what is happening to it, follow from the determination and media dissemination of that statistic. We need to be scrupulous about what it is and what it implies.

Does GNP give the same value, weight, and priority to building a hospital or research facility, to training engineers and other skilled personnel in the domestic United States, as it does to exporting the same facilities and services to Iran or Iraq? To a heart pacemaker as to a Saturday-night special or a nuclear bomb?

How do you measure productivity in the case of health care, where quality of service rather than quantity of output counts? Quality costs. It militates *against* productivity.

And what if we want, or need, low-"productivity" items? Can we limit our desires to products with the greatest yield? If cancer research is less profitable (productive) than raising tobacco, must we structure our priorities in terms of these surface criteria of productivity? How can one compare occupations and measure the productivity (or contribution) of the services of a life-insurance salesman, croupier, housewife, policeman, picketer, or ball player? How does one measure the productivity of a person who prefers leisure to the goods and services he could buy by working more? The less "productive" person brings the GNP down even though his or her happiness goes "up."

Are Americans better off today than last year, last generation, last century? How do we measure it? Do we have better food, health services and delivery, leisure, entertainment, or security against poverty, malnutrition, illness, and crime?

Economists have been trying to refine our GNP measures with "quality of life" indexes. The "measure of economic welfare" (MEW), developed by William Nordhaus and James Tobin, incorporates all consumption that contributes to human welfare, even if it is not included in the national income accounts—for example, voluntary leisure, and output that does not pass through the market. It *deducts* items that "do not directly contribute to a better life"—police protection and national defense, as well as the "negative externalities" connected with urbanization, pollution, and congestion.[7] Another measure, the physical quality of life index, developed by the Economic Development Council of Washington, D.C., in 1977, measures each country's rates of infant mortality, life expectancy, and literacy. Supply-sider Jude Wanniski endorses a still-to-be-developed gross national satisfaction index that would define as capital anything that is not used in consumption but continues to give satisfaction, including public investments in parks, roads, museums, beaches and libraries, landscapes and seascapes.[8]

The trouble with these efforts is not so much their roughness and apparent subjectivity—that is to be expected in their first stages of development—as the tendency to misconstrue them. They are offered not as refinements of the gross national product, but as alternatives that entail *tradeoffs* with the GNP.

Samuelson says this in so many words. The quality of life, he explains, calls for a tradeoff of GNP for the benefits of net economic welfare (NEW): higher taxes, more expensive electricity, slower growth, and lower productivity. People, "if they really wish to . . . can trade off quantity of goods for quality of life. . . . Public policies can choose to improve economic welfare, 'NEW'—if necessary, at the deliberate sacrifice of more GNP growth. Political economy must serve human wishes. There is no need for people to be chained to mere material growth unless they wish to be."[9]

While this formulation has its merits, it sacrifices any strategic advance that a net economic welfare index might provide. Worse yet, it *legitimizes* exactly what it tries to correct. The notion of a tradeoff has given antienvironmentalists their most potent arguments as they invoke the values of cost-effectiveness and productivity. On March 26, 1981, a Mobil advertisement in the *New York Times* questioned whether the once useful Clean Air Act, up for authorization in 1981, was suited to the needs of the 1980s in the light of past improvements, the oil embargo, and the electorate's "new emphasis on making the country more productive again. . . . *With the bill for foreign oil nearing $100 billion a year, inflation in excess of 10 percent, and some major industries in deep trouble,*" the nation could "*no longer afford the sky-high price of single-minded environmental zeal*" (italics in original), when marginal improvements cost much more. Clean air and water must submit to the logic of the margin; to the law of diminishing returns, not even absolute losses; and to the unassailable criterion of the GNP, which ignores nonmarketable goods, when the quality of life is surely *part* of our standard of living. There is more to our standard of living than spendable real income.

We can argue about definitions. But perhaps we can do better than call these benefits tradeoffs when deregulation, in the name of productivity, exposes us to nuclear pollution, acid rain, chemical wastes, and poisoned air.

POLLUTION: CAN WE WORK IT
INTO THE GNP?

Let us analyze just one dimension of the GNP. It is widely propounded and almost never refuted that a major reason for our halting GNP growth and productivity is the vast amount of labor and resources that government regulation has forced American industry to "divert" to cleaning up the air we breathe and the water we drink, to the "neglect" of "more vital" productive capital equipment. According to this argument, if we invested all the funds in more efficient, updated capital equipment, we could produce more steel and more automobiles cheaper and better than the Japanese and capture a larger share of the foreign markets. With a faster-growing GNP there would be a bigger pie and a bigger slice for everyone.

But what if the larger slice is rotten? Wouldn't each of us value and opt for a smaller slice with qualities of excellence?

The antienvironmentalist thesis implies that producing pollution-control equipment is wasteful and destructive to our life style. It keeps us from producing more machinery and equipment to produce more steel and cars that will be *paid for* by domestic or foreign consumers. Growth lets us all buy more things we must *pay for;* thus, we are living a better life.

What admirable simplicity! If one pays for something it has value. If one does not pay for it, it has no value and is not worth producing. A gas-guzzling, air-polluting automobile has appreciable value, not only when it is produced, but each day it is used, since it consumes gas and oil and spare parts and mechanical labor and Simoniz and auto insurance, all of which must be paid for. But pure drinking water, on which life and life-sustaining food depend, has zero value. And so does the equipment that preserves it. Pollution-control equipment is included in the GNP, but once only, when it is manufactured and sold. Its continuing daily contributions to our lives and health are never measured because clean air and water are free.

Well, you may argue, that's accurate. You only include each piece of machinery or equipment once in the GNP, when it's paid for. Why not the same for pollution-control equipment? The reason is obvious. Equipment for an oil refinery is included in GNP once, when it's paid for. But what it produces is also paid for and added to GNP as long as the equipment lasts. If cleaner air and cleaner water, like electricity, were metered as they were delivered to our communities, they would also be included in GNP as we paid for them, and antipollutants would then be considered productive.

Clearly, the bias we have introduced in constructing the GNP is toward productive machinery as measured by the dollars paid for their output—not the quality and real value delivered to the consumer. Yet can anyone maintain that an American car sold to a Japanese consumer (who does not buy our gas or insurance) raises our living standard more than the clean air and water produced by pollution-control equipment and delivered to us each day free of any direct charges—even though the charges are incorporated into the company's end products? Exactly that logic is built into the GNP upon which we make our most crucial economic decisions.

At this moment we are drastically curtailing our commitment to, and spending on, equipment designed to improve the air we breathe and the water we drink because its costs hurt our "growth." Business is agitating for a reduction of such environmental regulations (one would almost suspect that businessmen neither breathe nor drink) to "straighten out" the economy. Congressmen, other political leaders, and a portion of our citizenry see such "easing" as essential to restoring our growth, productivity, standard of living, and quality of life.

There may be some cost inefficiency in regulations involving environmental improvement, just as there is cost inefficiency in every other aspect of productive equipment. Some of the legislation may entail unnecessary, overambitious overkill. Bureaucratic delays entail costs and lost time that can delay or destroy projects. A company may wait three years and spend $300,000 to obtain the series of permits that will let it operate under the Clean Air Act. Agencies delay decisions on controversial nuclear power plants, oil refineries, and the like, and question the companies' predictions, monitoring data, and control equipment.[10]

It may be true that quality controls will curtail profits and even that honest efforts at quality control have been impeded as a result of overzealous administration. Yet is any other area more deserving of some waste in achieving a desirable or essential goal? Is it really more important to produce a car with better mileage and salability than to produce cleaner air and purer water? And can't we strive to do both? My objection is largely to this overwhelming, little-recognized bias in the structuring of GNP and productivity measures.

The distortion that favors undifferentiated quantitative materialism over quality-of-life measures should be modified and corrected. Let economists address this issue and design more useful statistics leading to better conclusions, better plans, and a better economy that delivers a superior life style to all. Economists can sharpen the intellectual precision required to achieve that goal. The GNP should be disaggregated and its components weighted; ways must be found to build *into* the GNP those products and services that help to create a better life, rather than merely to add them to the costs of production.

There are many ways to skin the cat once it is caught. Let me suggest one approach to "measuring" environmental control: citizens might pay the government each year for the cleaner air and water delivered to them, depending on and related to the amount of incremental dollars invested in equipment for pollution control and environmental purification. This would be not a tax, but a payment for the delivery of a useful public utility. Under these circumstances, the value of an improved human environment *would* enter into the GNP. The government, in turn, could use

229

the proceeds as an investment tax credit to stimulate capital equipment and/or research and development, or to further investment in pollution-control equipment as well.

This approach would redress the bias and give businessmen and economists the tools they need to construct the GNP. It would also provide the intellectual and psychological set not to criticize investment in cleaner air and purer water, but to measure, and so appreciate and encourage, the fruits of these investments.

The same approach could be extended to the weighting of safer cars, which are given no value in the GNP. Here again, a distorted focus has caused our policies to be misdirected.

We know that the profit incentive promotes indifference to pollution maximization. In fact, to pollute the environment is one of the easiest ways to lower costs, maximize profits, and even reduce prices to consumers. Productivity thrives on ignoring dangers to consumers or to our human biosphere.

If the businessman or economist feels it vital that we improve the quality of our oil and petrochemicals and not our air and water, when we can live without the former but not without the latter, it is only because the first is paid for, so that the businessman sees the incentive and the economist can measure the output. Thus we have arrived at the present topsy-turvy position. Let's forget the *free* quality air and the *free* purified water; let the consumer pay, so that the producer is eager to produce what is socially useful and statistically measurable. Let us revive our statistics and give them a more productive useful life.

If we don't do this and similar restructuring, we may be eliminating a valuable and vital program based on misleading assumptions and distorted logic. We will be eliminating something potentially great for all the wrong reasons.

PRODUCTIVITY AND PLANNING

Our productivity measures are in some ways as misleading as the GNP. Just as per capita GNP measures our standard of living, "productivity" measures our efficiency. Defined as dollar output per man-hour, it is arrived at by dividing the total GNP, or gross goods-and-services product, by the number of labor hours required to produce it. The more produced for each hour of the worker's time, the greater the productivity. Or, better yet, the higher the ratio of GNP to total man-hours, the greater the productivity. In contrast to growth, which means only more output, it means producing more, or as much, with less input, with fewer natural resources, less work, less plant and equipment.

Yet we can have a higher GNP with the same, or lower, productivity, if more inputs are used—more resources, labor, or capital—or if these inputs are less efficient or more costly; that is, if manpower is unskilled, or resources scarce, or interest rates high. We may even accept this outcome for some of our manpower policies. If unskilled workers are hired, productivity may decline, at least for a while, though total output and available goods increase because more workers are employed.

We can also have higher productivity with the same GNP or a lower one, hence a lower standard of living, because the total pie to be distributed is smaller. Productivity depends on many factors, including the economies of large-scale production, the size and skills of the work force, and technology or applied knowledge. If either human skill or technology is improved, output can grow even if capital stock per worker remains fixed. It depends also on the ability and flexibility to improve productivity, move people, and eliminate featherbedding without encountering resistance.

These processes, however, are self-limiting. Economies of scale or mass production reach a point of diminishing returns. Markets, or shares of market, become saturated. The marginal productivity of labor, which has little to do with individual productivity, limits the possibilities of potential growth. Once fewer and fewer workers are needed to produce a given output, greater labor productivity obviously results in unemployment. As the lessons of agriculture and other cases of overproduction have taught us, if the market can't absorb the added output at prices that generate at least as much total income, increased output per worker can lead to depression.

This is one of the Catch-22s of our economic system. The more efficient our productive methods, the more unemployment we create, which triggers all sorts of countervailing efforts. Unions and labor on work teams know this well; they have a stake in resisting productivity gains—workers because their jobs are threatened, union leaders because they will lose members. This resistance produces conflict and the iron law of unionism: the relentless and inflationary push for higher wages independent of productivity. Even in Japan union leaders have recently insisted that companies pay union dues for the robots they introduce. This demand proves that union leaders are more interested in the total dues they receive than in preserving jobs for their human members.

The iron law of unionism operates by a dynamic that is destructive and ultimately self-destructive. To increase his earnings, a worker should increase his productive output; otherwise he merely increases his own wage and forces prices up without helping to increase the total economic output or standard of living. In this inflationary process he gains nothing but the illusory psychic reward of a larger nominal paycheck. This may temporarily improve his standard vis-à-vis the rest of the work force, but his gains will be canceled out as others quickly push for catch-up wages. Since few, especially unions, are satisfied with merely catching up but want to leap ahead, this leapfrogging process inspires persistent inflation. As each sector maneuvers for a larger slice without increasing output, no one ends up better off. Any improvement in one's share is at the direct expense of another's.

On the other hand, increased productivity threatens to eliminate some positions, reducing the total number of employees needed to produce the requisite output. Obviously no union ever wants this situation! Hence the inevitable conflict: the simultaneous push for *higher* wages and *lower* productivity, the formula for inevitable inflation.

This tendency is reinforced by the need of union leaders themselves to deliver increases for their members each year irrespective of productivity achievements. Rewards are related not to results but to the collective threat and power of unions to disrupt and inconvenience, to hold up production.

One wonders what our stage of economic development would be today had the farm workers of the eighteenth and nineteenth centuries organized into unions dedicated to these goals. The Industrial Revolution could never have gotten off the ground—or off the farm. That revolution took off because farm output increased dramatically, freeing workers to move into new and growing business ventures to build a larger national product.

As that transformation shows, increased productivity *in the long run* benefits all. People were, and may be, displaced and dislocated in the process. But this process, painful as it is temporarily for some, brings about progress and an improving life style for all; whereas stagnation leads to further stagnation and a diminished life style for all. Unions may succeed in resisting worker dislocation as a result of increased productivity and invention, which displace older equipment and modes of work organization. But the inevitable export of jobs to cheaper and more efficient foreign producers and the economic stagnation that such strategies produce result in the very displacement that the unions are trying to prevent.

Nowhere is the ineffectuality of this process more apparent than in the results of cost-of-living adjustments in the private sector. By some poetic justice, the unhappy choice of accepting either wage cuts or job cuts has fallen first to the auto industry, the very industry that initiated these adjustments after several years of post–World War II struggle with its unions. When in 1950 Chrysler instituted cost-of-living indexing, the move was hailed as a sign of pioneering industrial policy. In a sense it was. It ended a years-old round of industrial disputes. From 1946 on, after pressing vainly for governmental anti-inflationary measures, the larger CIO unions in the auto, steel, electrical-equipment, and meat-packing industries had conducted a series of strikes to win wage increases about equal to the price of inflation.[11] Although even then it was apparent that wage increases were no protection against inflation, since prices did not stabilize, indexing seemed "capable" of keeping auto workers happy and their living standard ever rising, regardless of their output or of the effect these contracts would have on their employers' competitive standing.

In fact, what they initiated was, and had to be, a fool's paradise. It is a tribute to the supremacy of the American auto industry at the time, and to the vast competitive edge it enjoyed, that the move seemed to work at all. But all it did in those years of prosperity, high industrial profits, and full employment was institutionalize the same round of wage-and-price spirals that had gone before, only this time without strikes and conflict.

So it is only natural that the industry that accepted this contract, which was mathematically contradictory over any significant period, should have been the one forced to lay off the largest number of union members, the one not only to lose its competitive edge when foreign car markets intruded upon American auto sales, but to jeopardize its ability to survive. Management and labor, who entered this Faustian compact of promising to pay for what they should not and ultimately could not pay for, were finally called to an accounting.

JAPAN: THE REAL SECRET OF SUCCESS

Germany and Japan have shown both productivity and wage increases that outstripped ours in the 1970s. After adjustments for inflation, wages increased by 63 percent in Germany and 54 percent in Japan, against 11 percent for the United States.[12]

The immediate reason is obvious. A Japanese auto worker produces an average of seventy-four cars in the time it takes an American to produce eleven! Workers keep at the job consistently, without strikes, demands for increased wages, pensions, vacations. Their unions do not resist modernization, change, or productivity improvements.

This much-envied application and docility does not stem from individual or even cultural differences, or from the homogeneity of the work force. It lies in the structure of incentives. Japanese workers have lifetime employment and seniority-based wages. (Their wages are also significantly lower than those of American workers—a tradeoff for job security.) One might expect that guaranteed tenure and seniority would militate against hard work, just as guaranteed raises in unions tend to. But these incentives have quite another effect: technical progress threatens neither jobs nor raises. In fact, the worker has a direct economic stake in maximizing his own productivity and embracing change, because half the typical worker's wages come in the form of semiannual bonuses that are contingent upon profits.[13]

The incentives of job security and profit-based wages are almost the opposite of our own system of indexing and wage—not job—security. The American worker has little stake in his or her company's success. His raises are guaranteed, not linked to productivity, and his income is guaranteed, in periods of unemployment, by a combination of company, union, and government benefits. Since little in this environment relates his rewards to his contributions, it is hard to induce increased effort or cooperation when technical innovations or productivity changes are introduced.

Not that all our productivity problems can be laid at the door of labor. In the service sector, productivity is lower—and harder to define, much of it not being quantifiable. Management productivity and the organization of work are also critical, particularly in our older companies as they become increasingly bureaucratized and develop layers of administration. In certain private utilities, with their guaranteed profits and government-regulated increases (which really constitute a form of indexing), there is little or no incentive to keep costs low. These firms contribute to inflation through their monopoly and guaranteed return on investment. In a utility company like Consolidated Edison of New York, is not the incentive to be less efficient, to undertake less effort, to make room for higher salaries and more employees, administrators and executives, more total assets and personnel, to enhance the power of top management? You find the same patterns in our banks and in the defense industry.

Nor can we forever extol the virtues of the Japanese labor force and the myths of employer-worker fealty. The actual course of Japanese capital-labor relations has had a rocky history, with its share of labor disputes. Moreover, even the model worker cannot compete with the productivity of capital. One new piece of industrial machinery can produce more than fifty dedicated Japanese workers.

How, then, have Japan and other countries managed to avoid the fate and the fears of our own? One answer is government planning. In direct contradiction to the claims of some of our own business leaders, wage improvement, better quality control, and higher productivity can all be achieved with government involvement more active than ours, and are being achieved in economies that are far more heavily regulated than ours.

The United States is by far the least regulated of all industrialized countries. Others generally have a large nationalized government sector, especially in utilities, steel, and autos. Germany has its Volkswagen, France its Renault, Britain its steel industry. Many foreign governments are also involved in central planning. The government is often the main source of capital investment funds, and can control as it lends. The most extreme case (short of the socialist examples) is Japan, where most investment funds directly or indirectly flow through government channels. Social-welfare legislation and environmental protection are also typically stronger in these countries.

It is thus trivial to warn of the inevitable pitfalls of government regulation when other countries with greater degrees of intervention are flourishing in terms of productivity. Regulations in themselves have no inherent relationship to economic growth or decline. They can be managed to stimulate economic growth, as they are in Japan, or to slow expansion along the lines of the no-growth school. It all depends on one's goals.

Japan again is a sterling example. Unlike the United States, which has enormous domestic natural resources and fertile and productive agricultural farmland, Japan has few natural resources and must even import virtually all of its oil. Yet it succeeds in controlling inflation far better than does the United States. It enjoys a very positive balance of payments in contrast to our enormous negative balance of payments. It resists the international competition for funds, keeping interest rates low to protect the domestic economy. These differences are attributable to management and planning by the government leadership. Government and business, and labor as well, have a far less adversarial relationship than they do in America.

The Japanese tradition of government's fostering and often leading and setting goals for development has a long history. Japan joined the industrial race late; in the late nineteenth century she sent her students abroad and began to copy Western technology. The government aggressively pushed development, building railroads and utilities, putting heavy taxes on the gains in land value that resulted from agricultural innovation, and permitting a few energetic, wealthy families to develop vast industrial empires while the population was made to work hard to earn a living. In a few decades, without relying on net foreign investment and loans, Japan became a first-ranking military and industrial power, by-passing the laborious processes of discovery and invention as she learned from the West by imitation. After World War II, the process was deliberately accelerated, not only by our foreign aid but by Truman's Point Four program of 1949, which promised to share our technical knowledge with underdeveloped countries. From 1953 to 1973, Japan grew at a rate more than twice the average of ten North American and European countries and great-ly exceeded the rate of any one of them. Although that rate must level off, Japan's long-term growth rate is expected to continue to surpass our own. [14]

That spectacular record need not be attributed to labor, al-though labor cooperation is a strong component. But we can for-get the homogeneity, reliability, and loyalty of the labor force when, as has been pointed out, one good piece of capital equip-ment can outperform tens and hundreds of hard-working, dedicat-ed employees. More important is the fact that Japan, like Germany, started after World War II with relatively new produc-tive facilities—ironically, with our assistance—and (again like Germany) was not required or inclined to address any meaningful part of its productive energies to noncapital-building defense spending. Its high savings rate, 22 percent of personal after-tax income, compared with our 5.5 percent, prepares individuals for retirement while providing funds for public and private invest-ment. [15] It allocates 18 percent of its GNP to investment in fixed capital, as against 6 percent for the United States. And it does not tax capital gains. [16]

On top of that, the Japanese, to a degree that Germany does not match, understand economics, planning, and marginality. They understand targeting to achieve what they want. Govern-ment serves as an integral part of business, functioning as com-mercial banker, investment banker, manpower mobilizer, protectionist, and subsidizer. Together with business, govern-ment targets an industry that seems to offer opportunity. Then it provides the funds at unusually attractive subsidized rates, grants a monopoly to one firm, or at most an oligopoly to a few, so that

237

it or they will achieve the immediate benefits of mass production—with the latest equipment and without the resistance to
technologically superior productive improvements that might dramatically reduce the number of needed employees and that in other cases and locales lead to massive union resistance. Thus the
company can sell all its output in Japan. Without competition
and with low-cost capital, it can produce the greatest output with
the least fixed overhead, and become the lowest-cost, and, by definition, most efficient producer. At that point it can immediately
compete effectively for the overseas markets.

The government, to achieve this end, which it sees as desirable
and socially useful in that it provides domestic employment (a
present-day form of mercantilism), does whatever it must to be
helpful. It provides (often hidden) subsidies, such as lower interest
costs and higher payouts, to the company for the other products
that it may purchase from it, so that the company becomes more
profitable at a lower break-even point. With lower unit costs, the
firm can then sell more cheaply abroad, despite the high shipping
costs to distant places. It can outprice all its rivals and, in a sort of
self-fulfilling prophecy, thereby take the lion's share of the market.

Of course, Japan negotiates with the United States and other
countries to reduce its exports in a constant charade that works,
remarkably enough, in the meanwhile maintaining its own array
of onerous import barriers so that the same outside competitors
cannot get even a fair shot at competing in its market to reduce
their own unit prices and thus make themselves more competitive.

The Japanese understand basic economics. And their government, together with the business community, translates that understanding into actions that achieve the goals it desires. In this
way it can and will, absent countervailing actions on the part of
the United States or the Common Market, take a major, even pre-
dominant, share of any market that it chooses to pursue.

At the same time, and by virtue of its strategic position and
power, the government is in a position to provide a variety of incentives to achieve quality controls. It can order steel mills to reduce air pollution without providing detailed regulations. If the

firms do not voluntarily comply, they will soon be in trouble with the banks.

Finally, Japan seems to be more amenable to making long-term investment and to lower returns on investment in order to achieve and establish its goals of market dominance, in contrast to American executives who are trained to look at the short-term bottom line. In 1979, the average net return on investment in Japan amounted to 10.3 percent; in the United States the figure for that year was 16.9 percent. "If one excludes the losses of our mismanaged automobile and steel industries, the latter figure would be still higher," writes Wassily Leontief. "In other words, the Japanese companies are ready to expand so long as they can expect to recover in full the new investment over seven years, while their American counterparts will not move unless they can count on profits after four-and-a-half years."[17]

To be sure, our companies are crippled by high interest rates that not only hinder investment but dictate the projects to be risked. Our government policies not only reduce the rate of return on capital, reducing the marginal productivity of labor in the process, but neglect to sponsor new companies which provide the majority of new jobs and the lion's share of our major innovations—over 50 percent between 1953 and 1973, and over twenty-four times as many, per research dollar, as the large companies, according to an Office of Management and Budget study. So wedded are cabinet-level officials to their present habits and patronage patterns that they strenuously protested a recent proposal to grant a token 1 percent of the research funds of government agencies with large ($100 million plus) R&D budgets to small companies grossing less than $25 million a year.[18]

If we are to emulate Japan's productivity, we must recognize that it has been achieved despite government intervention and regulation more stringent than ours, despite wages growing faster than ours, and despite the strict quality controls that we abhor. The key has been strategic and intelligent planning based on sound economics. If we are to address ourselves to the solution of our problems, we must orient ourselves to targeted planning in pursuit of specific social goals.

NOTES

1. William M. Batten, "A Time of Opportunity, a Time of Danger," *The Economy of 1981: A Bipartisan Look,* New York Stock Exchange, 1981.

2. Samuelson, *Economics,* 11th ed., 671.

3. Daniel Yankelevich, *Economic Policy and the Question of Political Will,* New York, Public Agenda Foundation, 1980, 22–24.

4. Arthur Housburg (President, Con Ed), "The Politicos' Contribution to Electric Rates," *New York Times,* May 15, 1981, A30; "Utility Rates: New Political Dynamite," *U.S. News and World Report,* April 30, 1979, 45; *Statistical Abstract,* 1979, 100th ed., Table 1319., 754.

5. Thurow, *Zero-Sum Society,* 39.

6. Craig Bond Hatfield, "Big Oil's Not the Foe," *New York Times,* February 18, 1981, A31.

7. Lipsey and Steiner, *Macroeconomics,* 90; Samuelson, *Economics,* 11th ed., 3.

8. Jude Wanniski, *The Way the World Works,* New York, Simon and Schuster, 1978, 58–59, 66–67.

9. Samuelson, *Economics,* 11th ed., 3, 185.

10. Neil Orloff, "Rethinking Environmental Law," *New York Times,* May 10, 1981, Sec. 3, 3; "Supporters of Regulatory Reforms Moving to Trim Agencies' Powers," by Martin Tolchin, *New York Times,* July 13, 1981.

11. Faulkner, *American Economic History,* 718–19.

12. "The U.S. Wage Woes," *New York Times,* March 8, 1981, Sec. 3, 18F.

13. Thurow, *Zero-Sum Society,* 84.

14. Samuelson, *Economics,* 11th ed., 665; Lipsey and Steiner, *Macroeconomics,* 416.

15. Steve Lohr, "In Tokyo, Anxiety Over Growth," *New York Times International Economic Survey,* February 14, 1982, 32.

16. Peterson, "No More Free Lunch," 58.

17. Wassily Leontief, "Supply Side May Not Be on America's Side," *New York Times,* April 5, 1981, Sec. 4, E20.

18. "Government Opposes R&D Percentage for Small Businesses," *Electronic Design,* August 6, 1981, 50; "Entrepreneurs Set the Pace in New Technologies," *Medical Device Regulatory Briefcase,* vol. 5, no. 6, June 1980, 1.

12

Planning: Strategies for Growth

If we are to mobilize our resources for planning that will not dominate, it is essential that we set up agencies that will diagnose and suggest solutions to be carried out by other, existing government departments and agencies, so that the agencies themselves do not acquire a vested interest in their own expansion and thereby intrude on private-sector freedom.

Some fear that such measures would lead to a planned economy, with government subsidizing weak, politically targeted spending programs, and with heavy-handed regulation. Ironically, this seems to have been the pattern of our current government sponsorship. It is certainly no necessary outcome if the planning agency is designated as a catalyst for, and not the state "owner" or administrator of, the social programs it suggests. A committee appointed by the president to develop plans that the president and Congress would translate into legislative programs is hardly a totalitarian nightmare.

GOALS, PRIORITIES, AND POLITICAL SCHIZOPHRENIA

The first premise of our guiding economic philosophy is that we obviously have goals. We also have priorities, or hierarchies, in the urgency of their achievement. These tenets seem simple enough, even trite, but they are rarely adopted in public policy. For if we adopt such a perspective, we must look first at long-term goals and not dally with political expediency or the desire for political self-preservation that pull us in contrary and inconsistent directions.

If we don't define our goals, we can't establish priorities. And if we don't establish priorities, we often try to accomplish everything at once, with the result that we generate conflicting, contradictory actions that are counterproductive to our most critical efforts.

Why, for example, do the traditional counterinflationary programs of inducing recession, increasing unemployment, and slowing growth no longer efficiently work? Economists have always been confident about such actions, and elementary logic supports their validity. These proven remedies no longer work because we have introduced *counter*-counterinflationary programs that automatically come into play to neutralize the counterinflationary programs we are trying to activate. Our policies are so schizophrenic, trying to achieve everything at once, that our actions contradict our desired objectives.

If our goal is to defeat inflation, that goal calls for government action that will really let us lower prices. We must establish the *priority,* so that, even if lower prices may and undoubtedly will hurt people's incomes—for instance the farmer's—short-term pain must be tolerated for the sake of the longer-term objective of more stable prices and a healthier total economy. This objective calls for lowering or eliminating the supports that keep prices up or at least keep them from falling.

But our policy follows quite the opposite tack. We recognize that farmers need more income to stay even with inflation. So the government raises farm price supports, ensuring the persistence of inflation.

In the same vein, the government fritters away money and credit availability in mutually contradictory measures. In spring 1980, terrified at the prospect of inflation at 17 percent, it instituted severe monetary controls and restrictions on consumer spending to slow down consumer demand and bring prices down. Yet just as its policy appeared to be taking hold, it suddenly saw that what it sought to induce was actually occurring. Consumer spending was slowing down, as was the economy, but to such a degree that the administration was frightened by the slowdown or recession, a condition that of course is never popular, and that the government, had it had any sense of perspective, should have known from the start would occur and be unpopular. So it immediately took contradictory actions. It made consumer credit readily available, assuring the complete uselessness of its earlier and potentially effective counterinflationary actions. In summer 1981, under Reagan, it seemed that almost the same pattern was being repeated, as periodic spurts in the money supply canceled out the effects of interest rates that month after month reached unprecedented heights.

To defeat inflation, some costs, some wages, some prices must not only stop rising, but must go down, to offset others that will inevitably continue to rise. To this end, government must actually encourage and stimulate such a trend. It should not act, as it usually does, to protect and insulate everyone from such a possibility: farmers with price supports, Social Security recipients with indexing that even exceeds the inflation rate, government employees with wage increases. These acts and many others not only support and ensure continuing inflation, but—because they entail spending and deficits and in turn push up interest rates (a cost that goes into almost every single product)—give inflation another push. If the government did let prices fall or took steps to push them down, it would *quickly* halt inflation!

Unless we establish goals and set a specific order of priorities to achieve them, we will continue, as did the Carter administration with its indecisiveness, to introduce contradictory and conflicting policies and actions that offset each other and often prove more damaging in the end than if nothing had been done. Because of this vacillation, the economic planning and policies of Carter's administration—and, in fact, of the entire professional economic community—forfeited credibility.

Reagan has been doing the same with defense spending. His initial priority was to check inflation and cut spending and taxes. He could not do all this and at the same time fulfill all the Pentagon's fantasies. He, too, is lashing out in all directions and neutralizing his first efforts.

The process began with a vengeance in spring 1981, with colossal deficit projections, treasury yields breaking record after record, and a "surprising" (such were the headlines) jump in the money supply. The failure even to approach a balanced budget, as increased defense spending offset budget cuts, precipitated an almost catastrophic rise in interest rates, which in turn raised the cost of funding the government's spending and debt to a point at which the increased cost quickly equaled almost half the painful social-program budget cuts. By almost completely negating the value of these hard-won economies, that expense jeopardized the benefits and viability of the Reagan tax cuts, which were designed to stimulate the economy as well as fight inflation through so-called supply-side economics. These tax incentives, coupled with the higher tax revenues that would result from the Laffer-curve effect of stimulated economic activity on the GNP, were to constitute the smaller slice of an ever-growing pie that would service the government's fiscal needs.

It could have worked. Had defense spending not been recklessly increased, Reagan's commitment to a balanced budget would have had an excellent chance of achieving its desired results. So much for *half*-baked plans. As it is, Reagan has since had to rescind some of his vaunted cutbacks through tax increases euphemistically termed revenue-enhancement.

The inability to set priorities also explains the enthusiastic rush to accept any seemingly new approach to economic problems—for example, the supply-side solution—in the face of continuing and escalating failure. Any theory that promises instant success gathers a following quickly, especially if it is served up as a curve—a Laffer curve, yet. It is the hope of the new burying the disgust with the old.

We cannot fulfill all goals at once. The values our goals embody may themselves be in conflict. Or they may compete with each other for limited resources or in decisions on what goods and services are to be produced and distributed. These decisions require tradeoffs. Any attempt to disregard this reality is counterproductive, and ultimately destructive of the very goals and objectives that idealists hope to accomplish.

THE LIMITS OF MACROECONOMIC POLICY

Current macroeconomic planning suffers from three major inadequacies. First, its strategies are mutually contradictory because they are not targeted. Second, it is indecisive about priorities, failing to choose which aspects of the business cycle and of GNP spending to address first. Finally, its countercyclical policies are not linked to the pursuit of long-term goals.

First, it must be recognized that macroeconomic planning is limited by the self-contradictory or self-equilibrating nature of economic processes. Economic events and policies themselves produce several effects, some of which can modify or even cancel out the effects of these policies.

Take these examples:

Full employment leads to inflation.

Full employment leads to recession.

As full employment and capacity utilization are approached, the incremental demand for more workers pushes wages up without increasing productivity, while the increased demand generated by high wages pushes prices up.

Yet in the slightly longer run, full employment and capacity utilization can lead to unemployment because an oversupply is produced. This is the internal dynamic of the business cycle.

Increased productivity leads to prosperity.

Increased productivity leads to unemployment and depression.

If the market cannot absorb the *added* output that improved productivity creates, the *same* output can be produced by fewer workers and some workers will eventually be displaced.

Increased savings lead to increased investment and prosperity.

Increased savings lead to reduced consumption and recession.

Part of the benefits of saving and investment are offset by reduced consumption.

High interest rates boost the value of the dollar abroad.

High interest rates lead to overvaluation of the dollar and a balance-of-payments deficit.

High interest rates lead to recession at home.

Recession comes about both because consumers buy more imports, reducing demand for domestic products, and because high interest rates discourage investment at home.

Low interest rates produce inflation; high interest rates check inflation. (Federal Reserve Board assumptions).

High interest rates produce inflation.

If investors and consumers continue to borrow, the increased cost will be built into the price of the product, while sustained demand, even if it is just to pay interest costs, will boost its prices further.

A tight money supply, or slow money growth, will raise interest rates.

A tight money policy makes money less and less available: increased competition for the more limited money supply raises its price—the cost of money or the interest rate.

A loose money supply policy, or fast growth of the money supply, will push up interest rates.

Easy money feeds inflation, forcing the federal government to raise interest rates and so harness borrowing and the money supply. The expectation that rapid money growth will accelerate inflation itself causes lenders to insist on a higher rate of return, or interest rate, in order to protect themselves against a deterioration of their "real" return.

Which causal sequence holds? Take, for example, demand and supply schedules, in which increased demand should lead to higher prices and increased supply to lower prices. Actually, the relationships are far more complicated. An increase in demand may reduce prices, or an increase in supply raise them. The intervening variable is elasticity. Yet economists, laymen, and especially politicians often defend one side of the question without taking these intervening factors into account.

In the area of monetary policy, in terms of a simple supply-demand model an increase in money should lead to lower interest rates. Instead we find that, with an unexpected increase in money supply, the prime rate rises, and the discount rate goes up to "check" the increase in money supply.

With our balance-of-payments policies, high interest rates support the dollar abroad yet shake the equilibrium of the domestic economy, both because of exorbitant interest rates and the impact on the price of exports, which become competitively prohibitive, generate domestic unemployment, and upset our balance of payments.

To address all problems at once is a virtual impossibility—like going forward and backward at the same time. Simultaneously slowing the economy to reduce inflation, and speeding it up to reduce unemployment is impossible. We *cannot* deal with these problems exclusively through macroeconomic strategies. The result, when we do that, only wreaks havoc, as side effects dampen or even cancel out these diffuse strategies. This is why a diffuse supply-side strategy will not in and of itself achieve its intended goal. We must deal with these problems on the microeconomic level through precisely targeted incentives. We can speed up *some* segments to increase employment and slow down *other* segments to reduce the level of inflation. By the same token, diffuse efforts

247

to cut the budget cannot work. Cutbacks in welfare and cutbacks in training and employment programs simply cannot be lumped together as reform measures. One program addresses the demand side, the other the supply side of the equation.

To give a few examples of potentially anti-inflationary policies that *would* employ the logic of the margin:

• *Social Security should be just that:* insurance against the contingency of starvation or confinement in a poorhouse that once attended poverty in old age. As insurance, it should be no more than a protection against that threat. It should not be an extra payment to those for whom, fortunately, society has provided enough opportunity and material wealth that they do not require it (see chapter 5).

• *Indexing,* if this inflationary measure must be used at all, *should not be across-the-board,* but should be targeted at the components that are producing inflation or the populations that suffer from it. Most Social Security recipients, who own their own homes, are not affected by mortgage rates and warrant no increase in benefits when these rates are high (see chapter 5).

• *Old age and disability payments should be taxed.* Our present regulations allow a doctor who retires after suffering a heart attack to live in his own home on investment income plus other pension and insurance plans, including Keogh and IRA, while collecting disability benefits keyed to his former substantial earnings. A chronic schizophrenic who, with drugs and doctors' assistance, manages to work for twenty to thirty years and suffers a nervous breakdown, gets nothing.
His work experience does not qualify him for disability insurance. On the contrary, it proves he can work, and he is defined as "mildly" or "moderately" disabled on a scale of three. To be "severely" disabled on that scale of three, the person must require hospitalization; otherwise, his taxes have gone merely to subsidize the doctor's retirement. Since the physician, despite his lost po-

tential income, is well provided for, taxing his benefits would release some funds for others and remove some of the financial
strains on the system.

• *A sales or value-added tax should be imposed* as a direct means to
check demand and encourage savings. This tax is hardly as regressive as critics make it appear, and it has been widely adopted in
socialist countries, as well as in much of Western Europe. To
shield the poor, food and other necessities can be exempted from
taxation.

• *When single nonrecurring events produce shortages and high prices,* as
often happens in the case of foods—the increase in the wholesale
price index in August 1980 as a result of drought is one example—*emergency aid should be directed at the source,* not passed along
and built in permanently through cost-of-living adjustments and
price increases to create a multiplier inflationary effect.

• *The present measures of harsh contraction of business credit and activity, or inflationary fiscal and monetary strategies, each confront only one
horn of the dilemma.* Credit rationing, especially if targeted at consumers, would have the same effect without the consequences of
high interest rates, which exaggerate inflation and the severity of
ensuing decline (see chapter 8).

• Under present policies, *farmers' parity simply increases the levels of
price supports,* passing these increases along to everyone down the
line, with tremendous inflationary impact. The much-heralded
cancellation of dairy price supports in the spring of 1981 was a
stopgap that did not in any way modify the system of virtually
automatic semiannual price increases.

By law, dairy prices are pegged at 80 percent of parity, a figure
based on the purchasing power of farmers in 1914. That price is
adjusted twice a year, in April and October. By 1981 the prices of
dairy products had risen over 40 percent in three years, well above
the inflation rate as measured by the indexes of which they are a
critical component. They cost the government $1.8 billion in
1980–81. With guaranteed price supports, farmers are not only

immune to the vagaries of the market but produce large surpluses that the government is committed to buy up at inflated prices and store.[1] *Instead, government supports for farmers should go directly to the farmers, reimbursing* them *without raising the support prices,* which only flow a higher price to each consumer and affect the CPI, with its far-reaching consequences for all prices.

• *If the goal is to increase the quantity of a given crop* and thereby reduce its price to the consumer, *the farmer can be paid directly a bonus subsidy* of, say, $1 a bushel. Or, if government wants to assure farmers a decent minimum income, it can adjust their tax rates or even introduce negative tax rates, so that in a bad year the government provides the farmer some minimal "decent" income. This approach, directed at farmers income and not their prices, would not build price inflation into farm products and would at the same time ensure farmers' security. It could even be used to provide profit incentives for farmers to produce specific crops that have been defined as socially desirable.

• *Defense spending is intrinsically as inflationary as are transfer payments* and for much the same reason. Both consume our resources without adding to our productive output or standard of living (see chapters 4 and 7).

We can economize on defense spending without raising the issues of effective negotiation and diplomacy or the requisite level of overkill that our national defense program demands. The trouble with defense is not money, but muddling. The psychology that anything goes results in both sloppy cost estimates and in sloppy planning and strategy. Our embarrassments in Iran and Afghanistan did not stem from military weakness, nor did their resolution hinge on our military strength. The conflict in El Salvador raises the same issues as the Vietnam War, and threatens the same domestic conflict. Again without debating the ideological merits of another war, we may ask: If it is not worth the necessary sacrifice—*a shift to a war economy*—is it, even on economic grounds, worth fighting?

Our defense program combines a religious approach to spending with a secular, expedient approach to recruitment. The armed forces, seeking ever more tantalizing incentives for trainees, lure many who are not employable elsewhere and whose commitment to a military career is dubious. In Detroit, the erstwhile guaranteed reservoir of jobs for local untrained manpower, the only remaining hope for unskilled high-school graduates, now cut off from work in the auto industry, is the military.

It is high time that we displaced a mercenary army and turned to a peacetime military draft. We would regain a cross-section of our population, cut down sharply on escalating military personnel costs, restore some measure of efficiency, and offer training to the less-skilled who could then return, with the benefits of discipline and further education, to the civilian sector. Not least, we would reduce the burden of the deficit and of defense spending, which is now the most inflationary component of our budget.

None of these proposals takes a new approach to government. They simply apply common sense and some supply-side logic to old and trusted measures that need to be dusted off. We would do well, in fact, to review some old ideas before adopting the supply-side nostrums professed, or some of the ruinous Thatcher policies now practiced in England.

Macroeconomic policies have consistently failed to focus on which aspects of the business cycle and of GNP to target. We should, for example, take another look at old-fashioned Keynesian principles. Some supply-side economists, along with other critics of the welfare system, tend to stereotype Keynesianism, equating it with loose credit, government spending to solve all ills, and huge deficits that permanently increase government taxes. Yet true Keynesian economics has seldom been applied. It was supposed to be a two-sided strategy, with government filling in the demand gap in depression and stepping out of the picture when crisis subsided. It even implied creating surpluses when the demand side was overheated to counteract the disequilibrium by slowing down the other side.

Despite lip-service to Keynesianism, government has not followed this policy. Had it done so, government spending would have followed a countercyclical pattern, rising when business slowed and declining with recovery, rather than reaching new higher plateaus as a percent of GNP after every recession (see chapters 4 and 9).

We should consider surplus-side as well as supply-side economics as a means of curing inflation. Just as deficit spending is a recognized remedy for curing recession by stimulating demand, so a budget surplus is one of the more effective remedies for curing inflation, because it smothers demand that would otherwise escalate. The logic of Keynesian economics prevails!

We require no *a priori* commitment to a balanced budget *or* to deficit spending. More important than either surpluses or deficits are the incentives that will produce the desired multiplier effect. A deficit *at the appropriate time* is healthy fiscal policy. More government outlay than income helps cushion recession. As tax receipts decline in an economic slowdown, while welfare and unemployment expenditures rise, the budget is bound to be unbalanced.

The key to appropriate strategy is the use government makes of its fiscal weapons and tax policy to stimulate or restrain activity in the private economy. Success will depend on the spending priorities it establishes through policies that carry out longer-term social goals. The resources it uses as incentives should have a multiplier effect in the private economy that is greater and, ideally, several times greater, than if government merely threw a given amount of money, or the equivalent, tax forgiveness, at the problem.

In other words, government, by its policies or programs, should maximize the cost-benefit effect of a given specific deficit amount, not merely count up the deficit in dollar terms. Small differences, signals to the private sector, can make large differences—jawboning small declines in interest rates, or diminishing the borrowing costs for specific projects, particularly priority projects. Pursuing such a course requires no new philosophy of government. The government has already initiated such incentives as the investment tax credit, has favored attractive interest rates for veterans, for FHA housing, for farm crops. It has even engaged in such counterproductive measures as paying farmers to keep acreage idle.

Our supply-side and monetary strategies operate at cross purposes because they address different phases of the business cycle. Supply-side measures (much like Keynesian measures) are antidepression strategies. Tax cuts, easy fiscal policy, low interest rates, and investment incentives are all addressed to reviving the economy. They are also anti-inflationary to the extent that they encourage investment more than consumption yet keep demand at levels high enough to spark business optimism.

Our monetary policy, however, has robbed the supply-side model of its essential ingredient, low interest rates. The result is that its chance for success is diminished or destroyed. In polar opposition to supply-side measures, our monetary policy stresses tightly controlled money supply growth, a stringent anti-inflationary strategy, reducing GNP growth, creating depression in its wake. By restricting available money and keeping interest rates high, it curtails capital spending (which is crowded out, in any case, by unrelenting government spending) and chokes off the demand side completely. With business operating at 60 percent of capacity, there can be no motive to invest.

• *Our present countercyclical policies are not linked to the pursuit of long-range goals.* There is a tendency, when things are going well, to become buoyant, to believe that conditions will persist indefinitely. The function of mature leadership is to recognize the fallacy of this all-too-human failing, following the prescience of Joseph in Egypt, who saw that seven good years would be followed by seven bad.

The government can ease the volatility and violence of disequilibrium by acting as a countercyclical force not only in crises but in periods of normalcy. We have reached a stage where poverty resulting from nature's parsimony should be extinct. To prepare for shortages and for recession, the government should store food during periods of plenty so that it will be available to the people in hard times, evening out the price volatility and fluctuations of disequilibrium. The government can exercise a psychological countervailing power as well as an economic one. The populace would be braced by the knowledge that "this, too, shall pass."

By contrast, the present warehousing of grain serves not the country but the special interest farming groups. It is linked to parity policy, whose function is to keep the price of wheat high (not stable); to carrying out transactions like the Russian wheat sales that are calculated to support and even raise prices; and to promises to use grain reserves for export only so that domestic prices for grain will not be permitted to fall. The result is rationing by price elasticity, by large price increases that leave many, especially those at the lower end of the economic ladder, compelled to do without.

• *The Strategic Oil Reserve should exist as more than a fiction.* No effort is being made to augment our reserves despite an oil glut and temporarily attractive prices. At a time when we should be planning for free energy independence, our government appears to be waiting for a crisis.

• *Even more urgently do we need unemployment policies that mesh with our long-term goals.* We must see that what Reagan calls the social safety net, and what Roosevelt stressed in his 1944 address to Congress—a decent job, health care, food, and education—are provided without the inflationary, debilitating, and, in the end, sterile consequences of our benefit programs. Our policies have followed the Depression tradition of providing basic income security without adequately developing such job-creating and constructive programs as the WPA and CCC. Now that we no longer suffer depression of the same magnitude, we can look to more productive alternatives in job creation and job training that overcome the present built-in limitations and resistance. This problem will not be resolved merely by social spending cutbacks that weed out the inefficiencies of the system. In fact, some of these cutbacks may make inequities even more inevitable, if the distribution of benefits becomes increasingly policitized and operates to favor people who have know-how, while eliminating the naive.

Welfare may be cheaper than creating a more skilled labor force, which is one reason why welfare policies persist. But jobs and manpower training are the only productive solution for the individual and society. My own endorsement is for government-subsidized, if need be heavily subsidized, apprenticeships in private industry. The long-term benefits have a multiplier effect, creating taxpayers rather than tax consumers and giving people a sense of self-worth and pride, while welfare subsidies only waste and drain our resources. *Work* can be subsidized to prevent layoffs; unemployment benefits should be prorated in terms of tenure on the job; and funds can be provided for retraining workers in a company or an industry (see chapter 6).

But more than that, we desperately need policies that coordinate subsistence and employment programs. We cannot afford to make do, as we do, with separate and fragmented agencies involved with welfare, surplus labor, the constructive use of the variously disabled, job training, and job creation. Nor can we limit ourselves to the futile alternatives of either tolerating unconscionably high levels of unemployment or granting emergency assistance. These are short-term answers to problems that must be dealt with in the broader context of long-term social planning.

TOWARD A HUMANISTIC-INDUSTRIAL COMPLEX

Let us start by defining our direction as one that moves us from a military-industrial to a humanistic-industrial complex. There are certain goods and services that we can all agree we need in greater measure. Some are so basic to our well-being that we can define them as part of our national interest. They include:

EDUCATION
We must upgrade our educational efforts to meet the growing challenge of Japan and other nations in mathematics, science, engineering, and vocational training.

ENERGY
We need both
NEW SOURCES of energy and
CONSERVATION EFFORTS—superior motors and redesigned equipment.

In the field of
MEDICAL RESEARCH
We need basic research in such critical areas as:
CANCER PREVENTION, TREATMENT, and CURES,
AGING and DEGENERATIVE DISEASES, and
HEART DISEASE.
In the related area of
HEALTH SERVICES TO SOCIETY
We must work to provide both more
DOCTORS and
MORE EFFICIENT AND INEXPENSIVE PATIENT
CARE.
We must also produce more, better, and safer
INDIVIDUAL and MASS TRANSPORTATION, entailing
FEWER DEATHS,
LESS POLLUTION,
LESS ENERGY WASTE.
We must rebuild and enhance our deteriorating INFRA-
STRUCTURE, our bridges, roads, tunnels, sewer systems, and
ports.

To create the proper incentives, we should favor those owners and workers in enterprises engaged in the most socially useful work. Tax incentives in these targeted areas, by permitting the highest after-tax yields, would permit employers in these industries to pay their workers higher wages and adopt socially beneficial quality and environmental controls.

By the same token, we must recognize that certain economic activities cannot be left to the free play of market forces alone, without guidance and regulation. Some are socially useful but too costly to be assumed by voluntary effort alone. Some are not only too costly but too *important* to be left to the private sector with its necessary emphasis on profits—necessary, of course, because the private firm that ignores the profit criterion destroys itself, and hence its own capacity for further useful activity.

In such essential areas, business may anticipate only an indirect, remote payoff, since a high degree of intellectual and financial risk of failure is involved. One such area is defense. Other areas include research and development in atomic and other forms of energy; space travel and exploration; medical research on illnesses like cancer and heart disease; population control and optimal population growth; and pollution control. Here the public good is most effectively pursued through direct strategic intervention rather than by exclusive reliance on free markets. For these areas we need massive all-out efforts, even overkill, to achieve our goals. Throwing dollars at certain problems that are amenable to solution, expending funds along with the best intellectual power and dedicated effort we can muster, is a strategy that *does* work.

Through these activities, we want to ensure for each human being a better quality of life—freedom from famine and hunger, from war and nuclear holocaust, from plague and disease, from environmental destruction, from air and water pollution, from over-all diminishing satisfaction.

We want to ensure a different kind of freedom—freedom from self-destruction, from external arbitrary tyranny. For our future generations of children we want to ensure the right to a good life, and the realization of their potential and the riches that this earth can offer. We want to minimize the tragedy of wasted human resources and grant each individual economic dignity, the right to earn his way and take pride in some social contribution.

Such an approach does not commit us to a zero-sum game, which entails redistribution within a fixed and static frame; it *will* require the sacrifice of present benefits for the sake of future rewards. There is always a tradeoff between current consumption and sacrifice for the future. As our ubiquitous production-possibility models show, just as the frontier of economic growth may move outward, its curve illustrates the tradeoffs—between guns and butter, between public and private spending, between consumption and investment. We cannot expand in all directions at once. Progress is a function of commitment to the desired change, the commitment of present resources to a better future. Our axiom might be: the greater the present sacrifice, the more rapid the advance toward that goal and the more certain its achievement.

This delaying of immediate gratification-consumption strategy holds as much for a developed people requiring a quantum jump in the development of energy resources as it does for a developing nation on the verge of what Robert Heilbroner calls "the great ascent." If you help underdeveloped countries merely with exported food or consumer goods, and do nothing to impel social and attitudinal change, you may improve the present life style of the people, but you will do little to help them take off on their ascent. You will create parasites, not self-sustaining individuals. Similarly, if, on the domestic front, you provide the poor with income maintenance and don't encourage work, so that they can move toward their own individual takeoff, you create dependents without solving their problems.

As the analogy to economic development suggests, the way out of our crisis lies in shifting priorities from the maintenance of a domestic colony to a focus on capital formation and the encouragement of self-reliance. The former is a permanent drain, entailing a permanent sacrifice. The latter has at least a net benefit: investment in capital goods makes possible more of *both* goods— consumption and capital—in the future.

This is an optimistic strategy for growth, not merely for redistribution. It entails paying the premiums necessary to ensure growth and the generation of renewed productivity and job creation to produce the larger pie from which all may better partake.

• A presidential and congressional Office of Essential or Critical Priorities should be set up and charged with the functions of defining socially desirable national goals, whether "profitable" or not, and assessing their place and cost in relation to other critical variables. Several years ago Mark Shepherd, Jr., Chairman of Texas Instruments, suggested the establishment of a Board for National Objectives that would initiate ideas and the development of a long-range viewpoint among political leaders. The board would include former political leaders and representatives of labor, management, and the general public. With all the commissions in existence, there is none so far that has systematically defined a national plan or set of goals, or that has had the kind of input that could effect significant change.

• To help carry out these priorities, an *American Service Corps* should launch a national jobs program, gearing its activities to the long-term goals of the Office of Critical Priorities and providing one constructive approach to the problem of wasted human resources. It would deal with the various issues related to youth unemployment, individuals on welfare, recruits from the population of older citizens. Needless to say, the program would absorb many of the unemployed, so that the jobless rate would be reduced and with it the fears and often harmful policy reactions that that emotional statistic tends to generate.

The American Service Corps would be an extension of the draft—a form of universal national service that is not confined to military training. Like the Peace Corps, it would be an alternative or supplement to the military draft, but it would be domestic. Like VISTA, it would engage in public-service activities at home, except that it would be not volunteer work, but service owed to the country, and it would function not as a kind of supplementary social work, but in a variety of services and occupations deemed socially useful. As an employer of last resort, it would keep people from being wasted, absorb the unemployed into training programs, put the reservoir of surplus labor to work. In order not to compete with the private sector, it would operate with low wages, as the draft did, and possibly with a maximum wage, as the CETA programs have. Moreover, oriented to socially defined and not strictly economic (that is, profit-making) priorities, it would provide a constructive training program and a vehicle for performing desired social tasks.

Such an agency could promote apprenticeship programs (see chapter 6) and provide scholarships for trade skills and job training or retraining, in a simple extension of the scholarships the federal government has provided for college and graduate education. Indeed, scholarship funds for vocational training programs can provide social benefits as great as those derived from college and graduate education. Future professional elites, who look forward to ample income, should be helped with college loans rather than with outright subsidies when we are confronted with such massive training needs for the hard-to-employ.

• When we evaluate our employment policies and their effort on unemployment figures, we should analyze also the real impact of bringing down unemployment through indiscriminate stimulative policies. *A macroeconomic approach that tries to draw upon every last marginally productive worker only produces inflation without providing any real benefits* in terms of increased meaningful production.

What we must analyze in all such cases is the incremental cost—the marginal increase required to employ each less productive, less experienced, less trained, perhaps even less reliable or less disciplined person. What fiscal and/or monetary stimulus is required to bring about the next one-quarter of a percent reduction in unemployment (or so-called "unemployment")? What would be the inflationary impact? And how much real productivity, in terms of GNP increase, is added as you draw upon the less skilled? Such analysis, it need hardly be added, should be applied to measuring the inflationary impact of any government action.

• Lest it seem that I am trying to develop a pool of low-level inexpensive labor, let me add that *these strategies should extend to professional training.* If we are to address supply-side economics seriously, it must be applied consistently and geared also to increasing the pool of skilled and professional labor in critical fields.

Medicine now suffers a severe shortage of doctors. One of the major causes of the ever-rising costs of drugs, hospitals, and doctors is an almost total lack of economic price competition. The American Medical Association maintains a licensed, tightly rationed professional monopoly while trying to persuade us, in the face of reality, that we already have too many doctors.

Instead of permitting these subsidized medical costs to mount, or allowing cruel retrenchments on services that the poor can neither afford nor forgo, the supply of services to poor communities should be expanded through scholarships linked to field service in poor areas. These scholarships would have a broader purpose than providing opportunity for bright and indigent students, opportunities that would only increase competition for a limited pool of positions. It would require an expansion of available openings in medical school.

If necessary, some autonomous agency could be set up. The need for medical personnel in the military, which existing ROTC fellowships do not fill, can provide such an opportunity. What if a military medical school were to train personnel to meet its own needs? Volunteers to such an effort would serve for ten years in the military service, then would be free to work as physicians in the civilian sector. This approach can be extended to programs serving the poor or elderly. The only ones likely to object, and they have done this effectively so far, are the members of the medical profession, which has thrived on the combined inflationary strategies of restricted supplies and subsidized demand (Medicare and Medicaid) and stoutly resisted all other government aid to medicine, such as the building or expansion of medical schools and facilities to satisfy the rising subsidized demand. Here, as in other fields, professional monopolies should be resisted, at the very least with the sponsorship of greater opportunity for the education of future competitors.

These cases show how government intervention can be used, not to create a socialistic state, but to recreate and implement the conditions of more perfect competition. We must restore a situation in which supply meets demand, the only sane situation in which medical services can be applied with efficiency and economy.

• *A targeted manpower policy must abandon global Phillips-curve concepts,* which mask a variety of disparate elements in confusing aggregate statistics, and address these problems in terms of microeconomic factors. Were the unemployment level alone and its tradeoff the only factor in inflation, the problem could never have reached its recent dimensions. Union demands, medical costs, the professional fees of doctors, lawyers, accountants, and advertising men, all adding to production and consumption costs, are also responsible for inflation and even for our decline in productivity as measured. To develop unemployment policies based upon noninflationary principles, we must recognize that, with many socially useful projects remaining to be carried out, a marginal increase in one sector will not have the same inflationary impact that it might in another.

The present "targeting" of certain aid to high-unemployment areas is not an adequate approach. It creates "make-work" jobs, is easily politicized, and often supplants local funding of the same jobs. Geographic targeting is a beginning, but it does not address long-term goals or social needs.

• By the same token, *revitalization cannot be achieved with diffuse supply-side strategies; with untargeted tax incentive programs and faster depreciation allowances; with grants providing greater employment* so that Tiffany (yes) can expand with massive public funding; *with the subsidies* that have made the New York State Jobs Incentive program a failure by paying employers to hire workers whom they would have hired anyway and giving out millions to thriving companies building offices in boom neighborhoods. Productivity cannot be defined solely in terms of a particular country's or company's idea of a desirable rate of return on capital. The notion of capital as an abstraction unrelated to any particular substance, whose only important property is yield, is potentially inimical to planning in terms of social value. It results only in GNP measures of progress. If the government is to move the country out of its impasse, it must consider, independently of businessmen's definitions, how and how much it will contribute to increasing productivity, and how a socially useful though presently unprofitable product can be encouraged through the introduction of appropriate incentives that enhance profitability, reduce the cost of doing business, and diminish risk.

THE DILEMMA OF DIMINISHING DEMAND

Another reason why revitalization cannot be confined to the indiscriminate stimulus of industry is the condition of diminishing demand, or the saturated markets that an affluent society approaches. Many people have *almost* everything they want in terms of products—houses, cars, second homes, color televisions, kitchen appliances. Many more have most of the products they desire. Still others have a more limited, less pressing demand for most essentials and for many discretionary products. Even low-income families have cars, televisions, and radios that provide the same entertainment to the poor and the wealthiest.

As a result, product demand is diminished as our productive and distributive efforts improve and increase in relation to a much more slowly expanding population. We are faced with an over-abundance of labor and/or a lower wage value of labor—again, not because labor has declined in technical efficiency, but, on the contrary, because fewer can produce more than is demanded. We arrive at the condition in which the application of additional labor to a relatively fixed capital base will yield enhanced returns on capital, but will yield diminishing returns when the employer considers adding another unit of labor.

If various demands decline because productivity is so effective that it eradicates scarcity, while markets become saturated (as has occurred in the auto industry), the value of labor's input is worth little or becomes even worthless. It is as if laborers working to produce more air could not sell it because of its abundance. Irrespective of labor's productivity in this undertaking, of its hard work, dedication, long hours, superior tools, and the scientific brilliance that labor applies, these efforts will yield nothing to labor, since the demand will be absent and the product worthless in the marketplace.

In Marxist analysis, the capitalist solution to this problem was (and is) constantly expanding markets through imperialism and war. For a while that seemed true, and in some respects, it still has a ring of credibility, what with our increased defense spending, arms sales, alarmist politicians, and obsession with the balance of payments. Why, indeed, can't a country benefit from (be elated by) a trade deficit? It gets the products it needs and does not consume its own precious resources. In any case, defense spending has not helped our economy's productivity, and has drained its resources and the strategic margin of scientific talent.

Another barren "solution" has been the endless force-feeding of consumption nourished by our television culture, a condition that Galbraith complained about in *The Affluent Society*. Given the fact that society had met so many of its private needs, he contended, the time was ripe for more public spending.

I concur with that line of analysis to a limited degree. But Galbraith has limited the means that can be used to achieve the same goal. Rather than by direct public spending, societal goals can be achieved by channeling these funds to the private sector, relying, as Friedrich Hayek saw, on competitiveness and the variety, spontaneity, and vitality of private industry. Countless "orphan" industries, in the development of medical products and in other new technical fields, are now neglected because their potential profit is uncertain. They are ideal targets for programs to stimulate industrial and job development, for economic stimuli that act as *positive* incentives that would offset, without eliminating, the costs that (often needed) regulation imposes on potential profitability. That is the road I envision toward the creation of a humanistic-industrial complex.

A true revitalization program will require some drastic and painful policies. It cannot afford the political expedient of shoring up troubled industries like autos and steel, which keep raising prices anyway, or of subsidizing the inefficiencies of mismanaged or failing companies. It means exposing us to foreign and domestic competition by phasing out tariffs and import quotas that benefit a few unions but drag down productivity and generate inflation. It means overhauling (not completely eliminating) regulation in order to set priorities determined by government, rather than by its several agencies, each with different goals that put industry under crossfire. The government should set its own priorities when there are conflicts between, say, energy and environment. Revitalization means tax incentives for research, development, and innovation, which have suffered from low investment and thus slowed the rate of technological change. Such incentives are especially important for smaller companies, the key source of new industrial ideas and of new jobs. Funds doled out in this area have been meager, and predicated on zero-sum assumptions, taking from universities to give to business. This is no way to *expand* R&D.

Current programs, using the rhetoric of reindustrialization, have been subsidizing dying industries, covering the mistakes of large companies, and supporting an entire range of expensive energy programs ranging from nuclear energy to synthetic fuels to gasohol and coal gasification and other favored projects, all of which use costly technologies and are run by large corporations.

Innovation, however, comes not from preserving the technology of old industries, but from allowing new technologies to emerge unpredictably from small enterprising companies that usually compete without any government support. The key industries of tomorrow lie in the applications of microprocessors and other semiconductor devices, in the fields of bioengineering and energy, in lasers and medical instruments. Arising constantly in the interstices of our established corporate structures, these new ventures belie the rigid monolithic models of both Galbraith's technostructure and the Marxists' advanced-monopoly capitalism. Government should channel these enterprises, with their visions of the future, to its own definitions of social need, rather than commit itself to the sponsorship of either mammoth dying industries, or just any small business, as it does under the Small Business Administration umbrella. And it can do so through a spectrum of projects that straddle apprenticeships, employment, educational funding and loans (another area short-sightedly cut back), research, and product development as they are planned for long-term goals.

Once that decision is made, certain otherwise futile questions become answerable. How do we create a new frontier in a country like the United States, which enjoys largely fulfilled demand? For what, indeed, do we need additional capital formation? Clearly, for new, socially useful, and desired products that can be invented and produced through the guidance of politicoeconomic planning. Then more manpower can be released for research and development that will accomplish socially useful ends that might, on economic grounds alone, be neglected.

Scientists and entrepreneurs can then occupy their time with projects whose payoff may be indeterminate in everything except the one certain outcome—namely, that these scientists and entrepreneurs are constructively occupied and hence warrant the support that will be required to fulfill their basic, recurring demands. And further, they may eventually discover, invent, or create new products and services deemed useful to society—substitutes for our diminishing natural resources, cancer cures, environmental improvements—that will once again regenerate demand through these new creations.

Research is analogous to the building of capital in the early stages of a country's economic development. Initially, agricultural methods and productivity must be improved to free the manpower needed to build capital goods. Then, as capital goods start to come on stream, more manpower can be freed to produce still more capital goods and continually upgrade the people's standard of living through increased productivity.

Similarly, an industrialized society reaches the point where it can move people and resources from the direct productive stream to the research stream in order to bring about constructive solutions to such problems as energy. At that point, society can move to create new and better products through such efforts, ever increasing the creation of new and superior technology and products, and thus continuously improving the quality of life and standard of living of its members.

Indeed, given that commitment, even more radically "conservative" measures might be taken that the Reaganomites have not yet dared to institute, such as the reduction or even elimination of the corporate income tax to encourage investment. Such stimulus should not be across the board; it should be targeted at areas of greatest social need.

This is not to claim that by such measures the unemployment-inflation tradeoff problem will be solved and the goal of full employment realized. To prevent wage-and-demand inflation, a reservoir of unemployed should be available who can be hired without pushing up the whole wage curve.

But the question is misconstrued if labor, or even reserve labor, is considered as one solid, monolithic bloc. The labor force is highly diverse and highly stratified; the early Marxist notion of a reserve army of the unemployed was valid only for a stage of capitalist development that we have long since passed. It is now relevant largely to some manufacturing and seasonal agricultural sectors, and to the secondary labor market. It has far less relevance to our tremendously differentiated technical, professional, and skilled work force, including the service sector of the postindustrial society. When we speak so glibly about these tradeoffs, or about a reserve labor pool, we rarely specify what we are talking about. Is it really the so-called undisciplined, unskilled, incapable, and intractable—those who pose our social problem—who are to be drawn upon for this purpose? When we talk about the reserve labor pool, are we saying anything about unemployed professionals, civil servants laid off during budget cuts, unemployed bureaucrats and intellectuals? Discussions of a reserve labor pool seldom mention these categories, because most of the lower-middle and middle-class can live on subsidies, unemployment benefits, savings, and family assistance. Moreover, professional and technical workers can shift occupations more easily than others.

Rather, the discussions focus on the very poor who constitute our economic burden, who may never work, or who stumble in and out of the work force at the discretion of those who happen to want to use them. Yet it is this sector of the population that we claim we want to train, and must, for our own economic survival, train, not only for their own benefit and their productivity, but because it is they who constitute our most important national problem, and they whom our subsidies have humiliated and made dependent.

Hence still another anomaly: we are claiming to train for productive work patterns and careers a population that we want to retain as a reserve labor pool. Yet if we train them, we risk creating not only full employment and inflation but expectations of stable careers when we need dilatory work habits on which a reserve labor pool depends. This is not what we claim. We maintain that we will be increasing productivity. If that were so, however, the threat of inflation would not be so acute.

Is it not time we stopped talking out of both sides of our mouths? Why must we say that at the level of "full employment" the increment of labor will push up prices without pushing up productivity, when we are still arguing about the definition of "full employment" or "acceptable unemployment" or, worse yet, what "the natural rate of unemployment" is, or even what productivity is? If we play at political semantics, we will only be embroiled in a futile dispute over how much tax money to spend on the unfortunate in varying degrees of desperation.

The only solution to this anomaly is to stop treating the work force as if it were one solid lump of manpower to be dealt with through macroeconomic policy, and to start treating each segment in isolation. This is why I have suggested very different strategies for the medical profession, for training the unskilled, for targeting new areas of development. Certainly, if we look at the problem in this way, we will find plenty of slack and room for increased employment and productivity.

The general notion of a flexible, elastic pool of labor does hold, for we cannot otherwise adapt our labor needs to technological evolution or to the cycles and fluctuations of our economy. Yet the most important factor in dealing with surplus labor is education. We cannot afford to create and perpetuate a permanent caste, not only of reserve labor but of individuals who have lost the incentive and capacity to work. To solve this problem we need a flexible and voluntary, and not necessarily indigent, reserve labor force.

There are some hopeful signs that this end can be achieved. Despite the increase in the numbers joining the labor force, the number of man-hours worked has not increased nearly as much as the number of workers employed. More workers undertake part-time or temporary employment, buying leisure for themselves. Some are young men who have not yet settled down to their life careers, who work in the secondary labor market where worker demand is flexible. Others prefer their freedom, have hopes for other careers or their own businesses, or simply want added discretionary income. Many may come from the "new culture" with its emphasis on freedom and autonomy, the segment of a generation that Charles Reich, Paul Goodman, and Theodore Roszak have described, which made room for the more ambitious, including upwardly mobile members of minority groups.

FAILING UTOPIA

There is much room for further refinement and improvement of the design for the equitable distribution of the nation's output and wealth. But the solution is not, by vote of the masses, to create a spurious equality. For by that method, instead of achieving our desired goal, we will have stunted the motives that spur innovation, change, and even, ironically, optimism, not to mention growth.

We can hope for even more. It may be that labor, some day, will work primarily on the basis of whether workers enjoy the duties of their jobs, rather than solely, or predominantly, for their wages. Their willingness to work will be based on something we might call their "Total Gratification Return"—a combination of wages, work involvement, and personal growth—rather than on wage gratification alone. To some degree, at least until recently, this has occurred in academia. With salaries that barely competed with those in union labor, college faculties (in a 1978 U.S. Department of Labor survey) ranked highest among the occupations in terms of job satisfaction, higher than lawyers and businessmen.

Eventually, too, we may reach that stage of social evolution in which the laborer who does the essential work, who descends into the mines, who does what no one else in society prefers to do, will be paid the most for his efforts, or, at any rate, more than the person who sits behind a desk. And deservedly so, because more are willing to work at a desk than to sully their hands or to do what is physically exacting or dangerous.

Not that these, or other changes or advances will solve all of humanity's problems. Our lives are marked by human failings, jealousies, disappointments, the unremitting passage of generations from youth to age, physical decay, and death. The state cannot, and should not, be expected to create utopia.

Yet that frame of limitation is not unyielding. Time after time, humanity has rebuilt itself upon the ashes of war and plague and famine. We have consistently staved off the Malthusian destiny of food exhaustion, and the desperate straits of war and starvation to which it would push us, through increases in agricultural productivity and changes in population control. Having learned to fly, we plan to colonize the interstellar spaces. We have, moreover, created a world in which, in many nations, even the poorest have an unparalleled standard of living in the variety and quality of everyday food, travel, free television entertainment, films, and free libraries, not to mention health facilities and medical care. Their environment is more varied than that of even the privileged up to the modern era, perhaps as late as a century ago.

Although the tragedy of the underclass should not be minimized, this perspective may be more useful than clichés of massive poverty in describing it. For the welfare state has been achieved, not only in a minimal standard of living, and not merely through the redistribution of property, but through the products of the acquisitive drive itself as it has spurred creativity and invention.

It is on that impulse that we must base our future growth. Like economic development, revitalization rests on the application of old and new technology to new problems, on the creatively destructive process of innovation, of technology constantly reshaping and improving upon itself, that Joseph Schumpeter saw as the essence of capitalism. Through that process, we have the capacity to develop substitutes for silver in photographic film. We can develop substitutes for gold in dentistry and for use in electronics and other fields. Once we address the energy problem with enough urgency, with the allocation of the dollar resources and the intelligent human resources we have, we will find energy substitutes and sources far superior to the fossil and nuclear energy on which we rely now. Once we direct our efforts, we can prolong our lives and restore our health through the miracles of medical technology.

If we are to avoid procrastinating and want to mobilize energetically to achieve our goals, we will have to develop belief in our ability to cause meaningful directed change. There are precedents enough in the dedicated efforts of the Manhattan Project, the development of synthetic rubber, our mobilization for World War II, our response to *Sputnik*. With the knowledge that we can make things happen, we can influence our destiny.

Like human knowledge, the frontier of innovation is a horizon, constantly receding before us. Yet in its pursuit we leave behind a record of expanding achievement. With intelligent planning and the appropriate incentives, that record will produce solutions to our worst economic and social problems, granting—in terms of material goods, education, health, and the sheer variety of experience available to us—a quality of life surpassing that of all preceding generations in the history of mankind.

NOTE

1. "New York Dairy Farmers Back Cut in Price Supports," *New York Times,* April 5, 1981, Sec. 1, 43.

Glossary

ATS account. Automatic transfer of savings. Arrangements whereby funds and transferred automatically from a person's savings account to his checking account to cover checks or maintain a balance.

Automatic stabilizers. Government taxes and spending that act as counter-cyclical agents without requiring specific intervention at those points in the cycle. For example, taxes increase in prosperity, checking consumption, while unemployment insurance increases in depression, maintaining consumption demand.

Balance-of-payments accounts. A summary or account of a country's international transactions, involving payments and receipts of foreign exchange.

Balance-of-payments deficit. A situation in which a country's receipts on current and capital account fall short of its payments (ignoring transactions by monetary authorities).

Balance-of-payments surplus. A situation in which a country's receipts on current and capital account exceed its payments (ignoring transactions by monetary authorities).

Balance of trade. The difference between the value of exports and the value of imports of visible items (goods).

Balanced budget. A situation in which current revenue equals current spending.

Bank runs. Panicky shifts by the public from bank deposits to currency.

Bill rate. The rate of return, adjusted to an annual basis, received by investors in United States Treasury bills.

Bond. An evidence of debt carrying a specified amount, a schedule of interest payments, and a date for redemption of the face value of the bond.

Budget deficit. Government expenditures in excess of tax receipts.

Budget surplus. Excess of federal revenues over spending.

Business cycles. Patterned fluctuations in the level of economic activity.

271

Capacity. The level of output that corresponds to the minimum level of short-run average total costs. Also called *plant capacity*.

Capital. A factor of production, defined to include all man-made aids to further production. Real capital refers to physical assets, including plant, equipment, and inventories. Money capital refers to equity capital and debt.

Capital-output ratio. The ratio of the value of capital to the annual value of output it produces.

Capital stock. The aggregate quantity of a society's capital goods.

Cartel. An organization of producers designed to reduce or eliminate competition among its members, usually through agreements to restrict output in an effort to achieve noncompetitive prices.

Central bank. A country's official bank, which the government sets up to help handle its transactions, regulate monetary policy (money supply and credit conditions), lend to and coordinate commercial banks, issue currency, and regulate foreign exchange. In the modern world the central bank is usually the sole money-issuing authority.

Certificate of deposit (CD). A negotiable time deposit carrying a higher interest rate than that paid on ordinary time deposits. Typically issued to business enterprises, negotiable CDs often have denominations of $100,000 or more and interest rates that depend upon money market conditions at time of issue.

Commercial bank. Privately owned, profit-seeking institutions that offer checking accounts. They provide a variety of financial services, particularly short-term business loans. They may offer time and savings deposits and engage in other types of banking activities.

Commercial loans. Short-term loans to businesses, usually for the financing of inventory.

Commercial paper. Short-term securities issued mainly by industrial corporations, utilities, finance companies, and bank-holding companies. The paper usually has a maturity of less than nine months and is sold at a discount.

Command economy. An economy in which decisions of the central political authorities exert the major influence on the allocation of resources.

Commodities. Marketable items produced to satisfy wants. Commodities may be goods, which are tangible, or services, which are intangible.

Consumption. The act of using commodities to satisfy wants.

Cost-push inflation. Inflation caused by increased costs rather than excess aggregate demand. The increased costs may stem from excessive wage demands by unions or price demands by large producers.

Credit. Loans made by lenders to borrowers. Examples are bank loans; corporate, municipal, and U.S. government bonds; doctors' bills; and charge accounts.

Credit crunch. A shortage of credit, or the ability of lending institutions to loan funds.

Credit instrument. A written statement that a person, business firm, or government will pay a specified amount of money either on demand or on a certain future date. Examples are promissory notes, bonds, and checks.

Credit rationing. Rationing of available funds among borrowers when there is excess demand for loans at prevailing interest rates.

Credit risk. The risk that the borrower may default.

Crowding-out effect. A reduction in private expenditure as a direct result of an increase in government expenditure.

Currency. Coins and paper money.

Currency in circulation. Currency outstanding, excluding the amount held by the U.S. Treasury and the Federal Reserve banks.

Currency outstanding. All U.S. coins and paper money issued, whether held by the U.S. Treasury, the Federal Reserve banks, or the public. It includes money held by persons and banks in foreign countries and some that has been lost or destroyed after issuance.

Debt management. Policies of the U.S. Treasury designed to influence economic activity by altering the maturity of the U.S. government debt.

Demand. Several distinct but closely related concepts:
1. *Quantity demanded;*
2. The whole relationship of the quantity demanded to variables that determine it, such as tastes, household income, distribution of income, population, price of the commodity, and prices of other commodities;
3. The *demand schedule;*
4. The *demand curve.*
The phrase "increase (or decrease) in demand" means a shift of the demand curve to the right (left), indicating an increase (decrease) in the quantity demanded at each possible price.

Demand curve. The graphic representation of the *demand schedule.*

Demand deposit. A bank deposit that is transferred by a check or withdrawn—converted into currency—on demand.

Demand for money. The total amount of money that the public wishes to hold for all purposes.

Demand-pull inflation. Inflation arising from excess aggregate demand.

Demand schedule. The relationship between the quantity demanded of a commodity and its price, other factors being equal.

Deposit creation. The ability of the commercial banking system to expand its deposits by several times the amount of an increase in its reserves. The process of creating deposits is called the multiple expansion process.

Deposit money. Money held by the public in the form of demand deposits with commercial banks.

Depository intermediary. A financial institution that creates deposits for savers and lends the money so acquired at interest to business firms and investors.

Depreciation. The wearing out of plant and equipment, machinery, and housing.

Depreciation of the exchange rate. A fall in the free-market value of domestic currency in terms of foreign currencies.

Depression. A period of very low economic activity with very high unemployment and high excess capacity.

Desired investment. The amount of expenditures for capital goods that enterprises plan to make. This may differ from the actual amount of investment because of unintended changes in inventories.

Devaluation of the exchange rate. A downward revision in the value at which a country's currency is pegged in terms of foreign currencies.

Discount rate. The rate charged by the Federal Reserve banks for the reserves lent to member commercial banks.

Discounted loan. A type of loan in which the amount received by the borrower is less than the principal amount of the loan. The interest paid consists of the difference between these two amounts.

Disintermediation. A reduction in the amount of deposits in financial institutions or intermediaries, generally as a result of rises in market interest rates, which pull funds out of depository institutions, whose rates paid on deposits are regulated.

Disposable income. Personal income less the amount paid in personal taxes; the household income available for spending and saving.

Elastic demand. The situation existing when for a given percentage change in price there is a greater percentage change in quantity demanded; elasticity greater than 1.

Elasticity of demand. A measure of the responsiveness of the quantity of a commodity demanded to a change in market price. Formula:

$$\frac{\text{percentage change in quantity demanded}}{\text{percentage change in price}}$$

Equilibrium conditions. The conditions that must be fulfilled for some economic variable, such as price or national income, to be in equilibrium.

Equilibrium national income. The level of national income at which aggregate expenditure (total planned spending) equals the economy's total output.

Equilibrium price. The price at which quantity demanded equals quantity supplied, i.e., at which no surpluses or shortages exist.

Equities. A type of asset providing a variable amount of income and with a variable sale price. The main examples of equities are corporation stock and the ownership of unincorporated enterprises.

Eurodollar deposits. Deposits, denominated in dollars, that are held in banks outside the United States, usually in overseas branches of American banks.

Excess demand. Shortage; a situation in which, at the given price, quantity demand exceeds quantity supplied.

Excess reserves. Bank reserves above the amount legally required.

Excess supply. Surplus; a situation in which, at the given price, quantity supplied exceeds quantity demanded.

Exchange rate. The price of a foreign currency in terms of a country's own money.

Expectational inflation. Inflation that occurs because decision-makers raise prices (so as to keep their relative prices constant) in the expectation that the price level is going to rise.

Externalities (also called third-party effects) Effects, either good or bad, on parties not directly involved in the production or use of a commodity.

Factors of production. Resources used to produce goods and services to satisfy wants. Land, labor, and capital are three basic categories of factors of production. Sometimes used synonymously with *inputs*.

Federal Deposit Insurance Corporation (FDIC). A federal deposit insurance system of which all banks belonging to the Federal Reserve System must be members, and which other qualifying banks may join. Each deposit in an insured bank is covered up to $100,000.

Federal funds sold. A member bank's deposits at the Federal Reserve bank that have been lent to another bank.

Federal funds rate. The interest rate at which banks lend their excess reserves to each other overnight. Although a market rate, it is affected by the policies of the Federal Reserve Board as it determines the level of reserves in the banking system.

Federal Open Market Committee. An important policy-making unit of the Federal Reserve System. Its membership includes the seven members of the board of governors of the Federal Reserve System plus the presidents of five of the Federal Reserve banks.

Federal Reserve Board. The seven-member board of governors of the Federal Reserve System. The Federal Reserve governors are appointed for fourteen-year terms by the president. The chairman is also appointed by the president.

Federal Reserve notes. The most common type of paper currency in use in the United States today. They are issued by the Federal Reserve banks and are liabilities of these banks.

Federal Reserve System. The division of the country into twelve Federal Reserve districts, each with its own Federal Reserve bank. The banks are headquartered in New York, Chicago, San Francisco, Philadelphia, Boston, Cleveland, St. Louis, Kansas City, Atlanta, Richmond, Dallas, and Minneapolis. They are coordinated by the seven-member board of governors of the Federal Reserve System in Washington, D.C. The Federal Reserve Board, with the twelve regional Federal Reserve banks, constitutes our American central bank.

Financial assets. Stocks, bonds, commercial paper, CDs, or similar claims to physical assets or money.

Financial intermediaries. Financial institutions, including commercial banks, that create deposits or other types of liquid debt to obtain funds which are invested in less liquid types of loans and securities.

Fiscal policy. The deliberate use of the government's revenue-raising and spending activities in an effort to influence the behavior of such macrovariables as the GNP and total employment.

Fixed costs. Costs that do no change with ouput. Sometimes called overhead costs.

Fixed factors. Factors of production that cannot be increased in the short run.

Float. The time lag between the writing of a check and the actual transfer or withdrawal of funds from the bank on which the check is written. Banks have use of the funds over this time span.

Foreign exchange (foreign media of exchange). Actual foreign currency or various claims on it, such as bank balances or promises to pay.

Free market economy. An economy in which the decisions of individual household and firms (as distinct from the central authorities) exert the major influence over the allocation of resources.

Free trade. International transactions unrestricted by quotas, tariffs, or direct controls.

Frictional unemployment. Short-term unemployment caused by the shifting of persons between jobs.

Full employment. Usually considered to exist when the rate of unemployment is between 4 and 5 percent. This allows for job shifting and for other types of frictional unemployment.

Full-employment balance. The budget deficit or surplus that would occur if national income were at its full employment level.

Full- (or high-) employment budget. Federal revenues and expenditures estimates at the level they would have reached if there were full employment. This budget is used as a measure of the ease or tightness of fiscal policy.

Gold standard. Government policy that defines its currency in terms of a given weight of gold and will convert its currency into gold at that rate on demand.

Gross national product (GNP). The sum of all values added in the economy. It is the sum of the values of all final goods and services produced in a country during the year and, which is the same thing, the sum of all factor incomes earned. Also called gross national income.

Gross national product deflator (GNP deflator). The index number used to adjust the GNP, measured in current dollars, for price level changes so that it is measured in constant dollars.

Hard-core unemployed. Persons unemployed at least six months.

High-powered money. The monetary base.

Holding company. A company that holds the controlling shares of stock of another company.

Household. All the people who live under one roof and who make, or are subject to others making for them, joint financial decisions.

Human capital. The capitalized value of productive investments in persons, i.e., of their earning capacity. Usually refers to investments resulting from spending on education, training, and health improvements.

Incomes policy. *Wage-price guidelines.*

Index numbers. Averages that measure changes in variables like price level and industrial production, expressed as percentages relative to a base period assigned the value 100.

Individual retirement account (IRA). Savings account (limited in amount) offering tax advantages for persons not covered by employer pension plans.

Inelastic demand. The situation in which change in price produces a less than proportionate change in quantity demanded; elasticity less than unity or 1.

Inflation. (1) A rising price level in the economy, signifying a decrease in the real value of a unit of money. (2) A phase of the business cycle in which price increases tend to be general and rapid. Inflation is usually measured by a rise in a price index covering a variety of goods.

Innovation. The introduction of inventions into methods of production.

Insolvent bank. A bank whose deposit liabilities plus borrowings are larger than its assets.

Interest. Payment for the use of money.

Interest rate. Price paid per dollar borrowed per year, often expressed as a percentage (e.g., 6 percent).

Interest risk. The risk that the price of a security will fall because of a rise in interest rates.

International Monetary Fund (IMF). An international organization whose main purpose is to help governments of countries experiencing balance-of-payments difficulty.

Invention. The discovery of something new, such as a new production technique or a new product.

Inventories. Stocks of raw materials, or of finished goods, held by firms to mitigate the effect of short-term fluctuations in production or sales.

Investment. Spending on the production of goods not for present consumption.

Investment goods. Capital goods such as plant and equipment plus inventories; production that is not sold for consumption purposes.

Labor. A factor of production, usually defined to include all physical and mental contributions that people make to economic activity.

Labor force. See *Work force.*

Laffer curve. Graph plotting the supply-side theory that lower tax *rates* may bring in higher tax *revenues* because low taxes stimulate business investment, creating jobs, raising incomes for both business and consumers and thus resulting in higher tax revenues. See also *Supply-side theory.*

Laissez faire. Literally, "let do"; a policy implying the absence of government intervention in a market economy.

Land. A factor of production. Usually defined to include natural resources or raw materials as well as "land."

Law of diminishing returns. A principle or hypothesis stating that when larger amounts of one resource are used in combination with a fixed amount of another resource, eventually both the marginal productivity and the average productivity of the variable resource will get smaller.

Leakages. Uses of the monetary base that lower the size of the money multiplier. The principal leakages result from expansions of currency in circulation, time deposits, and excess reserves.

Liquid assets. Assets that may be converted into money quickly and without loss in nominal value.

Liquidity preference. The desire to hold assets in the form of cash and cash equivalents.

Liquidity trap. A situation in which interest rates are so low that investment in securities is discouraged because of expectations that interest rates will rise and push down securities prices.

M1. Currency in circulation plus demand deposits (checking accounts), other checkable deposits (e.g., NOW and ATS accounts), and travelers' checks.

M2. M1 plus savings and small (under $100,000) time deposits at all depository institutions, plus money market mutual-fund balances, overnight repurchase agreements, and Eurodollars.

M3. M2 plus large ($100,000 plus) time deposits at all depository institutions, term repurchase agreements, and institutional negative only money market mutual-fund balances.

Macroeconomics. The study of the determination of economic aggregates, such as total output, total employment, and the price level.

Margin requirement. Percentage of the purchase price of stocks or bonds that a customer must pay in cash while putting up the stock as security against a loan for the balance.

Marginal cost (incremental cost). The increase in total cost resulting from raising output by one unit.

Marginal efficiency of capital (MEC). The marginal rate of return on a nation's capital stock. It is the rate of return on one additional dollar of net investment added to the capital stock.

Marginal product (MP). The proportionate change in output that results from using one more unit of a variable factor.

Marginal product of capital. The addition to annual income that a business firm expects for a dollar of additional investment.

Marginal propensity to consumer (MPC). The percentage of additional income that persons spend for consumption.

Marginal revenue. Change in a firm's total revenue resulting from the sale of one unit more.

Marginal revenue product. Additional revenue resulting from the last unit of a variable factor.

Marginal tax rate. The fraction of an additional dollar of income that is paid in taxes.

Marginal utility. The additional satisfaction obtained by a buyer from consuming one more unit of a good; the rate of change of utility with respect to consumption.

Market. 1. An area over which buyers and sellers negotiate the exchange of a well-defined commodity; 2. From the point of view of a household, the firms from which it can buy a well-defined product; 3. From the point of view of a firm, the buyers to whom it can sell a well-defined product.
3. From the point of view of a firm, the buyers to whom it can sell a well-defined product.

Marketable United States government security. One that can be transferred from one owner to another by sale.

Markup. The percentage or amount added to cost to determine price.

Maturity date. The date on which the principal value of a bond, loan, savings certificate, or similar debt instrument will be repaid to the lender.

Medium of exchange. Money used to purchase goods and services and to pay debts.

Mercantilist policies. Governmental policies aimed at maintaining an excess of exports over imports.

Microeconomic policy. Activities of the central authorities that change resource allocation and/or income distribution.

Microeconomics. The study of particular markets and sectors of the economy, as distinguished from *macroeconomics,* the study of national aggregates.

Misery index. The sum of the unemployment and inflation rates.

Mixed economy. Economy in which some decisions are made by firms and households and some by central authorities.

Monetarists. Economic school stressing monetary causes of cyclical fluctuations and inflations, opposing an active stabilization policy as unnecessary, and stressing monetary policy as more effective than fiscal policy.

Monetary policy. An attempt to influence the economy by operating on such monetary variables as money supply and interest rates.

Monetary aggregates. A type of target used to guide Federal Reserve policy. The principal monetary aggregates used are total member bank reserves, the *monetary base,* and *money supply.*

Monetary base. Total member bank reserve deposits with the Federal Reserve banks plus currency in circulation. The monetary base is also called high-powered money.

Monetary system. The institutional arrangements for supplying the economy with money.

Monetary theory of inflation. Attributes inflation to excessive increases in the money supply per unit of output.

Monetary twist. Federal Reserve open-market operations designed to change relative yields of short-term and long-term U.S. government securities. Important in the early 1960s.

Money creation (creation of bank deposits). The ability of the banking system *as a whole* (not of the individual bank) to create new money and credit through the "multiple expansion of bank deposits." If required reserves are, say, 10 percent, the banking system can loan or invest up to $10,000 in new money, or credit, for each $1,000 deposited, for a net gain of $9,000 in the money supply. The process operates this way: bank 1 keeps $100 on reserve, and lends out $900 of the deposited funds; bank 2 then keeps $90 in reserves and lends out $810; and so on. The maximum potential for money creation may or may not be realized, depending on the demand for credit, the demand for currency, the desire for excess reserves—"leakage" out of the banking system, etc. The legal limit to the expansion of deposits is the reciprocal of the reserve requirement; the actual expansion of deposits is measured by the *money multiplier*.

Money market certificates. A type of time deposit with a maturity of six months, a minimum denomination of $10,000, and a rate of interest equal to the six-month Treasury bill rate at time of issue.

Money market mutual fund. A type of investment company that holds CDs, large denomination Treasury bills, commercial paper, or other short-term credit instruments.

Money multiplier. The ratio of the amount of money to the monetary base. Also called the expansion ratio.

Money supply. The total quantity of money existing at any point in time. A measure of short-term liquidity and credit demand. For different measures or definitions of the money supply, as issued by the Federal Reserve Board in January 1982, see *M1, M2,* and *M3.*

Mutual fund. An open-end investment company that offers to sell an unlimited amount of its shares to obtain funds to invest—usually in corporation stock. The company redeems its shares on demand at a price that reflects the value of its asset holding.

National debt. The total amount of United States government securities outstanding. The federal government issues securities as a means of borrowing to meet its expenditures when the federal budget is in deficit.

National income (NI). The total amount of wages, proprietors' income, rental income, net interest, and corporation profits received per year. It is equal to gross national product less the cost of depreciation and less the total amount of indirect business taxes.

Natural rate of unemployment. The rate of unemployment consistent (due to frictional and structural causes) with full employment national income. In the Phelps-Friedman theory this is the rate of unemployment at which there is neither upward nor downward pressure on the price level.

Near money. Liquid assets easily convertible into money without risk of significant loss of value. They can be used as short-term stores of purchasing power but are not themselves media of exchange.

Neo-Keynesians or Keynesians. Economic school stressing changes in both aggregate expenditure and the money supply as causes of cyclical fluctuations and inflations, calling for active government stabilization policy and emphasizing fiscal policy as more effective than monetary policy.

NOW account. Savings account at a thrift institution on which checks can be drawn.

Open-market operations. The purchase and sale on the open market by the central bank of securities (usually short-term government securities).

Opportunity cost. The cost of using resources for a certain purpose, measured by the benefit or revenues given up by not using them in their best alternative use.

Outputs. The quantities of goods and services produced.

Per capita GNP. GNP divided by total population. Also called GNP per person.

Perfect competition. A market form in which all firms are price takers and in which there is freedom of entry into and exit from the industry.

Personal income. Income earned by individuals before allowances for personal income taxes paid or payable.

Phillips curve. Originally a relation between the percentage of the labor force unemployed and the rate of change of money wages. It can also be expressed as relation between the unemployment rate and the inflation rate, or between actual national income as a proportion of potential national income and the inflation rate.

Point of diminishing average productivity. The level of output at which average product reaches a maximum.

Point of diminishing marginal productivity. The level of output at which marginal product reaches a maximum.

Potential GNP. The GNP that could be produced if unemployment were kept down to 4 percent of the labor force. Also called *full-employment national income.*

Price index. A measure of changes in prices in general.

Price parity. The ratio of prices farmers receive for products they sell to the prices they pay for products they buy, compared with some base period; a basic concept in U.S. farm policy.

Prime rate. The interest rate that commercial banks charge on short-term business loans to their best customers.

Private sector. That portion of an economy in which principal decisions are made by private units such as household and firms.

Production possibility boundary. A curve on a graph showing which alternative combination of commodities can just be obtained if all available productive resources are used. The boundary between attainable and unobtainable combinations of resources.

Productivity. Output per unit of input; often refers to labor productivity, or output per man-hour.

Productivity of capital. The increase in production resulting from the use of capital, after allowance for maintenance and replacement of the capital.

Profit. The difference between the value of output and the value of inputs.

Progressivity of taxation. The ratio of taxes to income as income increases. If the ratio decreases, the tax is termed regressive; if constant, the tax is proportional; if it increases, the tax is progressive.

Protectionism. Partial or full protection of domestic industries from foreign competition in domestic markets by use of tariffs or other means.

Public sector. That portion of an economy in which principal decisions are made by the central authorities.

Pure return on capital. The amount capital can earn on a riskless investment.

Quantity demanded. The amount of a commodity that households want to buy in a given time period. A movement up or down the demand curve in response to a rise or fall in price.

Quantity supplied. The amount of a commodity producers wish to sell in some time period. An increase (decrease) in quantity supplied refers to a movement up (down) the supply curve in response to a rise (fall) in price.

Quantity theory of money. A theory that predicts that the money value of national income changes in proportion to changes in the money supply. (The changes will be all in prices, if national income is at its full employment level.)

Rate of return on capital. Frequently used to refer to a specific capital good. The annual net income produced by a capital good, expressed as a percentage of the price of the good.

Rationing. Distribution that limits the maximum quantity of a good or service that a consuming unit can purchase or obtain. A contrast to "rationing" by price.

Real income. Purchasing power of a household's income; money income corrected for changes in price levels.

Real rate of interest. A rate of interest expressed in constant dollars. It is the money (nominal) rate of interest less the rate of inflation.

Real value of money. Purchasing power of money, varying inversely with prices.

Recession. A downswing in the level of economic activity. Department of Commerce definition: a recession occurs when real GNP falls for two successive quarters.

Refunding. When new United States government securities are offered to owners of maturing United States government securities.

Regulation Q. A Federal Reserve regulation that has prohibited the payment of interest on checking accounts and set interest rate ceilings for banks between 1933 to 1980. Legislation passed in 1980 allows interest on certain checking accounts and phases out interest-rate ceilings over a six-year period.

Required reserves. The percentage of a bank's deposits and other sources of funds that must be held in the form of liquid assets—currency or deposits with the central bank.

Reserve ratio. The fraction of deposits of the public that a bank holds in reserves.

Reserve requirements. See *required reserves*.

Resource allocation. The allocation of an economy's scarce resources among alternative uses.

Return to capital. The total amount available for payments to owners of capital; the sum of pure returns to capital, risk premiums, and economic profits.

Revaluation of the exchange rate. An increase in the value at which a country's currency is pegged in terms of foreign currencies; the opposite of devaluation.

Revenue sharing. A noncategorical grant in aid, in which some federal revenue is returned to state and local governments for unrestricted expenditure.

Risk premium. The return to capital necessary to compensate owners of capital for the risk of loss of their capital.

Saving. Household saving is disposable income not spent on domestic or imported consumption goods and services. Firm saving is profits not distributed to owners.

Savings bonds. A type of U.S. government security. They are nonmarketable and available in both appreciation and current-income forms.

Savings certificate. A type of time deposit. The owner receives a certificate showing the amount deposited, interest rate, maturity date, and other terms. They are sold only to individuals, nonprofit organizations, and fiduciaries.

Savings deposits. Interest-bearing time deposits with no set maturity date. The principal type is called passbook deposits. They cannot legally be withdrawn without written notice thirty days or more in advance, but they are usually convertible into currency or demand deposits.

Scarcity, or economic scarcity. The basic fact of life and economics, that all human and nonhuman resources are finite in quantity and that hard choices must therefore be made between even desirable alternatives about the production and distribution of these scarce resources. These choices entail tradeoffs or *opportunity costs.* The consequence is that even the best applied knowledge and technology can produce only limited maximal amounts of each economic good. The *production-possibility boundary* allots the maximum amounts of various combinations of these goods achievable under given conditions.

Search unemployment. Unemployment caused by people searching for a good job rather than accepting the first job they come across.

Selective credit controls. Controls that affect the use of a particular type of credit. Examples are margin requirements on loans for purchasing corporate stock, the regulation of interest rates on time deposits, and marginal reserve requirements on installment credit extended by some retailers, minimum down payments on mortgages, and others.

Short run. The period of time over which the quantity of some inputs cannot, as a practical matter, be varied.

Short-run equilibrium. Generally, equilibrium subject to fixed factors; for a competitive firm, the output at which market price equals marginal cost; for a competitive industry, the price and output at which industry demand equals short-term industry supply and all firms are in short-run equilibrium. Either profits or losses are possible.

Social cost (social opportunity cost). The value of the best alternative use of resources available to society, as valued by society.

Stagflation. The coexistence of high rates of unemployment with high, and sometimes rising, rates of inflation.

Structural rigidity inflation. The theory that downward inflexibility of money prices means that the adjustment of *relative* prices necessary in any changing economy will cause a rise in the average level of prices (i.e., an inflation).

Structural unemployment. Unemployment caused by changes in the structure of the economy or the nature of the work force. Structural changes may include the decline of old industries; changes in the work force may involve demographic change, such as the proportion of women in the work force, or changing skills. Structural unemployment may also result when such politico-economic arrangements as welfare payments and unemployment insurance, possibly competing with a potential worker's discretionary earnings after taxes and expenses of dressing and traveling to work are considered, result in disincentives to work.

Supply. Several related concepts:

1. *Quantity supplied;*

2. The whole relationship of the quantity supplied to variables that determine it, such as producers' goals, technology, price of the commodity, prices of other commodities, and prices of factors of production;

3. The *supply schedule;*

4. The *supply curve.* The phrase increase (decrease) in supply means a shift of the supply curve to the right (left), indicating an increase (decrease) in the quantity supplied at each possible price.

Supply curve. The graphic representation of the *supply schedule.*

Supply of effort (or total supply of labor). The total number of hours of work that the population is willing to supply.

Supply of money. See *money supply.*

Supply schedule. The relationship between the quantity supplied of a commodity and its price, other factors being equal. Various amounts of the commodity that will be supplied at different prices.

Supply-side theory, or supply-side economics. Theory derived from Say's law that supply creates its own demand. Maintains that government strategies that stimulate savings and investment, rather than consumption, will alleviate both depression, by creating jobs and spending power, and inflation, by augmenting the production and supply of goods to absorb that spending power. Partially complementary to, though often opposed to, Keynesian theory. Currently, supply-side economics, also described as Reaganomics, has come to mean reducing both corporate and individual taxes in order to encourage investment and stimulate the private sector to generate increased employment, productivity, and economic growth, so that, consistent with the *Laffer curve* theory, the amount of the tax cut, and even more, will be recovered in increased taxes derived from the growth of the economy.

Thrift institutions. Mutual savings banks, savings-and-loan associations, and credit unions.

Time deposits. Interest-bearing bank deposits. These include savings deposits, savings certificates, and certificates of deposit. Types having a stated maturity date usually cannot be withdrawn before maturity without penalty.

Transfer payments. Personal gifts and government welfare payments. Payments of money that are not made in return for any services or for the use of real property.

Treasury bill. A short-term, marketable United States government security sold at a discount. T-bills are typically issued in maturities of three months, six months, nine months, and one year. They are always sold by auction when issued.

Treasury note. A type of marketable U.S. government security having an initial maturity of one to ten years. There is no legal ceiling to the coupon rates on these notes.

Unemployment rate. Percentage of the work force that is unemployed. See also *search unemployment, structural unemployment.*

Value added. A method of accounting that deducts from the price of any good at any stage of production the costs of materials and intermediate products that have been purchased from other firms and are not produced at that particular stage of production. For example: the value added on the price of flour does not include the price that the miller paid for the wheat. It is the value added at each subsequent stage of production.

Value-added tax (VAT). A tax collected at each stage of production, from raw material to finished product, on the value added at that stage of production. On a loaf of bread, for example, VAT is collected on the farmer's wheat, on the miller's flour, on the baker's dough, and on the grocer's loaf of bread. But the tax on the miller's flour subtracts from its price the cost of the wheat purchased from the farmer, taxing only the value added at the miller's stage of production. And the tax on the loaf of bread deducts from its price the costs of all preceding stages of production, taxing only the last stage. Widely used in European Common Market countries.

Variable costs. Costs that vary directly with changes in output. Direct costs.

Variable factors. Factors of production whose quantities can be varied in the short run.

Velocity of circulation. Turnover of money. GNP divided by money supply. The higher the velocity, the higher the turnover. Also called *income velocity.*

Wage-price guidelines. Goals set by the federal government to limit increases in wages and prices.

Work force. The number of people employed or looking for work. Excludes individuals not looking for work (e.g., students, nonworking housewives, and the permanently unemployed), those unable to work, and "discouraged workers" who may have stopped looking for work because they feel they cannot find jobs.

Yield. Interest on a security as a percentage of its market price rather than (as in the case of a bond) face value.

Index